Microsoft® Office 365™

POWERPOINT® 2016

INTRODUCTORY

Microsoft® Office 365™
POWERPOINT® 2016

INTRODUCTORY

SUSAN L. SEBOK

SHELLY CASHMAN SERIES®

Australia • Brazil • Japan • Korea • Mexico • Singapore • Spain • United Kingdom • United States

Shelly Cashman Microsoft
PowerPoint 2016: Introductory
Susan L. Sebok

SVP, GM Skills & Global Product Management: Dawn Gerrain

Product Director: Kathleen McMahon

Senior Product Team Manager: Lauren Murphy

Associate Product Manager: Melissa Stehler

Senior Director, Development: Marah Bellegarde

Product Development Manager: Leigh Hefferon

Managing Content Developer: Emma F. Newsom

Developmental Editor: Deb Kaufmann

Product Assistant: Erica Chapman

Manuscript Quality Assurance: Jeffrey Schwartz, John Freitas, Serge Palladino, Susan Pedicini, Danielle Shaw, Susan Whalen

Senior Production Director: Wendy Troeger

Production Director: Patty Stephan

Senior Content Project Manager: Matthew Hutchinson

Manufacturing Planner: Julio Esperas

Designer: Diana Graham

Text Design: Joel Sadagursky

Cover Template Designer: Diana Graham

Cover image(s): Piotr Zajc/Shutterstock.com; Mrs. Opossum/Shutterstock.com

Compositor: Lumina Datamatics

Vice President, Marketing: Brian Joyner

Marketing Director: Michele McTighe

Marketing Manager: Stephanie Albracht

For product information and technology assistance, contact us at
Cengage Learning Customer & Sales Support, 1-800-354-9706

For permission to use material from this text or product,
submit all requests online at **www.cengage.com/permissions**
Further permissions questions can be e-mailed to
permissionrequest@cengage.com

Library of Congress Control Number: 2015961000

ISBN: 978-1-305-87079-6

Cengage Learning
20 Channel Center Street
Boston, MA 02210
USA

Cengage Learning is a leading provider of customized learning solutions with employees residing in nearly 40 different countries and sales in more than 125 countries around the world. Find your local representative at **www.cengage.com.**

Cengage Learning products are represented in Canada by Nelson Education, Ltd.

To learn more about Cengage Learning, visit **www.cengage.com.**
Purchase any of our products at your local college store or at our preferred online store **www.cengagebrain.com**

The material in this book was written using Microsoft Office 2016 and was Quality Assurance tested before the publication date. As Microsoft continually updates Office 2016 and Office 365, your software experience may vary slightly from what is seen in the printed text.

Microsoft® Office 365™
POWERPOINT® 2016

INTRODUCTORY

Contents

Microsoft **PowerPoint 2016**

MODULE ONE

Creating and Editing a Presentation with Pictures

MODULE TWO

Enhancing a Presentation with Pictures, Shapes, and WordArt

Productivity Apps for School and Work

Corinne Hoisington

Lochlan keeps track of his class notes, football plays, and internship meetings with OneNote.

Zoe is using the annotation features of Microsoft Edge to take and save web notes for her research paper.

Nori is creating a Sway site to highlight this year's activities for the Student Government Association.

Hunter is adding interactive videos and screen recordings to his PowerPoint resume.

© Rawpixel/Shutterstock.com

Being computer literate no longer means mastery of only Word, Excel, PowerPoint, Outlook, and Access. To become technology power users, Hunter, Nori, Zoe, and Lochlan are exploring Microsoft OneNote, Sway, Mix, and Edge in Office 2016 and Windows 10.

In this Module

Learn to use productivity apps!
Links to companion **Sways**, featuring **videos** with hands-on instructions, are located on www.cengagebrain.com.

Introduction to OneNote 2016

notebook | section tab | To Do tag | screen clipping | note | template | Microsoft OneNote Mobile app | sync | drawing canvas | inked handwriting | Ink to Text

As you glance around any classroom, you invariably see paper notebooks and notepads on each desk. Because deciphering and sharing handwritten notes can be a challenge, Microsoft OneNote 2016 replaces physical notebooks, binders, and paper notes with a searchable, digital notebook. OneNote captures your ideas and schoolwork on any device so you can stay organized, share notes, and work with others on projects. Whether you are a student taking class notes as shown in **Figure 1** or an employee taking notes in company meetings, OneNote is the one place to keep notes for all of your projects.

Figure 1: OneNote 2016 notebook

Each **notebook** is divided into sections, also called **section tabs**, by subject or topic.

Use **To Do tags**, icons that help you keep track of your assignments and other tasks.

Type on a page to add a **note**, a small window that contains text or other types of information.

Personalize a page with a **template**, or stationery.

Write or draw directly on the page using drawing tools.

Pages can include pictures such as **screen clippings**, images from any part of a computer screen.

Attach files and enter equations so you have everything you need in one place.

Creating a OneNote Notebook

OneNote is divided into sections similar to those in a spiral-bound notebook. Each OneNote notebook contains sections, pages, and other notebooks. You can use One-Note for school, business, and personal projects. Store information for each type of project in different notebooks to keep your tasks separate, or use any other organization that suits you. OneNote is flexible enough to adapt to the way you want to work.

When you create a notebook, it contains a blank page with a plain white background by default, though you can use templates, or stationery, to apply designs in categories such as Academic, Business, Decorative, and Planners. Start typing or use the buttons on the Insert tab to insert notes, which are small resizable windows that can contain text, equations, tables, on-screen writing, images, audio and video recordings, to-do lists, file attachments, and file printouts. Add as many notes as you need to each page.

Syncing a Notebook to the Cloud

OneNote saves your notes every time you make a change in a notebook. To make sure you can access your notebooks with a laptop, tablet, or smartphone wherever you are, OneNote uses cloud-based storage, such as OneDrive or SharePoint. **Microsoft OneNote Mobile app**, a lightweight version of OneNote 2016 shown in **Figure 2**, is available for free in the Windows Store, Google Play for Android devices, and the AppStore for iOS devices.

If you have a Microsoft account, OneNote saves your notes on OneDrive automatically for all your mobile devices and computers, which is called **syncing**. For example, you can use OneNote to take notes on your laptop during class, and then open OneNote on your phone to study later. To use a notebook stored on your computer with your OneNote Mobile app, move the notebook to OneDrive. You can quickly share notebook content with other people using OneDrive.

Figure 2: Microsoft OneNote Mobile app

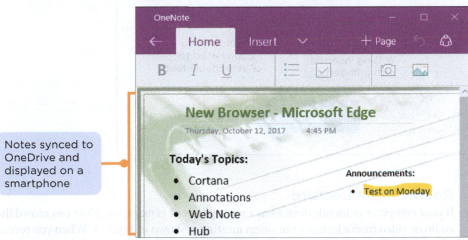

Notes synced to OneDrive and displayed on a smartphone

Taking Notes

Use OneNote pages to organize your notes by class and topic or lecture. Beyond simple typed notes, OneNote stores drawings, converts handwriting to searchable text and mathematical sketches to equations, and records audio and video.

OneNote includes drawing tools that let you sketch freehand drawings such as biological cell diagrams and financial supply-and-demand charts. As shown in **Figure 3**, the Draw tab on the ribbon provides these drawing tools along with shapes so you can insert diagrams and other illustrations to represent your ideas. When you draw on a page, One-Note creates a **drawing canvas**, which is a container for shapes and lines.

On the Job Now

OneNote is ideal for taking notes during meetings, whether you are recording minutes, documenting a discussion, sketching product diagrams, or listing follow-up items. Use a meeting template to add pages with content appropriate for meetings.

Figure 3: Tools on the Draw tab

Draw tab

Pens and highlighters are in the Tools group.

Insert rectangles and lines from the Shapes group.

Lines and shapes are in the Shapes group.

Make drawings using pens in the Tools group.

Insert text using the Type button in the Tools group.

Files syncing over the Internet

Microsoft OneDrive

OneNote Pages in the Notebook

Converting Handwriting to Text

When you use a pen tool to write on a notebook page, the text you enter is called **inked handwriting**. OneNote can convert inked handwriting to typed text when you use the **Ink to Text** button in the Convert group on the Draw tab, as shown in **Figure 4**. After OneNote converts the handwriting to text, you can use the Search box to find terms in the converted text or any other note in your notebooks.

Figure 4: Converting handwriting to text

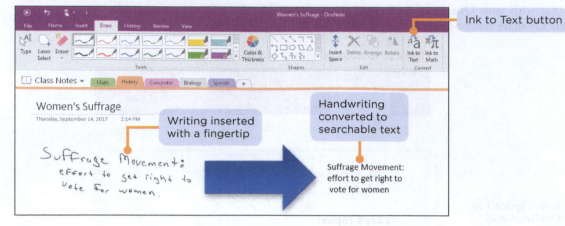

Ink to Text button

Women's Suffrage

Writing inserted with a fingertip

Handwriting converted to searchable text

Suffrage Movement: effort to get right to vote for women

On the Job Now

Use OneNote as a place to brainstorm ongoing work projects. If a notebook contains sensitive material, you can password-protect some or all of the notebook so that only certain people can open it.

Recording a Lecture

If your computer or mobile device has a microphone or camera, OneNote can record the audio or video from a lecture or business meeting as shown in **Figure 5**. When you record a lecture (with your instructor's permission), you can follow along, take regular notes at your own pace, and review the video recording later. You can control the start, pause, and stop motions of the recording when you play back the recording of your notes.

Figure 5: Video inserted in a notebook

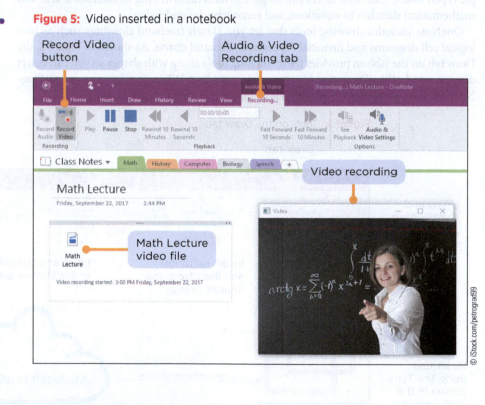

Record Video button

Audio & Video Recording tab

Video recording

Math Lecture video file

© iStock.com/petrograd99

Try This Now

Learn to use OneNote!
Links to companion **Sways**, featuring **videos** with hands-on instructions, are located on www.cengagebrain.com.

1: Taking Notes for a Week

As a student, you can get organized by using OneNote to take detailed notes in your classes. Perform the following tasks:

a. Create a new OneNote notebook on your Microsoft OneDrive account (the default location for new notebooks). Name the notebook with your first name followed by "Notes," as in **Caleb Notes**.
b. Create four section tabs, each with a different class name.
c. Take detailed notes in those classes for one week. Be sure to include notes, drawings, and other types of content.
d. Sync your notes with your OneDrive. Submit your assignment in the format specified by your instructor.

2: Using OneNote to Organize a Research Paper

You have a research paper due on the topic of three habits of successful students. Use OneNote to organize your research. Perform the following tasks:

a. Create a new OneNote notebook on your Microsoft OneDrive account. Name the notebook **Success Research**.
b. Create three section tabs with the following names:

- **Take Detailed Notes**
- **Be Respectful in Class**
- **Come to Class Prepared**

c. On the web, research the topics and find three sources for each section. Copy a sentence from each source and paste the sentence into the appropriate section. When you paste the sentence, OneNote inserts it in a note with a link to the source.
d. Sync your notes with your OneDrive. Submit your assignment in the format specified by your instructor.

3: Planning Your Career

Note: This activity requires a webcam or built-in video camera on any type of device.

Consider an occupation that interests you. Using OneNote, examine the responsibilities, education requirements, potential salary, and employment outlook of a specific career. Perform the following tasks:

a. Create a new OneNote notebook on your Microsoft OneDrive account. Name the notebook with your first name followed by a career title, such as **Kara - App Developer**.
b. Create four section tabs with the names **Responsibilities, Education Requirements, Median Salary**, and **Employment Outlook**.
c. Research the responsibilities of your career path. Using OneNote, record a short video (approximately 30 seconds) of yourself explaining the responsibilities of your career path. Place the video in the Responsibilities section.
d. On the web, research the educational requirements for your career path and find two appropriate sources. Copy a paragraph from each source and paste them into the appropriate section. When you paste a paragraph, OneNote inserts it in a note with a link to the source.
e. Research the median salary for a single year for this career. Create a mathematical equation in the Median Salary section that multiplies the amount of the median salary times 20 years to calculate how much you will possibly earn.
f. For the Employment Outlook section, research the outlook for your career path. Take at least four notes about what you find when researching the topic.
g. Sync your notes with your OneDrive. Submit your assignment in the format specified by your instructor.

Introduction to Sway

Sway site | responsive design | Storyline | card | Creative Commons license | animation emphasis effects | Docs.com

Expressing your ideas in a presentation typically means creating PowerPoint slides or a Word document. Microsoft Sway gives you another way to engage an audience. Sway is a free Microsoft tool available at Sway.com or as an app in Office 365. Using Sway, you can combine text, images, videos, and social media in a website called a **Sway site** that you can share and display on any device. To get started, you create a digital story on a web-based canvas without borders, slides, cells, or page breaks. A Sway site organizes the text, images, and video into a **responsive design**, which means your content adapts perfectly to any screen size as shown in **Figure 6**. You store a Sway site in the cloud on OneDrive using a free Microsoft account.

Figure 6: Sway site with responsive design

You can display a Sway presentation in a web browser.

Sway uses responsive design to make sure pages fit perfectly on any device.

Creating a Sway Presentation

You can use Sway to build a digital flyer, a club newsletter, a vacation blog, an informational site, a digital art portfolio, or a new product rollout. After you select your topic and sign into Sway with your Microsoft account, a **Storyline** opens, providing tools and a work area for composing your digital story. See **Figure 7**. Each story can include text, images, and videos. You create a Sway by adding text and media content into a Storyline section, or **card**. To add pictures, videos, or documents, select a card in the left pane and then select the Insert Content button. The first card in a Sway presentation contains a title and background image.

Figure 7: Creating a Sway site

Design and create Sway presentations.

Share and play published Sway sites.

Arrange content in a Storyline, which contains all the text, pictures, videos, and other media in a Sway presentation.

To add content, select a card, which is designed to hold a particular type of information.

After selecting a card, click the Insert Content button to add the content to the Sway presentation.

Adding Content to Build a Story

As you work, Sway searches the Internet to help you find relevant images, videos, tweets, and other content from online sources such as Bing, YouTube, Twitter, and Facebook. You can drag content from the search results right into the Storyline. In addition, you can upload your own images and videos directly in the presentation. For example, if you are creating a Sway presentation about the market for commercial drones, Sway suggests content to incorporate into the presentation by displaying it in the left pane as search results. The search results include drone images tagged with a **Creative Commons license** at online sources as shown in **Figure 8**. A Creative Commons license is a public copyright license that allows the free distribution of an otherwise copyrighted work. In addition, you can specify the source of the media. For example, you can add your own Facebook or OneNote pictures and videos in Sway without leaving the app.

On the Job Now

If you have a Microsoft Word document containing an outline of your business content, drag the outline into Sway to create a card for each topic.

Figure 8: Images in Sway search results

Select the source of media objects

Information about Creative Commons licenses

Storyline title

The Market for Commercial Drones

Drag an image to the picture placeholder box

Suggested images in the search results

Designing a Sway

Sway professionally designs your Storyline content by resizing background images and fonts to fit your display, and by floating text, animating media, embedding video, and removing images as a page scrolls out of view. Sway also evaluates the images in your Storyline and suggests a color palette based on colors that appear in your photos. Use the Design button to display tools including color palettes, font choices, **animation emphasis effects**, and style templates to provide a personality for a Sway presentation. Instead of creating your own design, you can click the Remix button, which randomly selects unique designs for your Sway site.

Publishing a Sway

Use the Play button to display your finished Sway presentation as a website. The Address bar includes a unique web address where others can view your Sway site. As the author, you can edit a published Sway site by clicking the Edit button (pencil icon) on the Sway toolbar.

Sharing a Sway

When you are ready to share your Sway website, you have several options as shown in **Figure 9**. Use the Share slider button to share the Sway site publically or keep it private. If you add the Sway site to the Microsoft **Docs.com** public gallery, anyone worldwide can use Bing, Google, or other search engines to find, view, and share your Sway site. You can also share your Sway site using Facebook, Twitter, Google+, Yammer, and other social media sites. Link your presentation to any webpage or email the link to your audience. Sway can also generate a code for embedding the link within another webpage.

Figure 9: Sharing a Sway site

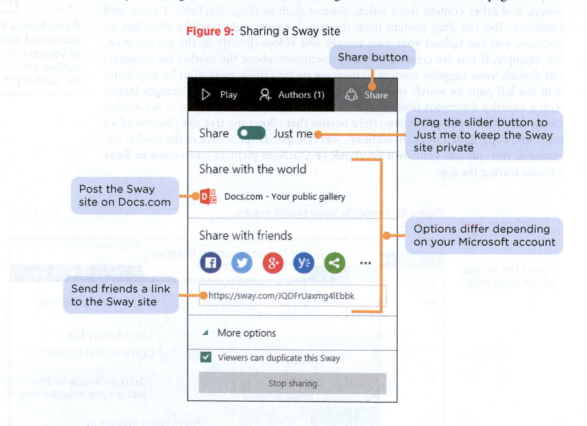

Try This Now

1: Creating a Sway Resume

Sway is a digital storytelling app. Create a Sway resume to share the skills, job experiences, and achievements you have that match the requirements of a future job interest. Perform the following tasks:

   a. Create a new presentation in Sway to use as a digital resume. Title the Sway Storyline with your full name and then select a background image.
   b. Create three separate sections titled **Academic Background, Work Experience**, and **Skills**, and insert text, a picture, and a paragraph or bulleted points in each section. Be sure to include your own picture.
   c. Add a fourth section that includes a video about your school that you find online.
   d. Customize the design of your presentation.
   e. Submit your assignment link in the format specified by your instructor.

2: Creating an Online Sway Newsletter

Newsletters are designed to capture the attention of their target audience. Using Sway, create a newsletter for a club, organization, or your favorite music group. Perform the following tasks:

   a. Create a new presentation in Sway to use as a digital newsletter for a club, organization, or your favorite music group. Provide a title for the Sway Storyline and select an appropriate background image.
   b. Select three separate sections with appropriate titles, such as Upcoming Events. In each section, insert text, a picture, and a paragraph or bulleted points.
   c. Add a fourth section that includes a video about your selected topic.
   d. Customize the design of your presentation.
   e. Submit your assignment link in the format specified by your instructor.

3: Creating and Sharing a Technology Presentation

To place a Sway presentation in the hands of your entire audience, you can share a link to the Sway presentation. Create a Sway presentation on a new technology and share it with your class. Perform the following tasks:

   a. Create a new presentation in Sway about a cutting-edge technology topic. Provide a title for the Sway Storyline and select a background image.
   b. Create four separate sections about your topic, and include text, a picture, and a paragraph in each section.
   c. Add a fifth section that includes a video about your topic.
   d. Customize the design of your presentation.
   e. Share the link to your Sway with your classmates and submit your assignment link in the format specified by your instructor.

Introduction to Office Mix

add-in | clip | slide recording | Slide Notes | screen recording | free-response quiz

To enliven business meetings and lectures, Microsoft adds a new dimension to presentations with a powerful toolset called Office Mix, a free add-in for PowerPoint. (An **add-in** is software that works with an installed app to extend its features.) Using Office Mix, you can record yourself on video, capture still and moving images on your desktop, and insert interactive elements such as quizzes and live webpages directly into PowerPoint slides. When you post the finished presentation to OneDrive, Office Mix provides a link you can share with friends and colleagues. Anyone with an Internet connection and a web browser can watch a published Office Mix presentation, such as the one in **Figure 10**, on a computer or mobile device.

Figure 10: Office Mix presentation

You can view a published Office Mix presentation in a browser on any device, even if PowerPoint is not installed.

Click to continue to the next slide.

Display a list of slides with titles.

Adding Office Mix to PowerPoint

To get started, you create an Office Mix account at the website mix.office.com using an email address or a Facebook or Google account. Next, you download and install the Office Mix add-in (see **Figure 11**). Office Mix appears as a new tab named Mix on the PowerPoint ribbon in versions of Office 2013 and Office 2016 running on personal computers (PCs).

Figure 11: Getting started with Office Mix

Download the Office Mix free add-in from mix.office.com.

Click the Get Office Mix button to download Office Mix and install it as a tab on the PowerPoint ribbon.

PowerPoint Gets Interactive

Get Office Mix ↓

Capturing Video Clips

A **clip** is a short segment of audio, such as music, or video. After finishing the content on a PowerPoint slide, you can use Office Mix to add a video clip to animate or illustrate the content. Office Mix creates video clips in two ways: by recording live action on a webcam and by capturing screen images and movements. If your computer has a webcam, you can record yourself and annotate the slide to create a **slide recording** as shown in **Figure 12**.

On the Job Now

Companies are using Office Mix to train employees about new products, to explain benefit packages to new workers, and to educate interns about office procedures.

Figure 12: Making a slide recording

Record your voice; also record video if your computer has a camera.

Use the Slide Notes button to display notes for your narration.

For best results, look directly at your webcam while recording video.

Choose a video and audio device to record images and sound.

Use inking tools to write and draw on the slide as you record.

When you are making a slide recording, you can record your spoken narration at the same time. The **Slide Notes** feature works like a teleprompter to help you focus on your presentation content instead of memorizing your narration. Use the Inking tools to make annotations or add highlighting using different pen types and colors. After finishing a recording, edit the video in PowerPoint to trim the length or set playback options.

The second way to create a video is to capture on-screen images and actions with or without a voiceover. This method is ideal if you want to show how to use your favorite website or demonstrate an app such as OneNote. To share your screen with an audience, select the part of the screen you want to show in the video. Office Mix captures everything that happens in that area to create a **screen recording**, as shown in **Figure 13**. Office Mix inserts the screen recording as a video in the slide.

On the Job Now

To make your video recordings accessible to people with hearing impairments, use the Office Mix closed-captioning tools. You can also use closed captions to supplement audio that is difficult to understand and to provide an aid for those learning to read.

Figure 13: Making a screen recording

Record the action on the screen within the red dashed outline.

Record audio while capturing your on-screen actions.

Select Area button

Inserting Quizzes, Live Webpages, and Apps

To enhance and assess audience understanding, make your slides interactive by adding quizzes, live webpages, and apps. Quizzes give immediate feedback to the user as shown in **Figure 14**. Office Mix supports several quiz formats, including a **free-response quiz** similar to a short answer quiz, and true/false, multiple-choice, and multiple-response formats.

Figure 14: Creating an interactive quiz

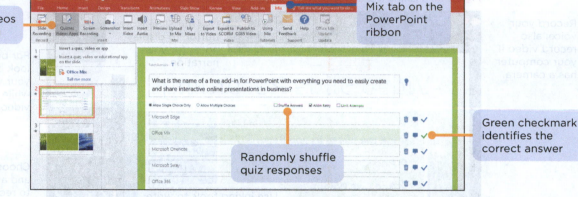

Sharing an Office Mix Presentation

When you complete your work with Office Mix, upload the presentation to your personal Office Mix dashboard as shown in **Figure 15**. Users of PCs, Macs, iOS devices, and Android devices can access and play Office Mix presentations. The Office Mix dashboard displays built-in analytics that include the quiz results and how much time viewers spent on each slide. You can play completed Office Mix presentations online or download them as movies.

Figure 15: Sharing an Office Mix presentation

Try This Now

Learn to use Office Mix!
Links to companion **Sways**, featuring **videos** with hands-on instructions, are located on www.cengagebrain.com.

1: Creating an Office Mix Tutorial for OneNote

Note: This activity requires a microphone on your computer.

Office Mix makes it easy to record screens and their contents. Create PowerPoint slides with an Office Mix screen recording to show OneNote 2016 features. Perform the following tasks:

a. Create a PowerPoint presentation with the Ion Boardroom template. Create an opening slide with the title **My Favorite OneNote Features** and enter your name in the subtitle.
b. Create three additional slides, each titled with a new feature of OneNote. Open OneNote and use the Mix tab in PowerPoint to capture three separate screen recordings that teach your favorite features.
c. Add a fifth slide that quizzes the user with a multiple-choice question about OneNote and includes four responses. Be sure to insert a checkmark indicating the correct response.
d. Upload the completed presentation to your Office Mix dashboard and share the link with your instructor.
e. Submit your assignment link in the format specified by your instructor.

2: Teaching Augmented Reality with Office Mix

Note: This activity requires a webcam or built-in video camera on your computer.

A local elementary school has asked you to teach augmented reality to its students using Office Mix. Perform the following tasks:

a. Research augmented reality using your favorite online search tools.
b. Create a PowerPoint presentation with the Frame template. Create an opening slide with the title **Augmented Reality** and enter your name in the subtitle.
c. Create a slide with four bullets summarizing your research of augmented reality. Create a 20-second slide recording of yourself providing a quick overview of augmented reality.
d. Create another slide with a 30-second screen recording of a video about augmented reality from a site such as YouTube or another video-sharing site.
e. Add a final slide that quizzes the user with a true/false question about augmented reality. Be sure to insert a checkmark indicating the correct response.
f. Upload the completed presentation to your Office Mix dashboard and share the link with your instructor.
g. Submit your assignment link in the format specified by your instructor.

3: Marketing a Travel Destination with Office Mix

Note: This activity requires a webcam or built-in video camera on your computer.

To convince your audience to travel to a particular city, create a slide presentation marketing any city in the world using a slide recording, screen recording, and a quiz. Perform the following tasks:

a. Create a PowerPoint presentation with any template. Create an opening slide with the title of the city you are marketing as a travel destination and your name in the subtitle.
b. Create a slide with four bullets about the featured city. Create a 30-second slide recording of yourself explaining why this city is the perfect vacation destination.
c. Create another slide with a 20-second screen recording of a travel video about the city from a site such as YouTube or another video-sharing site.
d. Add a final slide that quizzes the user with a multiple-choice question about the featured city with five responses. Be sure to include a checkmark indicating the correct response.
e. Upload the completed presentation to your Office Mix dashboard and share your link with your instructor.
f. Submit your assignment link in the format specified by your instructor.

Introduction to Microsoft Edge

Reading view | Hub | Cortana | Web Note | Inking | sandbox

Microsoft Edge is the default web browser developed for the Windows 10 operating system as a replacement for Internet Explorer. Unlike its predecessor, Edge lets you write on webpages, read webpages without advertisements and other distractions, and search for information using a virtual personal assistant. The Edge interface is clean and basic, as shown in **Figure 16**, meaning you can pay more attention to the webpage content.

Figure 16: Microsoft Edge tools

Forward button | New tab button | Web address in the Address bar | Add to favorites or reading list button | Back button | Reading view button | More button | Refresh (F5) button | Hub (Favorites, reading list, history, and downloads) button | Share Web Note button | Make a Web Note button

Browsing the Web with Microsoft Edge

One of the fastest browsers available, Edge allows you to type search text directly in the Address bar. As you view the resulting webpage, you can switch to **Reading view**, which is available for most news and research sites, to eliminate distracting advertisements. For example, if you are catching up on technology news online, the webpage might be difficult to read due to a busy layout cluttered with ads. Switch to Reading view to refresh the page and remove the original page formatting, ads, and menu sidebars to read the article distraction-free.

Consider the **Hub** in Microsoft Edge as providing one-stop access to all the things you collect on the web, such as your favorite websites, reading list, surfing history, and downloaded files.

Locating Information with Cortana

Cortana, the Windows 10 virtual assistant, plays an important role in Microsoft Edge. After you turn on Cortana, it appears as an animated circle in the Address bar when you might need assistance, as shown in the restaurant website in **Figure 17**. When you click the Cortana icon, a pane slides in from the right of the browser window to display detailed information about the restaurant, including maps and reviews. Cortana can also assist you in defining words, finding the weather, suggesting coupons for shopping, updating stock market information, and calculating math.

On the Job Now

Businesses started adopting Internet Explorer more than 20 years ago simply to view webpages. Today, Microsoft Edge has a different purpose: to promote interaction with the web and share its contents with colleagues.

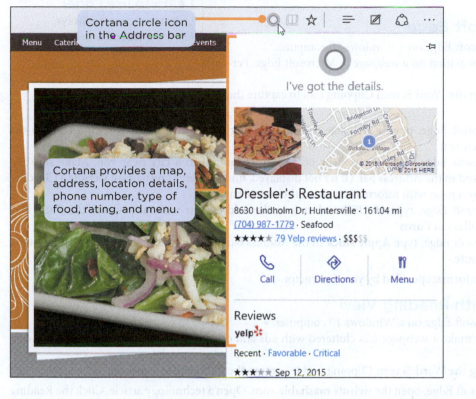

Cortana circle icon in the Address bar

I've got the details.

Cortana provides a map, address, location details, phone number, type of food, rating, and menu.

Dressler's Restaurant

8630 Lindholm Dr, Huntersville · 161.04 mi

(704) 987-1779 · Seafood

★★★★☆ 79 Yelp reviews · $$$$$

📞 Call   ◈ Directions   🍴 Menu

Reviews

yelp

Recent · Favorable · Critical

★★★☆☆ Sep 12, 2015

Annotating Webpages

One of the most impressive Microsoft Edge features are the **Web Note** tools, which you use to write on a webpage or to highlight text. When you click the Make a Web Note button, an **Inking** toolbar appears, as shown in **Figure 18**, that provides writing and drawing tools. These tools include an eraser, a pen, and a highlighter with different colors. You can also insert a typed note and copy a screen image (called a screen clipping). You can draw with a pointing device, fingertip, or stylus using different pen colors. Whether you add notes to a recipe, annotate sources for a research paper, or select a product while shopping online, the Web Note tools can enhance your productivity. After you complete your notes, click the Save button to save the annotations to OneNote, your Favorites list, or your Reading list. You can share the inked page with others using the Share Web Note button.

On the Job Now

To enhance security, Microsoft Edge runs in a partial sandbox, an arrangement that prevents attackers from gaining control of your computer. Browsing within the **sandbox** protects computer resources and information from hackers.

Figure 18: Web Note tools in Microsoft Edge

Inking toolbar with Web Note tools for making annotations

Writing and drawing created with the Pen tool

Highlighted text

Save a copy of the webpage with annotations

Typed note

Try This Now

1: Using Cortana in Microsoft Edge

Learn to use Edge!
Links to companion **Sways**, featuring **videos** with hands-on instructions, are located on www.cengagebrain.com.

Note: This activity requires using Microsoft Edge on a Windows 10 computer.

Cortana can assist you in finding information on a webpage in Microsoft Edge. Perform the following tasks:

a. Create a Word document using the Word Screen Clipping tool to capture the following screenshots.

- Screenshot A—Using Microsoft Edge, open a webpage with a technology news article. Right-click a term in the article and ask Cortana to define it.
- Screenshot B—Using Microsoft Edge, open the website of a fancy restaurant in a city near you. Make sure the Cortana circle icon is displayed in the Address bar. (If it's not displayed, find a different restaurant website.) Click the Cortana circle icon to display a pane with information about the restaurant.
- Screenshot C—Using Microsoft Edge, type **10 USD to Euros** in the Address bar without pressing the Enter key. Cortana converts the U.S. dollars to Euros.
- Screenshot D—Using Microsoft Edge, type **Apple stock** in the Address bar without pressing the Enter key. Cortana displays the current stock quote.

b. Submit your assignment in the format specified by your instructor.

2: Viewing Online News with Reading View

Note: This activity requires using Microsoft Edge on a Windows 10 computer.

Reading view in Microsoft Edge can make a webpage less cluttered with ads and other distractions. Perform the following tasks:

a. Create a Word document using the Word Screen Clipping tool to capture the following screenshots.

- Screenshot A—Using Microsoft Edge, open the website **mashable.com**. Open a technology article. Click the Reading view button to display an ad-free page that uses only basic text formatting.
- Screenshot B—Using Microsoft Edge, open the website **bbc.com**. Open any news article. Click the Reading view button to display an ad-free page that uses only basic text formatting.
- Screenshot C—Make three types of annotations (Pen, Highlighter, and Add a typed note) on the BBC article page displayed in Reading view.

b. Submit your assignment in the format specified by your instructor.

3: Inking with Microsoft Edge

Note: This activity requires using Microsoft Edge on a Windows 10 computer.

Microsoft Edge provides many annotation options to record your ideas. Perform the following tasks:

a. Open the website **wolframalpha.com** in the Microsoft Edge browser. Wolfram Alpha is a well-respected academic search engine. Type **US$100 1965 dollars in 2015** in the Wolfram Alpha search text box and press the Enter key.
b. Click the Make a Web Note button to display the Web Note tools. Using the Pen tool, draw a circle around the result on the webpage. Save the page to OneNote.
c. In the Wolfram Alpha search text box, type the name of the city closest to where you live and press the Enter key. Using the Highlighter tool, highlight at least three interesting results. Add a note and then type a sentence about what you learned about this city. Save the page to OneNote. Share your OneNote notebook with your instructor.
d. Submit your assignment link in the format specified by your instructor.

Office 2016 and Windows 10: Essential Concepts and Skills

Objectives

You will have mastered the material in this module when you can:

- Use a touch screen
- Perform basic mouse operations
- Start Windows and sign in to an account
- Identify the objects on the Windows 10 desktop
- Identify the apps in and versions of Microsoft Office 2016
- Run an app
- Identify the components of the Microsoft Office ribbon

- Create folders
- Save files
- Change screen resolution
- Perform basic tasks in Microsoft Office apps
- Manage files
- Use Microsoft Office Help and Windows Help

This introductory module uses PowerPoint 2016 to cover features and functions common to Office 2016 apps, as well as the basics of Windows 10.

Roadmap

In this module, you will learn how to perform basic tasks in Windows and PowerPoint. The following roadmap identifies general activities you will perform as you progress through this module:

1. SIGN IN to an account.
2. USE WINDOWS.
3. USE features in PowerPoint that are common across Office APPS.
4. FILE and folder MANAGEMENT.
5. SWITCH between APPS.
6. SAVE and manage FILES.

7. **CHANGE SCREEN RESOLUTION**.

8. **EXIT APPS**.

9. **USE ADDITIONAL** Office **APP FEATURES**.

10. **USE** Office and Windows **HELP**.

At the beginning of the step instructions throughout each module, you will see an abbreviated form of this roadmap. The abbreviated roadmap uses colors to indicate module progress: gray means the module is beyond that activity, blue means the task being shown is covered in that activity, and black means that activity is yet to be covered. For example, the following abbreviated roadmap indicates the module would be showing a task in the USE APPS activity.

1 SIGN IN | 2 USE WINDOWS | **3 USE APPS** | **4 FILE MANAGEMENT** | **5 SWITCH APPS** | **6 SAVE FILES**

7 CHANGE SCREEN RESOLUTION | **8 EXIT APPS** | **9 USE ADDITIONAL APP FEATURES** | **10 USE HELP**

Use the abbreviated roadmap as a progress guide while you read or step through the instructions in this module.

Introduction to the Windows 10 Operating System

Windows 10 is the newest version of Microsoft Windows, which is a popular and widely used operating system (Figure 1). An **operating system (OS)** is a set of programs that coordinate all the activities among computer or mobile device hardware.

Figure 1

The Windows operating system simplifies the process of working with documents and apps by organizing the manner in which you interact with the computer. Windows is used to run apps. An application, or **app**, consists of programs designed to make users more productive and/or assist them with personal tasks, such as creating presentations or browsing the web.

Using a Touch Screen and a Mouse

Windows users who have computers or devices with touch screen capability can interact with the screen using gestures. A **gesture** is a motion you make on a touch screen with the tip of one or more fingers or your hand. Touch screens are convenient because they do not require a separate device for input. Table 1 presents common ways to interact with a touch screen.

If you are using your finger on a touch screen and are having difficulty completing the steps in this module, consider using a stylus. Many people find it easier to be precise with a stylus than with a finger. In addition, with a stylus you see the pointer. If you still are having trouble completing the steps with a stylus, try using a mouse.

Table 1 Touch Screen Gestures

Motion	Description	Common Uses	Equivalent Mouse Operation
Tap	Quickly touch and release one finger one time.	Activate a link (built-in connection). Press a button. Run a program or an app.	Click
Double-tap	Quickly touch and release one finger two times.	Run a program or an app. Zoom in (show a smaller area on the screen, so that contents appear larger) at the location of the double-tap.	Double-click
Press and hold	Press and hold one finger to cause an action to occur, or until an action occurs.	Display a shortcut menu (immediate access to allowable actions). Activate a mode enabling you to move an item with one finger to a new location.	Right-click
Drag, or slide	Press and hold one finger on an object and then move the finger to the new location.	Move an item around the screen. Scroll.	Drag
Swipe	Press and hold one finger and then move the finger horizontally or vertically on the screen.	Select an object. Swipe from edge to display a bar such as the Action Center, Apps bar, and Navigation bar (all discussed later).	Drag
Stretch	Move two fingers apart.	Zoom in (show a smaller area on the screen, so that contents appear larger).	None
Pinch	Move two fingers together.	Zoom out (show a larger area on the screen, so that contents appear smaller).	None

Will the screen look different if you are using a touch screen?

The Windows and Microsoft Office interface varies slightly if you are using a touch screen. For this reason, you might notice that your Windows or PowerPoint screens looks slightly different from the screens in this book.

CONSIDER THIS

BTW
Pointer
If you are using a touch screen, the pointer may not appear on the screen as you perform touch gestures. The pointer will reappear when you begin using the mouse.

Windows users who do not have touch screen capabilities typically work with a mouse that has at least two buttons. For a right-handed user, the left button usually is the primary mouse button, and the right mouse button is the secondary mouse button. Left-handed people, however, can reverse the function of these buttons.

Table 2 explains how to perform a variety of mouse operations. Some apps also use keys in combination with the mouse to perform certain actions. For example, when you hold down the CTRL key while rolling the mouse wheel, text on the screen may become larger or smaller based on the direction you roll the wheel. The function of the mouse buttons and the wheel varies depending on the app.

Table 2	Mouse Operations		
Operation	**Mouse Action**	**Example***	**Equivalent Touch Gesture**
Point	Move the mouse until the pointer on the desktop is positioned on the item of choice.	Position the pointer on the screen.	None
Click	Press and release the primary mouse button, which usually is the left mouse button.	Select or deselect items on the screen or run an app or app feature.	Tap
Right-click	Press and release the secondary mouse button, which usually is the right mouse button.	Display a shortcut menu.	Press and hold
Double-click	Quickly press and release the primary mouse button twice without moving the mouse.	Run an app or app feature.	Double-tap
Triple-click	Quickly press and release the primary mouse button three times without moving the mouse.	Select a paragraph.	Triple-tap
Drag	Point to an item, hold down the primary mouse button, move the item to the desired location on the screen, and then release the mouse button.	Move an object from one location to another or draw pictures.	Drag or slide
Right-drag	Point to an item, hold down the right mouse button, move the item to the desired location on the screen, and then release the right mouse button.	Display a shortcut menu after moving an object from one location to another.	Press and hold, then drag
Rotate wheel	Roll the wheel forward or backward.	Scroll vertically (up and down).	Swipe
Free-spin wheel	Whirl the wheel forward or backward so that it spins freely on its own.	Scroll through many pages in seconds.	Swipe
Press wheel	Press the wheel button while moving the mouse.	Scroll continuously.	None
Tilt wheel	Press the wheel toward the right or left.	Scroll horizontally (left and right).	None
Press thumb button	Press the button on the side of the mouse with your thumb.	Move forward or backward through webpages and/or control media, games, etc.	None

*Note: The examples presented in this column are discussed as they are demonstrated in this module.

Scrolling

A **scroll bar** is a horizontal or vertical bar that appears when the contents of an area may not be visible completely on the screen (Figure 2). A scroll bar contains **scroll arrows** and a **scroll box** that enable you to view areas that currently cannot be seen on the screen. Clicking the up and down scroll arrows moves the screen content up or down one line. You also can click above or below the scroll box to move up or down a section, or drag the scroll box up or down to move to a specific location.

Figure 2

Keyboard Shortcuts

In many cases, you can use the keyboard instead of the mouse to accomplish a task. To perform tasks using the keyboard, you press one or more keyboard keys, sometimes identified as a **keyboard shortcut**. Some keyboard shortcuts consist of a single key, such as the F1 key. For example, to obtain help in many apps, you can press the F1 key. Other keyboard shortcuts consist of multiple keys, in which case a plus sign separates the key names, such as CTRL+ESC. This notation means to press and hold down the first key listed, press one or more additional keys, and then release all keys. For example, to display the Start menu, press CTRL+ESC, that is, hold down the CTRL key, press the ESC key, and then release both keys.

Starting Windows

It is not unusual for multiple people to use the same computer in a work, educational, recreational, or home setting. Windows enables each user to establish a **user account**, which identifies to Windows the resources, such as apps and storage locations, a user can access when working with the computer.

Each user account has a user name and may have a password and an icon, as well. A **user name** is a unique combination of letters or numbers that identifies a specific user to Windows. A **password** is a private combination of letters, numbers, and special characters associated with the user name that allows access to a user's account resources. An icon is a small image that represents an object; thus, a **user icon** is a picture associated with a user name.

When you turn on a computer, Windows starts and displays a **lock screen** consisting of the time and date (Figure 3). To unlock the screen, click the lock screen. Depending on your computer's settings, Windows may or may not display a sign-in screen that shows the user names and user icons for users who have accounts on the computer. This **sign-in screen** enables you to sign in to your user account and makes the computer available for use. Clicking the user icon begins the process of signing in, also called logging on, to your user account.

BTW

Minimize Wrist Injury

Computer users frequently switch between the keyboard and the mouse when developing PowerPoint slides; such switching strains the wrist. To help prevent wrist injury, minimize switching. For instance, if your fingers already are on the keyboard, use keyboard keys to scroll. If your hand already is on the mouse, use the mouse to scroll. If your hand is on the touch screen, use touch gestures to scroll.

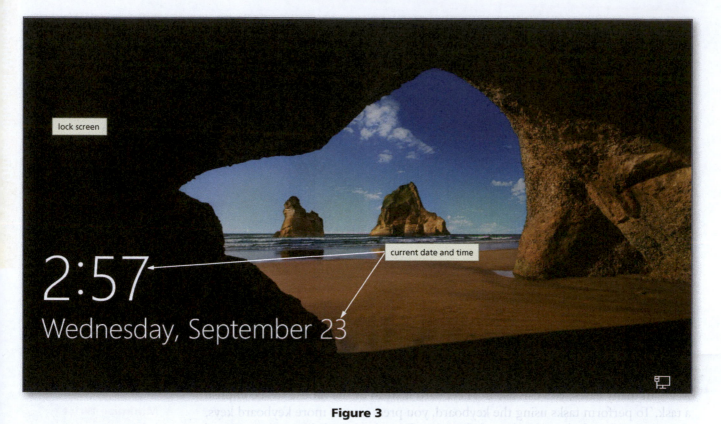

Figure 3

At the bottom of the sign-in screen is the 'Connect to Internet' button, 'Ease of access' button, and a Shut down button. Clicking the 'Connect to Internet' button displays a list of each network connection and its status. You also can connect to or disconnect from a network. Clicking the 'Ease of access' button displays the Ease of access menu, which provides tools to optimize a computer to accommodate the needs of mobility, hearing, and vision impaired users. Clicking the Shut down button displays a menu containing commands related to putting the computer or mobile device in a low-power state, shutting it down, and restarting the computer or mobile device. The commands available on your computer or mobile device may differ.

- The Sleep command saves your work, turns off the computer fans and hard drive, and places the computer in a lower-power state. To wake the computer from sleep mode, press the power button or lift a laptop's cover, and sign in to your account.
- The Shut down command exits running apps, shuts down Windows, and then turns off the computer.
- The Restart command exits running apps, shuts down Windows, and then restarts Windows.

To Sign In to an Account

1 SIGN IN | 2 USE WINDOWS | 3 USE APPS | 4 FILE MANAGEMENT | 5 SWITCH APPS | 6 SAVE FILES
7 CHANGE SCREEN RESOLUTION | 8 EXIT APPS | 9 USE ADDITIONAL APP FEATURES | 10 USE HELP

The following steps, which use SCSeries as the user name, sign in to an account based on a typical Windows installation. **Why?** *After starting Windows, you might be required to sign in to an account to access the computer or mobile device's resources.* You may need to ask your instructor how to sign in to your account.

①

- Click the lock screen (shown in Figure 3) to display a sign-in screen.
- Click the user icon (for SCSeries, in this case) on the sign-in screen, which depending on settings, either will display a second sign-in screen that contains a Password text box (Figure 4) or will display the Windows desktop (Figure 5).

Figure 4

Q&A Why do I not see a user icon?
Your computer may require you to type a user name instead of clicking an icon.

What is a text box?
A text box is a rectangular box in which you type text.

Why does my screen not show a Password text box?
Your account does not require a password.

- If Windows displays a sign-in screen with a Password text box, type your password in the text box.

②

- Click the Submit button (shown in Figure 4) to sign in to your account and display the Windows desktop (Figure 5).

Q&A Why does my desktop look different from the one in Figure 5?
The Windows desktop is customizable, and your school or employer may have modified the desktop to meet its needs. Also, your screen resolution, which affects the size of the elements on the screen, may differ from the screen resolution used in this book. Later in this module, you learn how to change screen resolution.

How do I type if my tablet has no keyboard?
You can use your fingers to press keys on a keyboard that appears on the screen, called an on-screen keyboard, or you can purchase a separate physical keyboard that attaches to or wirelessly communicates with the tablet.

Figure 5

The Windows Desktop

The Windows 10 desktop (shown in Figure 5) and the objects on the desktop emulate a work area in an office. Think of the Windows desktop as an electronic version of the top of your desk. You can perform tasks such as placing objects on the desktop, moving the objects around the desktop, and removing items from the desktop.

When you run an app in Windows 10, it appears on the desktop. Some icons also may be displayed on the desktop. For instance, the icon for the **Recycle Bin**, the location of files that have been deleted, appears on the desktop by default. A **file** is a named unit of storage. Files can contain text, images, audio, and video. You can customize your desktop so that icons representing programs and files you use often appear on your desktop.

Introduction to Microsoft Office 2016

Microsoft Office 2016 is the newest version of Microsoft Office, offering features that provide users with better functionality and easier ways to work with the various files they create. This version of Office also is designed to work more optimally on mobile devices and online.

Microsoft Office 2016 Apps

Microsoft Office 2016 includes a wide variety of apps, such as Word, PowerPoint, Excel, Access, Outlook, Publisher, and OneNote:

- **Microsoft Word 2016**, or Word, is a full-featured word processing app that allows you to create professional-looking documents and revise them easily.

- **Microsoft PowerPoint 2016**, or PowerPoint, is a complete presentation app that enables you to produce professional-looking presentations and then deliver them to an audience.

- **Microsoft Excel 2016**, or Excel, is a powerful spreadsheet app that allows you to organize data, complete calculations, make decisions, graph data, develop professional-looking reports, publish organized data to the web, and access real-time data from websites.

- **Microsoft Access 2016**, or Access, is a database management system that enables you to create a database; add, change, and delete data in the database; ask questions concerning the data in the database; and create forms and reports using the data in the database.

- **Microsoft Outlook 2016**, or Outlook, is a communications and scheduling app that allows you to manage email accounts, calendars, contacts, and access to other Internet content.

- **Microsoft Publisher 2016**, or Publisher, is a desktop publishing app that helps you create professional-quality publications and marketing materials that can be shared easily.

- **Microsoft OneNote 2016**, or OneNote, is a note taking app that allows you to store and share information in notebooks with other people.

Microsoft Office 2016 Suites

A **suite** is a collection of individual apps available together as a unit. Microsoft offers a variety of Office suites, including a stand-alone desktop app, Microsoft Office 365, and Microsoft Office Online. **Microsoft Office 365**, or Office 365, provides plans that allow organizations to use Office in a mobile setting while also being able to communicate and share files, depending upon the type of plan selected by the organization. **Microsoft Office Online** includes apps that allow you to edit and share files on the web using the familiar Office interface.

During the Office 365 installation, you select a plan, and depending on your plan, you receive different apps and services. Office Online apps do not require a local installation and can be accessed through OneDrive and your browser. **OneDrive** is a cloud storage service that provides storage and other services, such as Office Online, to computer and mobile device users.

CONSIDER THIS

How do you sign up for a OneDrive account?

- Use your browser to navigate to onedrive.live.com.
- Create a Microsoft account by clicking the Sign up button and then entering your information to create the account.
- Sign in to OneDrive using your new account or use it in PowerPoint to save your files on OneDrive.

Apps in a suite, such as Microsoft Office, typically use a similar interface and share features. Once you are comfortable working with the elements and the interface and performing tasks in one app, the similarity can help you apply the knowledge and skills you have learned to another app(s) in the suite. For example, the process for saving a file in PowerPoint is the same in Word, Excel, and some of the other Office apps. While briefly showing how to use PowerPoint, this module illustrates some of the common functions across the Office apps and identifies the characteristics unique to PowerPoint.

Running and Using an App

To use an app, you must instruct the operating system to run the app. Windows provides many different ways to run an app, one of which is presented in this section (other ways to run an app are presented throughout this module). After an app is running, you can use it to perform a variety of tasks. The following pages use PowerPoint to discuss some elements of the Office interface and to perform tasks that are common to other Office apps.

PowerPoint

PowerPoint is a full-featured presentation app that allows you to produce compelling presentations to deliver and share with an audience. A PowerPoint **presentation** also is called a **slide show**. PowerPoint contains many features to design, develop, and organize slides, including formatting text, adding and editing video and audio clips, creating tables and charts, applying artistic effects to pictures, animating graphics, and collaborating with friends and colleagues. You then can turn your presentation into a video, broadcast your slide show on the web, or create a photo album.

To Run an App Using the Start Menu and Create a Blank Presentation

1 SIGN IN | **2 USE WINDOWS** | 3 USE APPS | 4 FILE MANAGEMENT | 5 SWITCH APPS | 6 SAVE FILES | 7 CHANGE SCREEN RESOLUTION | 8 EXIT APPS | 9 USE ADDITIONAL APP FEATURES | 10 USE HELP

Across the bottom of the Windows 10 desktop is the taskbar. The taskbar contains the **Start button**, which you use to access apps, files, folders, and settings. A **folder** is a named location on a storage medium that usually contains related documents.

Clicking the Start button displays the Start menu. The **Start menu** allows you to access programs, folders, and files on the computer or mobile device and contains commands that allow you to start programs, store and search for documents, customize the computer or mobile device, and sign out of a user account or shut down the computer or mobile device. A **menu** is a list of related items, including folders, programs, and commands. Each **command** on a menu performs a specific action, such as saving a file or obtaining help. *Why? When you install an app, for example, the app's name will be added to the All apps list on the Start menu.*

The following steps, which assume Windows is running, use the Start menu to run PowerPoint and create a blank presentation based on a typical installation. You may need to ask your instructor how to run PowerPoint on your computer. Although the steps illustrate running the PowerPoint app, the steps to run any Office app are similar.

1
- Click the Start button on the Windows 10 taskbar to display the Start menu (Figure 6).

Figure 6

2
- Click All apps at the bottom of the left pane of the Start menu to display a list of apps installed on the computer or mobile device. If necessary, scroll to display the app you wish to run, PowerPoint 2016, in this case (Figure 7).

Figure 7

3
- If the app you wish to run is located in a folder, click or scroll to and then click the folder in the All apps list to display a list of the folder's contents.
- Click, or scroll to and then click the app name (PowerPoint 2016, in this case) in the list to run the selected app (Figure 8).

Figure 8

4

- Click the Blank Presentation thumbnail on the PowerPoint start screen to create a blank PowerPoint presentation in the PowerPoint window (Figure 9).

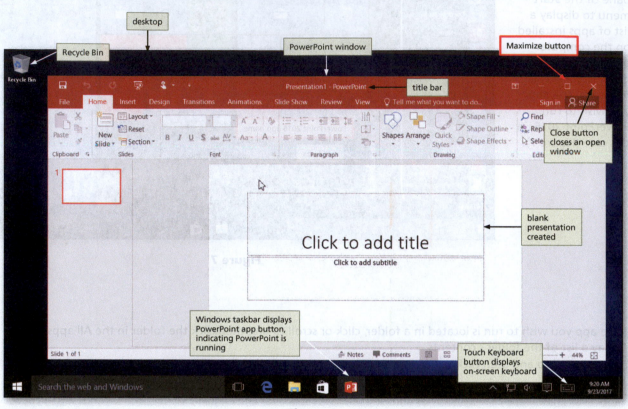

Figure 9

Q&A What happens when you run an app?

Some apps provide a means for you to create a blank presentation or document, as shown in Figure 8; others immediately display a blank presentation or document in an app window, such as the PowerPoint window shown in Figure 9. A **window** is a rectangular area that displays data and information. The top of a window has a **title bar**, which is a horizontal space that contains the window's name.

Other Ways

1. Type app name in search box, click app name in results list
2. Double-click file created in app you want to run

To Maximize a Window

1 SIGN IN | 2 USE WINDOWS | 3 USE APPS | 4 FILE MANAGEMENT | 5 SWITCH APPS | 6 SAVE FILES
7 CHANGE SCREEN RESOLUTION | 8 EXIT APPS | 9 USE ADDITIONAL APP FEATURES | 10 USE HELP

Sometimes content is not visible completely in a window. One method of displaying the entire contents of a window is to **maximize** it, or enlarge the window so that it fills the entire screen. The following step maximizes the PowerPoint window; however, any Office app's window can be maximized using this step. *Why?* *A maximized window provides the most space available for using the app.*

1

- If the PowerPoint window is not maximized already, click the Maximize button (shown in Figure 9) next to the Close button on the PowerPoint window's title bar to maximize the window (Figure 10).

Q&A What happened to the Maximize button?

It changed to a Restore Down button, which you can use to return a window to its size and location before you maximized it.

How do I know whether a window is maximized?
A window is maximized if it fills the entire display area and the Restore Down button is displayed on the title bar.

Figure 10

Other Ways

1. Double-click title bar   2. Drag title bar to top of screen

PowerPoint Window, Ribbon, and Elements Common to Office Apps

The PowerPoint window consists of a variety of components to make your work more efficient and presentations more professional: the window, ribbon, Tell Me box, mini toolbar, shortcut menus, Quick Access Toolbar, and Microsoft Account area. Most of these components are common to other Office apps and have been discussed earlier in this module. Other components, discussed in the following paragraphs and later in subsequent modules, are unique to PowerPoint.

The basic unit of a PowerPoint presentation is a **slide**. A slide may contain text and objects, such as graphics, tables, charts, and drawings. When you create a new presentation, the default **Title Slide** layout appears (shown in Figure 11). PowerPoint includes several other built-in standard layouts. All layouts except the Blank slide layout contain placeholders for text or other content such as pictures, charts, or videos. The title slide in Figure 11 has two text placeholders for the main heading, or title, and the subtitle.

Scroll Bars   You use a scroll bar to display different portions of a presentation in the document window. At the right edge of the document window is a vertical scroll bar. If a slide is too wide to fit in the document window, a horizontal scroll bar also appears at the bottom of the document window. On a scroll bar, the position of the scroll box reflects the location of the portion of the slide that is displayed in the document window.

Status Bar   The **status bar**, located at the bottom of the document window above the Windows taskbar, presents information about the presentation, the progress of current tasks, and the status of certain commands and keys; it also provides controls for viewing the presentation. As you type text or perform certain tasks, various indicators and buttons may appear on the status bar.

The left side of the status bar in Figure 11 shows the current slide number followed by the total number of slides in the presentation. The right side of the status bar includes buttons and controls you can use to change the view of a slide and adjust the size of the displayed slide.

BTW

Touch Keyboard
To display the on-screen touch keyboard, click the Touch Keyboard button on the Windows taskbar (shown in Figure 9). When finished using the touch keyboard, click the X button on the touch keyboard to close the keyboard.

Figure 11

Roland Seifert/Unsplash

Ribbon The ribbon, located near the top of the window below the title bar, is the control center in PowerPoint and other Office apps (Figure 12). The ribbon provides easy, central access to the tasks you perform while creating a presentation. The ribbon consists of tabs, groups, and commands. Each **tab** contains a collection of groups, and each **group** contains related commands. When you run an Office app, such as PowerPoint, it initially displays several main tabs, also called default or top-level tabs. All Office apps have a Home tab, which contains the more frequently used commands.

In addition to the main tabs, the Office apps display **tool tabs**, also called contextual tabs (Figure 13), when you perform certain tasks or work with objects such as pictures or tables. If you insert a picture in a PowerPoint presentation for example, the Picture Tools tab and its related subordinate Format tab appear, collectively referred to as the Picture Tools Format tab. When you are finished working with the picture, the Picture Tools Format tab disappears from the ribbon. PowerPoint and other Office apps determine when tool tabs should appear and disappear based on tasks you perform. Some tool tabs, such as the Table Tools tab, have more than one related subordinate tab.

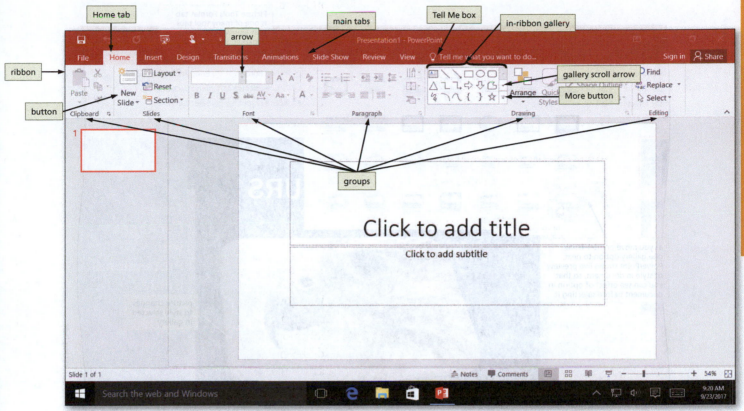

Figure 12

Figure 13

Items on the ribbon include buttons, boxes, and galleries (shown in Figure 12). A **gallery** is a set of choices, often graphical, arranged in a grid or in a list. You can scroll through choices in an in-ribbon gallery by clicking the gallery's scroll arrows. Or, you can click a gallery's More button to view more gallery options on the screen at a time.

Some buttons and boxes have arrows that, when clicked, also display a gallery; others always cause a gallery to be displayed when clicked. Most galleries support **live preview**, which is a feature that allows you to point to a gallery choice and see its effect in the presentation — without actually selecting the choice (Figure 14). Live preview works only if you are using a mouse; if you are using a touch screen, you will not be able to view live previews.

Figure 14

Some commands on the ribbon display an image to help you remember their function. When you point to a command on the ribbon, all or part of the command glows in a shade of gray, and a ScreenTip appears on the screen. A **ScreenTip** is an on-screen note that provides the name of the command, available keyboard shortcut(s), a description of the command, and sometimes instructions for how to obtain help about the command (Figure 15).

Figure 15

Some groups on the ribbon have a small arrow in the lower-right corner, called a **Dialog Box Launcher**, that when clicked, displays a dialog box or a task pane with additional options for the group (Figure 16). When presented with a dialog box, you make selections and must close the dialog box before returning to the presentation. A **task pane**, in contrast to a dialog box, is a window that can remain open and visible while you work in the presentation.

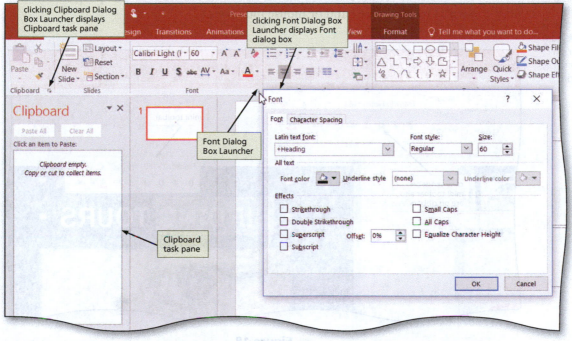

Figure 16

Tell Me Box   The **Tell Me box**, which appears to the right of the tabs on the ribbon, is a type of search box that helps you to perform specific tasks in an Office app (Figure 17). As you type in the Tell Me, the word-wheeling feature displays search results that are refined as you type. For example, if you want to center text in a slide, you can type "center" in the Tell Me box and then select the appropriate command. The Tell Me box also lists the last five commands accessed from the box.

Figure 17

Mini Toolbar   The **mini toolbar**, which appears automatically based on tasks you perform, contains commands related to changing the appearance of text in a presentation (Figure 18). If you do not use the mini toolbar, it disappears from the screen. The buttons, arrows, and boxes on the mini toolbar vary, depending on whether you are using Touch mode versus Mouse mode. If you right-click an item in the document window, PowerPoint displays both the mini toolbar and a shortcut menu, which is discussed in a later section in this module.

All commands on the mini toolbar also exist on the ribbon. The purpose of the mini toolbar is to minimize hand or mouse movement.

Roland Seifert/Unsplash

Figure 18

Quick Access Toolbar   The **Quick Access Toolbar**, located initially (by default) above the ribbon at the left edge of the title bar, provides convenient, one-click access to frequently used commands (shown in Figure 15). The commands on the Quick Access Toolbar always are available, regardless of the task you are performing. The Touch/Mouse Mode button on the Quick Access Toolbar allows you to switch between Touch mode and Mouse mode. If you primarily are using touch gestures, Touch mode will add more space between commands on menus and on the ribbon so that they are easier to tap. While touch gestures are convenient ways to interact with Office apps, not all features are supported when you are using Touch mode. If you are using a mouse, Mouse mode will not add the extra space between buttons and commands. The Quick Access Toolbar is discussed in more depth later in the module.

KeyTips   If you prefer using the keyboard instead of the mouse, you can press the ALT key on the keyboard to display **KeyTips**, or keyboard code icons, for certain commands (Figure 19). To select a command using the keyboard, press the letter or number displayed in the KeyTip, which may cause additional KeyTips related to the selected command to appear. To remove KeyTips from the screen, press the ALT key or the ESC key until all KeyTips disappear, or click anywhere in the app window.

Figure 19

Microsoft Account Area   In this area, you can use the Sign in link to sign in to your Microsoft account. Once signed in, you will see your account information, as well as a picture if you have included one in your Microsoft account.

To Display a Different Tab on the Ribbon

1 SIGN IN | 2 USE WINDOWS | **3 USE APPS** | 4 FILE MANAGEMENT | 5 SWITCH APPS | 6 SAVE FILES
7 CHANGE SCREEN RESOLUTION | 8 EXIT APPS | 9 USE ADDITIONAL APP FEATURES | 10 USE HELP

When you run PowerPoint, the ribbon displays nine main tabs: File, Home, Insert, Design, Transitions, Animations, Slide Show, Review, and View. The tab currently displayed is called the **active tab**.

The following step displays the Insert tab, that is, makes it the active tab. *Why? When working with an Office app, you may need to switch tabs to access other options for working with a presentation.*

1

- Click Insert on the ribbon to display the Insert tab (Figure 20).

🔎 **Experiment**

- Click the other tabs on the ribbon to view their contents. When you are finished, click Insert on the ribbon to redisplay the Insert tab.

Figure 20

Other Ways

1. Press ALT, press letter corresponding to tab to display   2. Press ALT, press LEFT ARROW or RIGHT ARROW until desired tab is displayed

To Collapse and Expand the Ribbon and Use Full Screen Mode

1 SIGN IN | 2 USE WINDOWS | **3 USE APPS** | 4 FILE MANAGEMENT | 5 SWITCH APPS | 6 SAVE FILES
7 CHANGE SCREEN RESOLUTION | 8 EXIT APPS | 9 USE ADDITIONAL APP FEATURES | 10 USE HELP

To display more of a slide or other item in the window of an Office app, some users prefer to collapse the ribbon, which hides the groups on the ribbon and displays only the main tabs, or to use **Full Screen mode**, which hides all the commands and just displays the slide. Each time you run an Office app, such as PowerPoint, the ribbon appears the same way it did the last time you used that Office app. The modules in this book, however, begin with the ribbon appearing as it did at the initial installation of Office or PowerPoint.

The following steps collapse, expand, and restore the ribbon in PowerPoint and then switch to Full Screen mode. *Why? If you need more space on the screen to work with your slide, you may consider collapsing the ribbon or switching to Full Screen mode to gain additional workspace.*

1

• Click the 'Collapse the Ribbon' button on the ribbon (shown in Figure 20) to collapse the ribbon (Figure 21).

Figure 21

Q&A What happened to the 'Collapse the Ribbon' button?

The 'Pin the ribbon' button replaces the 'Collapse the Ribbon' button when the ribbon is collapsed. You will see the 'Pin the ribbon' button only when you expand a ribbon by clicking a tab.

2

• Click Home on the ribbon to expand the Home tab (Figure 22).

Figure 22

Q&A Why would I click the Home tab?

If you want to use a command on a collapsed ribbon, click the main tab to display the groups for that tab. After you select a command on the ribbon and resume working in the presentation, the groups will be collapsed once again. If you decide not to use a command on the ribbon, you can collapse the groups by clicking the same main tab or clicking in the app window.

🔎 **Experiment**

• Click Home on the ribbon to collapse the groups again. Click Home on the ribbon to expand the Home tab.

3

• Click the 'Pin the ribbon' button on the expanded Home tab to restore the ribbon.
• Click the 'Ribbon Display Options' button to display the Ribbon Display Options menu (Figure 23).

Figure 23

4

- Click Auto-hide Ribbon to use Full Screen mode, which hides all the commands from the screen (Figure 24).
- Click the ellipsis to display the ribbon temporarily.
- Click the 'Ribbon Display Options' button to display the Ribbon Display Options menu (shown in Figure 23).
- Click 'Show Tabs and Commands' on the Ribbon Display Options menu to exit Full Screen mode.

Figure 24

Other Ways
1. Double-click a main tab on the ribbon	2. Press CTRL+F1

To Use a Shortcut Menu to Relocate the Quick Access Toolbar

1 SIGN IN | 2 USE WINDOWS | 3 USE APPS | 4 FILE MANAGEMENT | 5 SWITCH APPS | 6 SAVE FILES
7 CHANGE SCREEN RESOLUTION | 8 EXIT APPS | 9 USE ADDITIONAL APP FEATURES | 10 USE HELP

When you right-click certain areas of the PowerPoint and other Office app windows, a shortcut menu will appear. A **shortcut menu** is a list of frequently used commands that relate to an object. *Why? You can use shortcut menus to access common commands quickly.* When you right-click the status bar, for example, a shortcut menu appears with commands related to the status bar. When you right-click the Quick Access Toolbar, a shortcut menu appears with commands related to the Quick Access Toolbar. The following steps use a shortcut menu to move the Quick Access Toolbar, which by default is located on the title bar.

1

- Right-click the Quick Access Toolbar to display a shortcut menu that presents a list of commands related to the Quick Access Toolbar (Figure 25).

Figure 25

2
- Click 'Show Quick Access Toolbar Below the Ribbon' on the shortcut menu to display the Quick Access Toolbar below the ribbon (Figure 26).

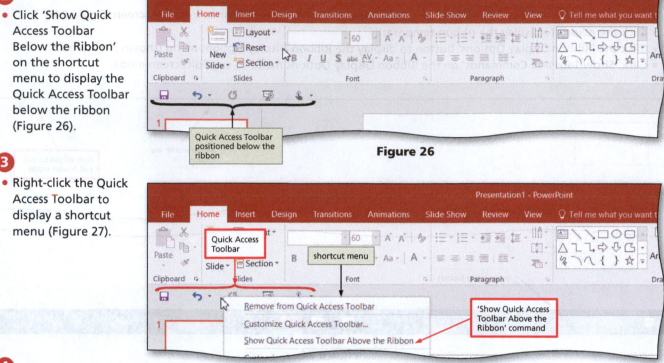

Figure 26

3
- Right-click the Quick Access Toolbar to display a shortcut menu (Figure 27).

Figure 27

4
- Click 'Show Quick Access Toolbar Above the Ribbon' on the shortcut menu to return the Quick Access Toolbar to its original position (shown in Figure 25).

Other Ways

1. Click 'Customize Quick Access Toolbar' button on Quick Access Toolbar, click 'Show Below the Ribbon' or 'Show Above the Ribbon'

To Customize the Quick Access Toolbar

1 SIGN IN | 2 USE WINDOWS | **3 USE APPS** | 4 FILE MANAGEMENT | 5 SWITCH APPS | 6 SAVE FILES
7 CHANGE SCREEN RESOLUTION | 8 EXIT APPS | 9 USE ADDITIONAL APP FEATURES | 10 USE HELP

The Quick Access Toolbar provides easy access to some of the more frequently used commands in the Office apps. By default, the Quick Access Toolbar contains buttons for the Save, Undo, and Redo commands. If your computer or mobile device has a touch screen, the Quick Access Toolbar also might display the Touch/ Mouse Mode button. You can customize the Quick Access Toolbar by changing its location in the window, as shown in the previous steps, and by adding more buttons to reflect commands you would like to access easily. The following steps add the Quick Print button to the Quick Access Toolbar in the PowerPoint window. *Why? Adding the Quick Print button to the Quick Access Toolbar speeds up the process of printing.*

1
- Click the 'Customize Quick Access Toolbar' button to display the Customize Quick Access Toolbar menu (Figure 28).

Q&A

Which commands are listed on the Customize Quick Access Toolbar menu?

It lists commands that commonly are added to the Quick Access Toolbar.

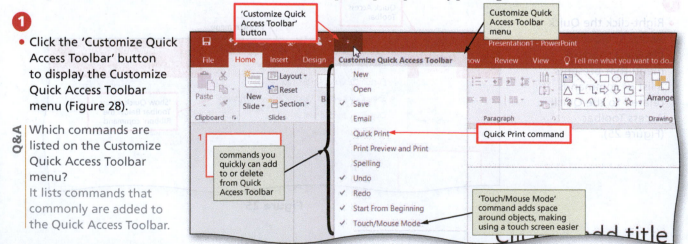

Figure 28

2

- If it is not selected already, click Quick Print on the Customize Quick Access Toolbar menu to add the Quick Print button to the Quick Access Toolbar (Figure 29).

Q&A
How would I remove a button from the Quick Access Toolbar?

You would right-click the button you wish to remove and then click 'Remove from Quick Access Toolbar' on the shortcut menu or click the 'Customize Quick Access Toolbar' button on the Quick Access Toolbar and then click the button name in the Customize Quick Access Toolbar menu to remove the check mark.

[Figure 29 — screenshot of PowerPoint showing Quick Print button added to Quick Access Toolbar, title text placeholder, and 'Click to add title' label]

Figure 29

To Enter Content in a Title Slide

1 SIGN IN | 2 USE WINDOWS | 3 USE APPS | 4 FILE MANAGEMENT | 5 SWITCH APPS | 6 SAVE FILES
7 CHANGE SCREEN RESOLUTION | 8 EXIT APPS | 9 USE ADDITIONAL APP FEATURES | 10 USE HELP

With the exception of a blank slide, PowerPoint assumes every new slide has a title. Many of PowerPoint's layouts have both a title text placeholder and at least one content placeholder. As you begin typing text in the title text placeholder, the title text also is displayed in the Slide 1 thumbnail in the Slides tab. The title for this presentation is Excellent Birding Apps and the subtitle text is Identify Birds Easily. The following step enters a presentation title and subtitle on the title slide. *Why? In general, every presentation should have a title to describe what the presentation will be covering, and the subtitle should support the title text and give additional details.*

1

- Click the 'Click to add title' label located inside the title text placeholder (shown in Figure 29) to select the placeholder.
- Type **Excellent Birding Apps** in the title text placeholder. Do not press the ENTER key because you do not want to create a new line of text (Figure 30).

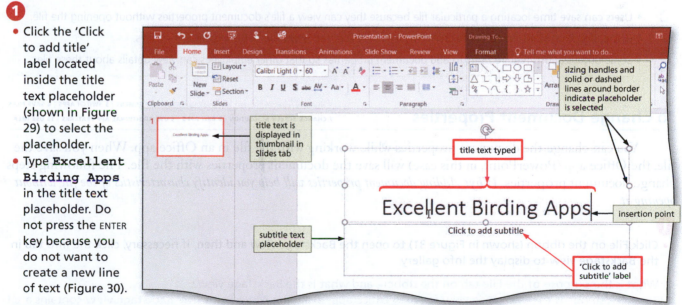

Figure 30

Q&A
What is the blinking vertical bar to the right of the text?

The blinking bar is the insertion point, which indicates where text, graphics, and other items will be inserted in the document. As you type, the insertion point moves to the right.

What if I make an error while typing?

You can press the BACKSPACE key until you have deleted the text in error and then retype the text correctly.

2

- Click the 'Click to add subtitle' label located inside the subtitle text placeholder (shown in Figure 30) to select the placeholder.
- Type **Identify Birds Easily** in the subtitle text placeholder. Do not press the ENTER key (Figure 31).

3

- Click outside the title text and subtitle text placeholders to deselect these slide elements.

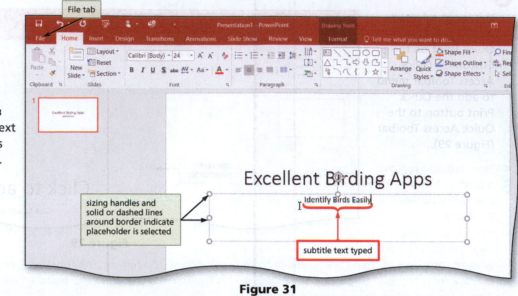

Figure 31

Document Properties

You can organize and identify your files by using **document properties**, which are the details about a file, such as the project author, title, and subject. For example, a class name or presentation topic can describe the file's purpose or content.

CONSIDER THIS

Why would you want to assign document properties to a presentation?

Document properties are valuable for a variety of reasons:

- Users can save time locating a particular file because they can view a file's document properties without opening the file.
- By creating consistent properties for files having similar content, users can better organize their files.
- Some organizations require users to add document properties so that other employees can view details about these files.

To Change Document Properties

1 SIGN IN | 2 USE WINDOWS | 3 USE APPS | **4 FILE MANAGEMENT** | 5 SWITCH APPS | 6 SAVE FILES
7 CHANGE SCREEN RESOLUTION | 8 EXIT APPS | 9 USE ADDITIONAL APP FEATURES | 10 USE HELP

You can change the document properties while working with the file in an Office app. When you save the file, the Office app (PowerPoint, in this case) will save the document properties with the file. The following steps change document properties. *Why? Adding document properties will help you identify characteristics of the file without opening it.*

1

- Click File on the ribbon (shown in Figure 31) to open the Backstage view and then, if necessary, click the Info tab in the Backstage view to display the Info gallery.

Q&A What is the purpose of the File tab on the ribbon, and what is the Backstage view?

The File tab opens the Backstage view for each Office app, including PowerPoint. The **Backstage view** contains a set of commands that enable you to manage documents and provides data about the documents.

What is the purpose of the Info gallery in the Backstage view?

The Info tab, which is selected by default when you click File on the ribbon, displays the Info gallery, where you can protect a presentation, inspect a presentation, and manage versions of a presentation, as well as view all the file properties, such as when the file was created.

- Click to the right of the Categories property in the Properties list and then type `CIS 101 Assignment` in the Categories text box (Figure 32).

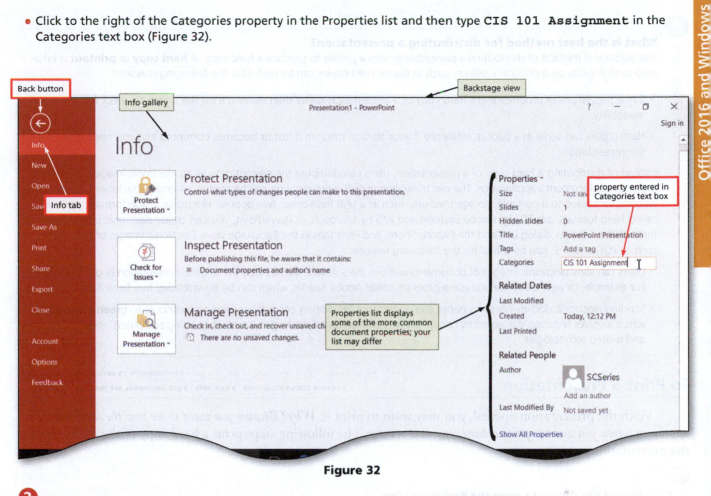

Figure 32

2
- Click the Back button in the upper-left corner of the Backstage view to return to the document window.

Printing, Saving, and Organizing Files

While you are creating a presentation, the computer or mobile device stores it in memory. When you save a presentation, the computer or mobile device places it on a storage medium, such as a hard disk, solid state drive (SSD), USB flash drive, or optical disc. The storage medium can be permanent in your computer, may be portable where you remove it from your computer, or may be on a web server you access through a network or the Internet.

A saved presentation is referred to as a file. A **file name** is the name assigned to a file when it is saved. When saving files, you should organize them so that you easily can find them later. Windows provides tools to help you organize files.

Printing a Presentation

After creating a presentation, you may want to print it. Printing a presentation enables you to distribute it to others in a form that can be read or viewed but typically not edited.

BTW

File Type
Depending on your Windows settings, the file type .pptx may be displayed immediately to the right of the file name after you save the file. The file type .pptx is a PowerPoint 2016 document.

CONSIDER THIS

What is the best method for distributing a presentation?

The traditional method of distributing a presentation uses a printer to produce a hard copy. A **hard copy** or **printout** is information that exists on a physical medium, such as paper. Hard copies can be useful for the following reasons:

- Some people prefer proofreading a hard copy of a presentation rather than viewing it on the screen to check for errors and readability.

- Hard copies can serve as a backup reference if your storage medium is lost or becomes corrupted and you need to recreate the presentation.

Instead of distributing a hard copy of a presentation, users can distribute the presentation as an electronic image that mirrors the original document's appearance. The electronic image of the presentation can be sent as an email attachment, posted on a website, or copied to a portable storage medium, such as a USB flash drive. Two popular electronic image formats, sometimes called fixed formats, are PDF by Adobe Systems and XPS by Microsoft. In PowerPoint, you can create electronic image files through the Save As dialog box and the Export, Share, and Print tabs in the Backstage view. Electronic images of documents, such as PDF and XPS, can be useful for the following reasons:

- Users can view electronic images of documents without the software that created the original presentation (e.g., PowerPoint). For example, to view a PDF file you use a program called Adobe Reader, which can be downloaded free from Adobe's website.

- Sending electronic documents saves paper and printer supplies. Society encourages users to contribute to **green computing**, which involves reducing the electricity consumed and environmental waste generated when using computers, mobile devices, and related technologies.

To Print a Presentation

1 SIGN IN | 2 USE WINDOWS | 3 USE APPS | **4 FILE MANAGEMENT** | 5 SWITCH APPS | 6 SAVE FILES
7 CHANGE SCREEN RESOLUTION | 8 EXIT APPS | 9 USE ADDITIONAL APP FEATURES | 10 USE HELP

With the presentation opened, you may want to print it. *Why? Because you want to see how the slide will appear on paper; you want to print a hard copy on a printer.* The following steps print a hard copy of the contents of the presentation.

1

- Click File on the ribbon to open the Backstage view.
- Click the Print tab in the Backstage view to display the Print gallery (Figure 33).

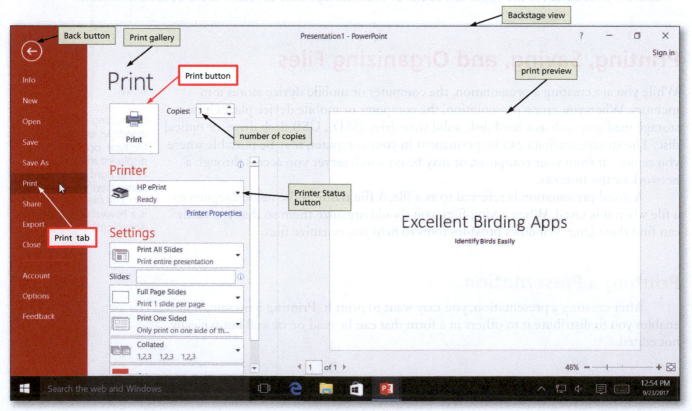

Figure 33

Q&A How can I print multiple copies of my presentation?
Increase the number in the Copies box in the Print gallery.

What if I decide not to print the presentation at this time?
Click the Back button in the upper-left corner of the Backstage view to return to the document window.

2

- Verify that the selected printer will print a hard copy of the presentation. If necessary, click the Printer Status button to display a list of available printer options and then click the desired printer to change the currently selected printer.

3

- Click the Print button in the Print gallery to print the presentation on the currently selected printer.
- When the printer stops, retrieve the hard copy (Figure 34).

Excellent Birding Apps
Identify Birds Easily

Figure 34

Q&A What if I want to print an electronic image of a presentation instead of a hard copy?
You would click the Printer Status button in the Print gallery and then select the desired electronic image option, such as Microsoft XPS Document Writer, which would create an XPS file.

Other Ways

1. Press CTRL+P

Organizing Files and Folders

A file contains data. This data can range from a research paper to an accounting spreadsheet to an electronic math quiz. You should organize and store files in folders to avoid misplacing a file and to help you find a file quickly.

If you are taking an introductory computer class (CIS 101, for example), you may want to design a series of folders for the different subjects covered in the class. To accomplish this, you can arrange the folders in a hierarchy for the class, as shown in Figure 35. The hierarchy contains three levels. The first level contains the storage medium,

| CIS 101 |

| Word | PowerPoint | Excel | Access | Outlook | Publisher | OneNote |

Figure 35

such as a hard drive. The second level contains the class folder (CIS 101, in this case), and the third level contains seven folders, one each for a different Office app that will be covered in the class (Word, PowerPoint, Excel, Access, Outlook, Publisher, and OneNote).

When the hierarchy in Figure 35 is created, the storage medium is said to contain the CIS 101 folder, and the CIS 101 folder is said to contain the separate Office folders (i.e., Word, PowerPoint, Excel, etc.). In addition, this hierarchy easily can be expanded to include folders from other classes taken during additional semesters.

The vertical and horizontal lines in Figure 35 form a pathway that allows you to navigate to a drive or folder on a computer or network. A **path** consists of a drive letter (preceded by a drive name when necessary) and colon, to identify the storage device, and one or more folder names. A hard drive typically has a drive letter of C. Each drive or folder in the hierarchy has a corresponding path.

By default, Windows saves documents in the Documents folder, music in the Music folder, photos in the Pictures folder, videos in the Videos folder, and downloads in the Downloads folder.

The following pages illustrate the steps to organize the folders for this class and save a file in a folder:

1. Create the folder identifying your class.
2. Create the PowerPoint folder in the folder identifying your class.
3. Save a file in the PowerPoint folder.
4. Verify the location of the saved file.

To Create a Folder

1 SIGN IN | 2 USE WINDOWS | 3 USE APPS | **4 FILE MANAGEMENT** | 5 SWITCH APPS | 6 SAVE FILES
7 CHANGE SCREEN RESOLUTION | 8 EXIT APPS | 9 USE ADDITIONAL APP FEATURES | 10 USE HELP

When you create a folder, such as the CIS 101 folder shown in Figure 35, you must name the folder. A folder name should describe the folder and its contents. A folder name can contain spaces and any uppercase or lowercase characters, except a backslash (\), slash (/), colon (:), asterisk (*), question mark (?), quotation marks ("), less than symbol (<), greater than symbol (>), or vertical bar (|). Folder names cannot be CON, AUX, COM1, COM2, COM3, COM4, LPT1, LPT2, LPT3, PRN, or NUL. The same rules for naming folders also apply to naming files.

The following steps create a class folder (CIS 101, in this case) in the Documents folder. *Why? When storing files, you should organize the files so that it will be easier to find them later.*

1
- Click the File Explorer button on the taskbar to run File Explorer.
- If necessary, double-click This PC in the navigation pane to expand the contents of your computer.
- Click the Documents folder in the navigation pane to display the contents of the Documents folder in the file list (Figure 36).

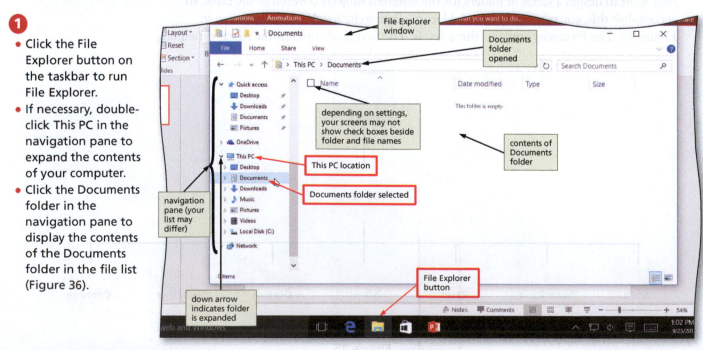

Figure 36

2

● Click the New folder button on the Quick Access Toolbar to create a new folder with the name, New folder, selected in a text box (Figure 37).

Q&A

Why is the folder icon displayed differently on my computer or mobile device?
Windows might be configured to display contents differently on your computer or mobile device.

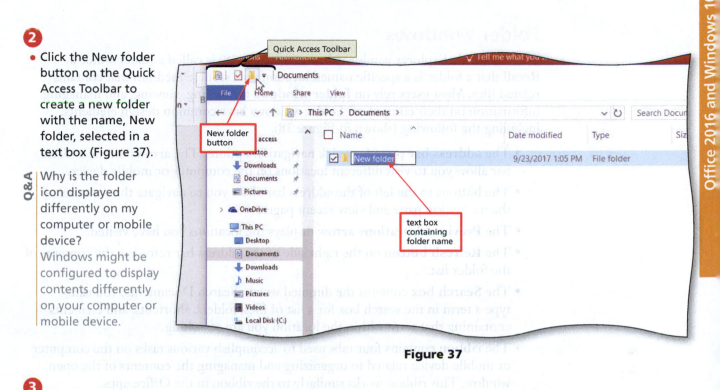

Figure 37

3

● Type **CIS 101** (or your class code) in the text box as the new folder name.

  If requested by your instructor, add your last name to the end of the folder name.

● Press the ENTER key to change the folder name from New folder to a folder name identifying your class (Figure 38).

Q&A

What happens when I press the ENTER key?
The class folder (CIS 101, in this case) is displayed in the file list, which contains the folder name, date modified, type, and size.

Figure 38

Other Ways

1. Press CTRL+SHIFT+N   2. Click New folder button (Home tab | New group)

Folder Windows

The File Explorer window (shown in Figure 38) is called a folder window. Recall that a folder is a specific named location on a storage medium that contains related files. Most users rely on **folder windows** for finding, viewing, and managing information on their computers. Folder windows have common design elements, including the following (shown in Figure 38).

- The **address bar** provides quick navigation options. The arrows on the address bar allow you to visit different locations on the computer or mobile device.
- The buttons to the left of the address bar allow you to navigate the contents of the navigation pane and view recent pages.
- The **Previous Locations arrow** displays the locations you have visited.
- The **Refresh button** on the right side of the address bar refreshes the contents of the folder list.
- The **Search box** contains the dimmed words, Search Documents. You can type a term in the search box for a list of files, folders, shortcuts, and elements containing that term within the location you are searching.
- The **ribbon** contains four tabs used to accomplish various tasks on the computer or mobile device related to organizing and managing the contents of the open window. This ribbon works similarly to the ribbon in the Office apps.
- The **navigation pane** on the left contains the Quick access area, the OneDrive area, the This PC area, and the Network area.
- The **Quick access area** shows locations you access frequently. By default, this list contains links only to your Desktop, Downloads, Documents, and Pictures.

To Create a Folder within a Folder

1 SIGN IN | 2 USE WINDOWS | 3 USE APPS | **4 FILE MANAGEMENT** | 5 SWITCH APPS | 6 SAVE FILES
7 CHANGE SCREEN RESOLUTION | 8 EXIT APPS | 9 USE ADDITIONAL APP FEATURES | 10 USE HELP

With the class folder created, you can create folders that will store the files you create using PowerPoint. The following step creates a PowerPoint folder in the CIS 101 folder (or the folder identifying your class). *Why? To be able to organize your files, you should create a folder structure.*

1

- Double-click the icon or folder name for the CIS 101 folder (or the folder identifying your class) in the file list to open the folder.
- Click the New folder button on the Quick Access Toolbar to create a new folder with the name, New folder, selected in a text box folder.
- Type **PowerPoint** in the text box as the new folder name.
- Press the ENTER key to rename the folder (Figure 39).

Figure 39

Other Ways

1. Press CTRL+SHIFT+N   2. Click New folder button (Home tab | New group)

To Expand a Folder, Scroll through Folder Contents, and Collapse a Folder

Folder windows display the hierarchy of items and the contents of drives and folders in the file list. You might want to expand a folder in the navigation pane to view its contents, scroll through its contents, and collapse it when you are finished viewing its contents. *Why? When a folder is expanded, you can see all the folders it contains. By contrast, a collapsed folder hides the folders it contains.* The following steps expand, scroll through, and then collapse the folder identifying your class (CIS 101, in this case).

- Double-click the Documents folder in the This PC area of the navigation pane, which expands the folder to display its contents and displays a black down arrow to the left of the Documents folder icon (Figure 40).

Figure 40

- Double-click the CIS 101 folder, which expands the folder to display its contents and displays a black down arrow to the left of the folder icon (Figure 41).

Experiment

- Drag the scroll box down or click the down scroll arrow on the vertical scroll bar to display additional folders at the bottom of the navigation pane. Drag the scroll box up or click the scroll bar above the scroll box to move the scroll box to the top of the navigation pane. Drag the scroll box down the scroll bar until the scroll box is halfway down the scroll bar.

Figure 41

- Double-click the folder identifying your class (CIS 101, in this case) to collapse the folder (Figure 42).

Q&A Why are some folders indented below others?
A folder contains the indented folders below it.

Figure 42

Other Ways

1. Point to display arrows in navigation pane, click arrow to expand or collapse
2. Select folder to expand or collapse using arrow keys, press RIGHT ARROW to expand; press LEFT ARROW to collapse

To Switch from One App to Another

The next step is to save the PowerPoint file containing the headline you typed earlier. PowerPoint, however, currently is not the active window. You can use the PowerPoint app button on the taskbar and live preview to switch to PowerPoint and then save the presentation in the PowerPoint window.

Why? By clicking the appropriate app button on the taskbar, you can switch to the running app you want to use. The following steps switch to the PowerPoint window; however, the steps are the same for any active Office app currently displayed as a button on the taskbar.

1

- Point to the PowerPoint app button on the taskbar to see a live preview of the open presentation(s) or the window title(s) of the open presentation(s), depending on your computer's configuration (Figure 43).

Q&A
What if I am using a touch screen?
Live preview will not work if you are using a touch screen. If you are using a touch screen and do not have a mouse, proceed to Step 2.

Figure 43

2

- Click the PowerPoint app button or the live preview to make the app associated with the app button the active window (Figure 44).

Q&A
What if multiple documents are open in an app?
Click the desired live preview to switch to the window you want to use.

Figure 44

Other Ways

1. Press ALT+TAB until app you wish to display is selected

To Save a File in a Folder

With the PowerPoint folder created, you can save the PowerPoint presentation shown in the document window in the PowerPoint folder. *Why? Without saving a file, you may lose all the work you have completed and will be unable to reuse or share it with others later.* The following steps save a file in the PowerPoint folder contained in your class folder (CIS 101, in this case) using the file name, Birding Apps.

1

● Click the Save button (shown in Figure 44) on the Quick Access Toolbar, which, depending on settings, will display either the Save As gallery in the Backstage view (Figure 45) or the Save As dialog box (Figure 46).

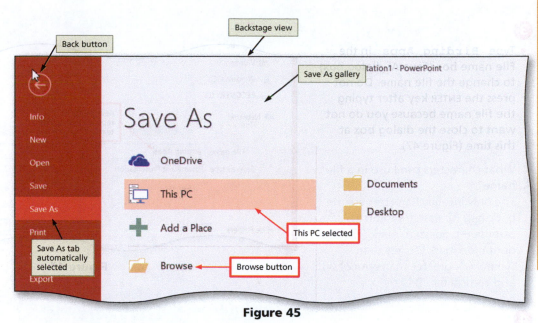

Figure 45

Q&A What if the Save As gallery is not displayed in the Backstage view?
Click the Save As tab to display the Save As gallery.

How do I close the Backstage view?
Click the Back button in the upper-left corner of the Backstage view to return to the PowerPoint window.

2

● If your screen displays the Backstage view, click This PC, if necessary, to display options in the right pane related to saving on your computer or mobile device; if your screen already displays the Save As dialog box, proceed to Step 3.

Q&A What if I wanted to save on OneDrive instead?
You would click OneDrive. Saving on OneDrive is discussed in a later section in this module.

● Click the Browse button in the left pane to display the Save As dialog box (Figure 46).

Q&A Why does a file name already appear in the File name box?

Figure 46

PowerPoint automatically suggests a file name the first time you save a presentation. The file name normally consists of the first few words contained in the presentation. Because the suggested file name is selected, you do not need to delete it; as soon as you begin typing, the new file name replaces the selected text.

3

- Type **Birding Apps** in the File name box (Save As dialog box) to change the file name. Do not press the ENTER key after typing the file name because you do not want to close the dialog box at this time (Figure 47).

Q&A

What characters can I use in a file name?

The only invalid characters are the backslash (\), slash (/), colon (:), asterisk (*), question mark (?), quotation mark ("), less than symbol (<), greater than symbol (>), and vertical bar (|).

new file name replaces highlighted text in File name box

Figure 47

4

- Navigate to the desired save location (in this case, the PowerPoint folder in the CIS 101 folder [or your class folder] in the Documents folder) by performing the tasks in Steps 4a and 4b.

4a

navigation pane

- If the Documents folder is not displayed in the navigation pane, drag the scroll bar in the navigation pane until Documents appears.
- If the Documents folder is not expanded in the navigation pane, double-click Documents to display its folders in the navigation pane.
- If your class folder (CIS 101, in this case) is not expanded, double-click the CIS 101 folder to select the folder and display its contents in the navigation pane (Figure 48).

Documents folder expanded

PowerPoint folder appears when CIS 101 folder is expanded

CIS 101 folder expanded

Figure 48

Q&A

What if I do not want to save in a folder?

Although storing files in folders is an effective technique for organizing files, some users prefer not to store files in folders. If you prefer not to save this file in a folder, select the storage device on which you wish to save the file and then proceed to Step 5.

PowerPoint folder

PowerPoint folder currently contains no files

PowerPoint folder selected

Save button

4b

- Click the PowerPoint folder in the navigation pane to select it as the new save location and display its contents in the file list (Figure 49).

Figure 49

⑤

- Click the Save button (Save As dialog box) to save the presentation in the selected folder in the selected location with the entered file name (Figure 50).

Q&A

How do I know that the file is saved?
While an Office app such as PowerPoint is saving a file, it briefly displays a message on the status bar indicating the amount of the file saved. In addition, the file name appears on the title bar.

Figure 50

Other Ways

1. Click File on ribbon, click Save As tab in Backstage view, click This PC, click Browse button, type file name (Save As dialog box), navigate to desired save location, click Save button

2. Press F12, type file name (Save As dialog box), navigate to desired save location, click Save button

How often should you save a presentation?

It is important to save a presentation frequently for the following reasons:

- The presentation in memory might be lost if the computer is turned off or you lose electrical power while an app is running.

- If you run out of time before completing a project, you may finish it at a future time without starting over.

CONSIDER THIS

Navigating in Dialog Boxes

Navigating is the process of finding a location on a storage device. While saving the Birding Apps file, for example, Steps 4a and 4b navigated to the PowerPoint folder located in the CIS 101 folder in the Documents folder. When performing certain functions in Windows apps, such as saving a file, opening a file, or inserting a picture in an existing presentation, you most likely will have to navigate to the location where you want to save the file or to the folder containing the file you want to open or insert. Most dialog boxes in Windows apps requiring navigation follow a similar procedure; that is, the way you navigate to a folder in one dialog box, such as the Save As dialog box, is similar to how you might navigate in another dialog box, such as the Open dialog box. If you chose to navigate to a specific location in a dialog box, you would follow the instructions in Steps 4a and 4b.

To Minimize and Restore a Window

1 SIGN IN | **2 USE WINDOWS** | 3 USE APPS | 4 FILE MANAGEMENT | 5 SWITCH APPS | 6 SAVE FILES

7 CHANGE SCREEN RESOLUTION | 8 EXIT APPS | 9 USE ADDITIONAL APP FEATURES | 10 USE HELP

Before continuing, you can verify that the PowerPoint file was saved properly. To do this, you will minimize the PowerPoint window and then open the CIS 101 window so that you can verify the file is stored in the CIS 101 folder on the hard drive. A **minimized window** is an open window that is hidden from view but can be displayed quickly by clicking the window's button on the taskbar.

In the following example, PowerPoint is used to illustrate minimizing and restoring windows; however, you would follow the same steps regardless of the Office app you are using. *Why? Before closing an app, you should make sure your file saved correctly so that you can find it later.*

The following steps minimize the PowerPoint window, verify that the file is saved, and then restore the minimized window.

①

- Click the Minimize button on the PowerPoint window title bar (shown in Figure 50) to minimize the window (Figure 51).

Q&A Is the minimized window still available?
The minimized window, PowerPoint in this case, remains available but no longer is the active window. It is minimized as a button on the taskbar.

- If the File Explorer window is not open on the screen, click the File Explorer button on the taskbar to make the File Explorer window the active window.

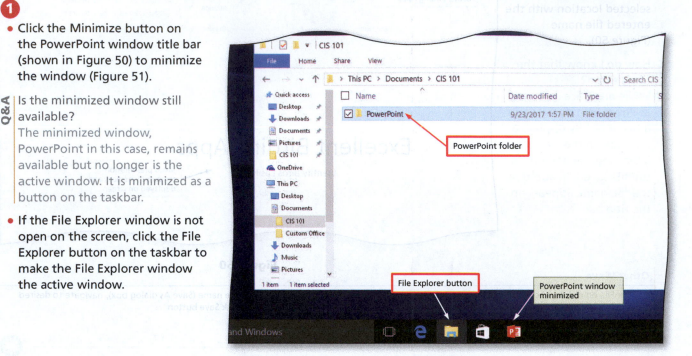

Figure 51

②

- Double-click the PowerPoint folder in the file list to select the folder and display its contents (Figure 52).

Q&A Why does the File Explorer button on the taskbar change?
A selected app button indicates that the app is active on the screen. When the button is not selected, the app is running but not active.

③

- After viewing the contents of the selected folder, click the PowerPoint app button on the taskbar to restore the minimized window (as shown in Figure 50).

Figure 52

Other Ways

1. Right-click title bar, click Minimize on shortcut menu, click taskbar button in taskbar button area
2. Press WINDOWS+M, press WINDOWS+SHIFT+M
3. Click PowerPoint app button on taskbar to minimize window. Click PowerPoint app button again to restore window.

To Save a File on OneDrive

One of the features of Office is the capability to save files on OneDrive so that you can use the files on multiple computers or mobile devices without having to use an external storage device, such as a USB flash drive. Storing files on OneDrive also enables you to share files more efficiently with others, such as when using Office Online and Office 365.

In the following example, PowerPoint is used to save a file on OneDrive. *Why? Storing files on OneDrive provides more portability options than are available from storing files in the Documents folder.*

You can save files directly on OneDrive from within an Office app. The following steps save the current PowerPoint file on OneDrive. These steps require that you have a Microsoft account and an Internet connection.

1
- Click File on the ribbon to open the Backstage view.
- Click the Save As tab in the Backstage view to display the Save As gallery.
- Click OneDrive in the left pane to display OneDrive saving options or a Sign In button, if you are not signed in already to your Microsoft account (Figure 53).

Figure 53

2
- If your screen displays a Sign In button (shown in Figure 53), click it to display the Sign in dialog box (Figure 54).

Q&A
What if the Sign In button does not appear?
If you already are signed into your Microsoft account, the Sign In button will not be displayed. In this case, proceed to Step 3.

- Follow the instructions on the screen to sign in to your Microsoft account.

Figure 54

3

- If necessary, in the Backstage view, click OneDrive in the left pane in the Save As gallery to select OneDrive as the save location.
- Click the Documents, or similar, folder in the right pane to display the Save As dialog box (Figure 55).

Q&A Why does the path in the OneDrive address bar in the Save As dialog box contain various letters and numbers?
The letters and numbers in the address bar uniquely identify the location of your OneDrive files and folders.

Figure 55

4

- Click the Save button (Save As dialog box) to save the file on OneDrive.

To Sign Out of a Microsoft Account

If you are using a public computer or otherwise wish to sign out of your Microsoft account, you should sign out of the account from the Account gallery in the Backstage view. Signing out of the account is the safest way to make sure that nobody else can access online files or settings stored in your Microsoft account. *Why? For security reasons, you should sign out of your Microsoft account when you are finished using a public or shared computer. Staying signed in to your Microsoft account might enable others to access your files.*

The following steps sign out of a Microsoft account from PowerPoint. You would use the same steps in any Office app. If you do not wish to sign out of your Microsoft account, read these steps without performing them.

1 Click File on the ribbon to open the Backstage view.

2 Click the Account tab to display the Account gallery (Figure 56).

3 Click the Sign out link, which displays the Remove Account dialog box. If a Can't remove Windows accounts dialog box appears instead of the Remove Account dialog box, click the OK button and skip the remaining steps.

Q&A Why does a Can't remove Windows accounts dialog box appear?
If you signed in to Windows using your Microsoft account, then you also must sign out from Windows, rather than signing out from within PowerPoint. When you are finished using Windows, be sure to sign out at that time.

4 Click the Yes button (Remove Account dialog box) to sign out of your Microsoft account on this computer or mobile device.

Q&A Should I sign out of Windows after removing my Microsoft account?
When you are finished using the computer, you should sign out of Windows for maximum security.

5 Click the Back button in the upper-left corner of the Backstage view to return to the presentation.

Figure 56

Screen Resolution

Screen resolution indicates the number of pixels (dots) that the computer uses to display the letters, numbers, graphics, and background you see on the screen. When you increase the screen resolution, Windows displays more information on the screen, but the information decreases in size. The reverse also is true: as you decrease the screen resolution, Windows displays less information on the screen, but the information increases in size.

Screen resolution usually is stated as the product of two numbers, such as 1366 × 768 (pronounced "thirteen sixty-six by seven sixty-eight"). A 1366 × 768 screen resolution results in a display of 1366 distinct pixels on each of 768 lines, or about 1,050,624 pixels. Changing the screen resolution affects how the ribbon appears in Office apps and some Windows dialog boxes. Figure 57, for example, shows the PowerPoint ribbon at screen resolutions of 1366 × 768 and 1024 × 768. All of the same commands are available regardless of screen resolution. The app (PowerPoint, in this case), however, makes changes to the groups and the buttons within the groups to accommodate the various screen resolutions. The result is that certain commands

Figure 57 (a) Ribbon at 1366 × 768 Resolution

Figure 57 (b) Ribbon at 1024 × 768 Resolution

may need to be accessed differently depending on the resolution chosen. A command that is visible on the ribbon and available by clicking a button at one resolution may not be visible and may need to be accessed using its Dialog Box Launcher at a different resolution.

Comparing the two ribbons in Figure 57, notice the changes in content and layout of the groups and galleries. In some cases, the content of a group is the same in each resolution, but the layout of the group differs. For example, the same gallery and buttons appear in the Slides groups in the two resolutions, but the layouts differ. In other cases, the content and layout are the same across the resolution, but the level of detail differs with the resolution.

To Change the Screen Resolution

1 SIGN IN | 2 USE WINDOWS | 3 USE APPS | 4 FILE MANAGEMENT | 5 SWITCH APPS | 6 SAVE FILES
7 CHANGE SCREEN RESOLUTION | 8 EXIT APPS | 9 USE ADDITIONAL APP FEATURES | 10 USE HELP

If you are using a computer to step through the modules in this book and you want your screen to match the figures, you may need to change your screen's resolution. *Why?* *The figures in this book use a screen resolution of 1366 × 768.* The following steps change the screen resolution to 1366 × 768. Your computer already may be set to 1366 × 768. Keep in mind that many computer labs prevent users from changing the screen resolution; in that case, read the following steps for illustration purposes.

1

- Click the Show desktop button, which is located at the far-right edge of the taskbar, to display the Windows desktop.
- Right-click an empty area on the Windows desktop to display a shortcut menu that contains a list of commands related to the desktop (Figure 58).

Q&A
Why does my shortcut menu display different commands?
Depending on your computer's hardware and configuration, different commands might appear on the shortcut menu.

Figure 58

2

- Click Display settings on the shortcut menu to open the Settings app window. If necessary, scroll to display the 'Advanced display settings' link (Figure 59).

Figure 59

3

- Click 'Advanced display settings' in the Settings app window to display the advanced display settings.
- If necessary, scroll to display the Resolution box (Figure 60).

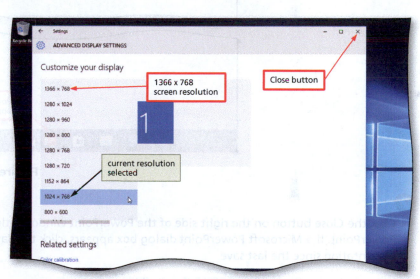

Figure 60

4

- Click the Resolution box to display a list of available screen resolutions (Figure 61).
- If necessary, scroll to and then click 1366 x 768 to select the screen resolution.

Q&A What if my computer does not support the 1366 x 768 resolution?
Some computers do not support the 1366 x 768 resolution. In this case, select a resolution that is close to the 1366 x 768 resolution.

Figure 61

5

- Click the Apply button (Advanced Display Settings window), shown in Figure 60, to change the screen resolution and a confirmation message (Figure 62).
- Click the Keep changes button to accept the new screen resolution.
- Click the Close button (shown in Figure 61) to close the Settings app window.

Figure 62

Other Ways

1. Click Start button, click Settings, click System, click Display, click 'Advanced display settings,' select desired resolution in Resolution box, click Apply button, click Keep changes button

2. Type `screen resolution` in search box, click 'Change the screen resolution,' select desired resolution in Resolution box, click Apply button, click Keep changes button

To Exit an App with One Document Open

When you exit an Office app, such as PowerPoint, if you have made changes to a file since the last time the file was saved, the app displays a dialog box asking if you want to save the changes you made to the file before it closes the app window. *Why? The dialog box contains three buttons with these resulting actions: the Save button saves the changes and then exits the app, the Don't Save button exits the app without saving changes, and the Cancel button closes the dialog box and redisplays the file without saving the changes.*

If no changes have been made to an open presentation since the last time the file was saved, the app will close the window without displaying a dialog box.

The following steps exit PowerPoint. You would follow similar steps in other Office apps.

1

- If necessary, click the PowerPoint app button on the taskbar to display the PowerPoint window on the desktop (Figure 63).

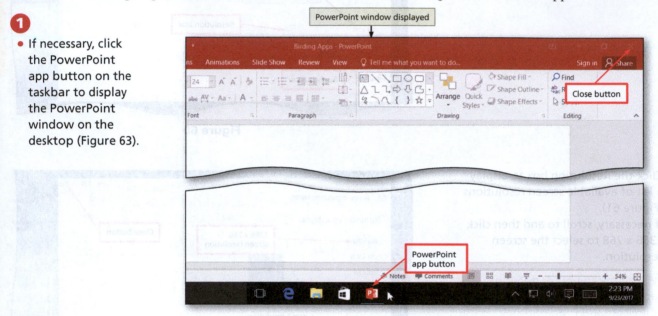

Figure 63

2

- Click the Close button on the right side of the PowerPoint window title bar to close the presentation and exit PowerPoint. If a Microsoft PowerPoint dialog box appears, click the Save button to save any changes made to the presentation since the last save.

Q&A What if I have more than one presentation open in PowerPoint?

You could click the Close button for each open presentation. When you click the last open document's Close button, you also exit PowerPoint. As an alternative that is more efficient, you could right-click the PowerPoint app button on the taskbar and then click 'Close all windows' on the shortcut menu to close all open documents and exit PowerPoint.

Other Ways

1. Right-click PowerPoint app button on Windows taskbar, click 'Close all windows' on shortcut menu
2. Press ALT+F4

To Copy a Folder to OneDrive

To back up your files or easily make them available on another computer or mobile device, you can copy them to OneDrive. The following steps copy your CIS 101 folder to OneDrive. If you do not have access to a OneDrive account, read the following steps without performing them. *Why? It often is good practice to have a backup of your files so that they are available in case something happens to your original copies.*

1

- Click the File Explorer button on the taskbar to make the folder window the active window.
- Navigate to the CIS 101 folder (or your class folder) in the Documents folder.
- Click Documents in the This PC area of the navigation pane to display the CIS 101 folder in the file list.

Q&A What if my CIS 101 folder is stored in a different location?
Use the navigation pane to navigate to the location of your CIS 101 folder. The CIS 101 folder should be displayed in the file list once you have located it.

- Click the CIS 101 folder in the file list to select it (Figure 64).

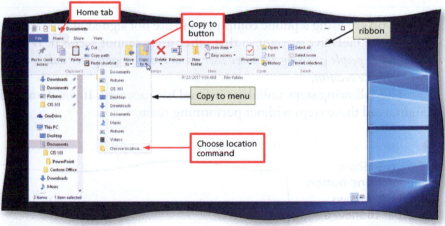

Figure 64

2

- Click Home on the ribbon to display the Home tab.
- Click the Copy to button (Home tab | Organize group) to display the Copy to menu (Figure 65).

Figure 65

3

- Click Choose location on the Copy to menu to display the Copy Items dialog box.
- Click OneDrive (Copy Items dialog box) to select it (Figure 66).

Figure 66

4

- Click the Copy button (Copy Items dialog box) to copy the selected folder to OneDrive.
- Click OneDrive in the navigation pane to verify the CIS 101 folder displays in the file list (Figure 67).

Q&A | Why does a Microsoft OneDrive dialog box appear when I click OneDrive in the navigation pane? If you are not currently signed in to Windows using a Microsoft account, you will manually need to sign in to a Microsoft account to save files to OneDrive. Follow the instructions on the screen to sign in to your Microsoft account.

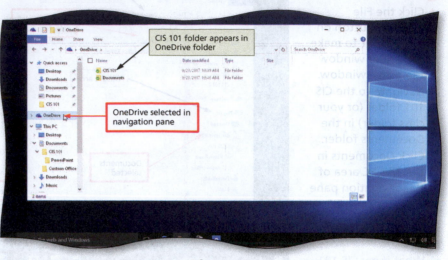

CIS 101 folder appears in OneDrive folder

OneDrive selected in navigation pane

Figure 67

Other Ways

1. In File Explorer, select folder to copy, click Copy button (Home tab | Clipboard group), display contents of OneDrive in file list, click Paste button (Home tab | Clipboard group)

2. In File Explorer, select folder to copy, press CTRL+C, display contents of OneDrive in file list, press CTRL+V

To Unlink a OneDrive Account

1 SIGN IN | 2 USE WINDOWS | 3 USE APPS | **4 FILE MANAGEMENT** | 5 SWITCH APPS | 6 SAVE FILES
7 CHANGE SCREEN RESOLUTION | 8 EXIT APPS | **9 USE ADDITIONAL APP FEATURES** | 10 USE HELP

If you are using a public computer and are not signed in to Windows with a Microsoft account, you should unlink your OneDrive account so that other users cannot access it. *Why? If you do not unlink your OneDrive account, other people accessing the same user account on the computer will be able to view, remove, and add to files stored in your OneDrive account.*

The following steps unlink your OneDrive account. If you do not wish to sign out of your Microsoft account, read these steps without performing them.

1

- Click the 'Show hidden icons' button on the Windows taskbar to show a menu of hidden icons (Figure 68).

OneDrive icon (your OneDrive icon may look different)

'Show hidden icons' button

menu of hidden icons appears

Figure 68

2
- Right-click the OneDrive icon (shown in Figure 68) to display a shortcut menu (Figure 69).

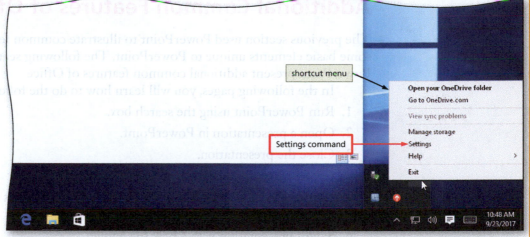

Figure 69

3
- Click Settings on the shortcut menu to display the Microsoft OneDrive dialog box (Figure 70).

Figure 70

4
- If necessary, click the Settings tab. (Some versions require you click an Account tab instead.)
- Click the Unlink OneDrive button (Microsoft OneDrive dialog box) to unlink the OneDrive account (Figure 71).
- When the Microsoft OneDrive dialog box appears with a Welcome to OneDrive message, click the Close button.
- Minimize the File Explorer window.

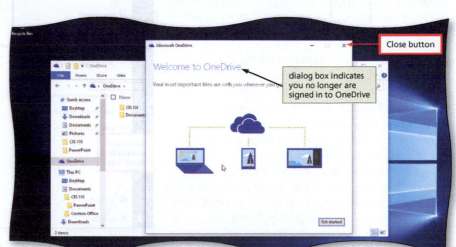

Figure 71

Break Point: If you wish to take a break, this is a good place to do so. To resume at a later time, continue to follow the steps from this location forward.

Additional Common Features of Office Apps

The previous section used PowerPoint to illustrate common features of Office and some basic elements unique to PowerPoint. The following sections continue to use PowerPoint present additional common features of Office.

In the following pages, you will learn how to do the following:

1. Run PowerPoint using the search box.
2. Open a presentation in PowerPoint.
3. Close the presentation.
4. Reopen the presentation just closed.
5. Create a blank PowerPoint presentation from Windows Explorer and then open the file.
6. Save a presentation with a new file name.

To Run an App Using the Search Box

1 SIGN IN | 2 USE WINDOWS | 3 USE APPS | 4 FILE MANAGEMENT | 5 SWITCH APPS | 6 SAVE FILES
7 CHANGE SCREEN RESOLUTION | 8 EXIT APPS | 9 USE ADDITIONAL APP FEATURES | 10 USE HELP

The following steps, which assume Windows is running, use the search box to run PowerPoint based on a typical installation; however, you would follow similar steps to run any app. *Why? Some people prefer to use the search box to locate and run an app, as opposed to searching through a list of all apps on the Start menu.* You may need to ask your instructor how to run PowerPoint on your computer.

1

- Type **PowerPoint 2016** as the search text in the search box and watch the search results appear in the search results (Figure 72).

Q&A Do I need to type the complete app name or use correct capitalization?

No, you need to type just enough characters of the app name for it to appear in the search results. For example, you may be able to type Powerpoint or powerpoint, instead of PowerPoint 2016.

What if the search does not locate the PowerPoint app on my computer?

You may need to adjust the Windows search settings. Search for the word, index; click 'Indexing Options Control panel'; click the Modify button (Indexing Options dialog box); expand the Local Disk, if necessary; place a check mark beside all Program Files entries; and then click the OK button. It may take a few minutes for the index to rebuild. If it still does not work, you may need to click the Advanced button (Indexing Options dialog box) and then click the Rebuild button (Advanced Options dialog box).

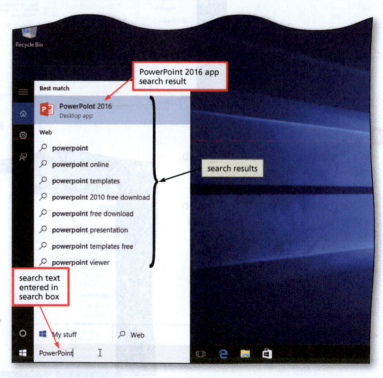

Figure 72

2

- Click the app name, PowerPoint 2016 in this case, in the search results to run PowerPoint and display the PowerPoint start screen.
- Click the Blank Presentation thumbnail on the PowerPoint start screen (shown earlier in this module in Figure 8) to create a blank presentation and display it in the PowerPoint window.
- If the PowerPoint window is not maximized, click the Maximize button on its title bar to maximize the window (Figure 73).

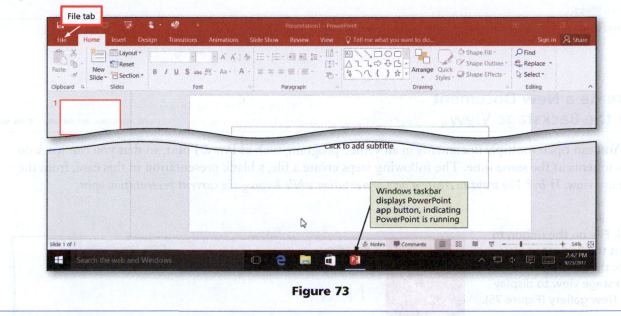

Figure 73

To Open an Existing File

1 SIGN IN | 2 USE WINDOWS | 3 USE APPS | 4 FILE MANAGEMENT | 5 SWITCH APPS | 6 SAVE FILES
7 CHANGE SCREEN RESOLUTION | 8 EXIT APPS | **9 USE ADDITIONAL APP FEATURES** | 10 USE HELP

As discussed earlier, the Backstage view contains a set of commands that enable you to manage documents and data about the documents. *Why? From the Backstage view in PowerPoint, for example, you can create, open, print, and save documents. You also can share documents, manage versions, set permissions, and modify document properties. In other Office apps, the Backstage view may contain features specific to those apps.* The following steps open a saved file, specifically the Birding Apps file, that recently was saved.

1

- Click File on the ribbon (shown in Figure 73) to open the Backstage view and then click the Open tab in the Backstage view to display the Open gallery in the Backstage view.
- Click This PC to display recent folders accessed on your computer.
- Click the Browse button to display the Open dialog box.
- If necessary, navigate to the location of the file to open (PowerPoint folder in the CIS 101 folder).
- Click the file to open, Birding Apps in this case, to select the file (Figure 74).

Figure 74

2

• Click the Open button (Open dialog box) to open the file (shown earlier in the module in Figure 50). If necessary, click the Enable Content button.

Q&A
Why did a Security Warning appear?
The Security Warning appears when you open an Office file that might contain harmful content. The files you create in this module are not harmful, but you should be cautious when opening files from other people.

Other Ways

1. Press CTRL+O   2. Navigate to file in File Explorer window, double-click file name

To Create a New Document
from the Backstage View

1 SIGN IN | 2 USE WINDOWS | 3 USE APPS | 4 FILE MANAGEMENT | 5 SWITCH APPS | 6 SAVE FILES
7 CHANGE SCREEN RESOLUTION | 8 EXIT APPS | 9 USE ADDITIONAL APP FEATURES | 10 USE HELP

You can open multiple documents in an Office program, such as PowerPoint, so that you can work on the documents at the same time. The following steps create a file, a blank presentation in this case, from the Backstage view. *Why? You want to create a new presentation while keeping the current presentation open.*

1

• Click File on the ribbon to open the Backstage view.

• Click the New tab in the Backstage view to display the New gallery (Figure 75).

Q&A
Can I create documents through the Backstage view in other Office apps?
Yes. If the Office app has a New tab in the Backstage view, the New gallery displays various options for creating a new file.

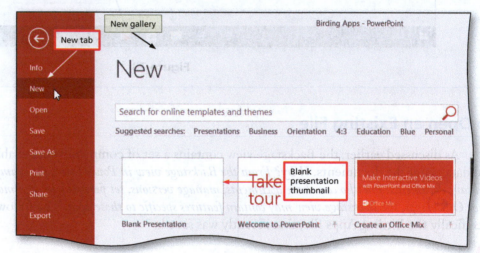

Figure 75

2

• Click the Blank Presentation thumbnail in the New gallery to create a new presentation (Figure 76).

Figure 76

Other Ways

1. Press CTRL+N

To Enter Text in a Presentation

The next PowerPoint presentation identifies the Best Rates for birding tours. The following step enters the first line of text in a slide.

① Type **Birding Tours on Sale** in the title text placeholder.

② Type **Book now for best rates** in the subtitle text placeholder (Figure 77).

③ Click outside the title text and subtitle text placeholders to deselect these slide elements.

Figure 77

To Save a File in a Folder

The following steps save the second presentation in the PowerPoint folder in the class folder (CIS 101, in this case) in the Documents folder using the file name, Best Rates.

① Click the Save button on the Quick Access Toolbar, which depending on settings, will display either the Save As gallery in the Backstage view or the Save As dialog box.

② If your screen displays the Backstage view, click This PC, if necessary, to display options in the right pane related to saving on your computer; if your screen already displays the Save As dialog box, proceed to Step 4.

③ Click the Browse button in the left pane to display the Save As dialog box.

④ Type **Best Rates** in the File name box (Save As dialog box) to change the file name. Do not press the ENTER key after typing the file name because you do not want to close the dialog box at this time.

⑤ If necessary, navigate to the desired save location (in this case, the PowerPoint folder in the CIS 101 folder [or your class folder] in the Documents folder). For specific instructions, perform the tasks in Steps 4a and 4b in the previous section in this module titled To Save a File in a Folder.

⑥ Click the Save button (Save As dialog box) to save the presentation in the selected folder on the selected drive with the entered file name.

To Close a File Using the Backstage View

1 SIGN IN | 2 USE WINDOWS | 3 USE APPS | 4 FILE MANAGEMENT | 5 SWITCH APPS | 6 SAVE FILES
7 CHANGE SCREEN RESOLUTION | 8 EXIT APPS | 9 USE ADDITIONAL APP FEATURES | 10 USE HELP

Sometimes, you may want to close an Office file, such as a PowerPoint presentation, entirely and start over with a new file. You also may want to close a file when you are done working with it. *Why? You should close a file when you are done working with it so that you do not make inadvertent changes to it.* The following steps close the current active PowerPoint file, that is, the Best Rates presentation, without exiting PowerPoint.

1
- Click File on the ribbon to open the Backstage view (Figure 78).

2
- Click Close in the Backstage view to close the open file (Best Rates, in this case) without exiting the active app (PowerPoint).

Q&A
What if PowerPoint displays a dialog box about saving?
Click the Save button if you want to save the changes, click the Don't Save button if you want to ignore the changes since the last time you saved, and click the Cancel button if you do not want to close the presentation.

Can I use the Backstage view to close an open file in other Office apps, such as Excel and Word?
Yes.

Figure 78

Other Ways

1. Press CTRL+F4

To Open a Recent File Using the Backstage View

1 SIGN IN | 2 USE WINDOWS | 3 USE APPS | 4 FILE MANAGEMENT | 5 SWITCH APPS | 6 SAVE FILES
7 CHANGE SCREEN RESOLUTION | 8 EXIT APPS | 9 USE ADDITIONAL APP FEATURES | 10 USE HELP

You sometimes need to open a file that you recently modified. *Why? You may have more changes to make, such as adding more content or correcting errors.* The Backstage view allows you to access recent files easily. The following steps reopen the Best Rates file just closed.

1
- Click File on the ribbon to open the Backstage view.
- Click the Open tab in the Backstage view to display the Open gallery (Figure 79).

2
- Click the desired file name in the Recent list, Best Rates in this case, to open the file.

Q&A
Can I use the Backstage view to open a recent file in other Office apps, such as Word and Excel?
Yes, as long as the file name appears in the list of recent files.

Figure 79

Other Ways

1. Click File on ribbon, click Open tab in Backstage view, click This PC, click Browse button, navigate to file (Open dialog box), click Open button

To Create a New Blank Document from File Explorer

File Explorer provides a means to create a blank Office document without running an Office app. The following steps use File Explorer to create a blank PowerPoint presentation. *Why? Sometimes you might need to create a blank presentation and then return to it later for editing.*

1
- Click the File Explorer button on the taskbar to make the folder window the active window.
- If necessary, double-click the Documents folder in the navigation pane to expand the Documents folder.
- If necessary, double-click your class folder (CIS 101, in this case) in the navigation pane to expand the folder.
- Click the PowerPoint folder in the navigation pane to display its contents in the file list.
- With the PowerPoint folder selected, right-click an open area in the file list to display a shortcut menu.
- Point to New on the shortcut menu to display the New submenu (Figure 80).

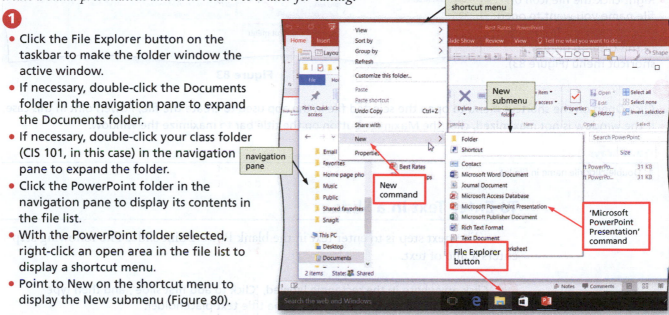

Figure 80

2
- Click 'Microsoft PowerPoint Presentation' on the New submenu to display an icon and text box for a new file in the current folder window with the file name, New Microsoft PowerPoint Presentation, selected (Figure 81).

Figure 81

3
- Type **Recommended Travel Agents** in the text box and then press the ENTER key to assign a new file name to the new file in the current folder (Figure 82).

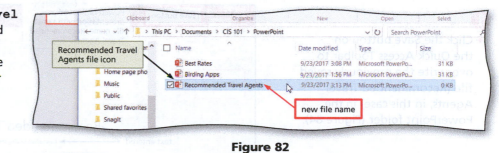

Figure 82

To Run an App from File Explorer and Open a File

Previously in this module, you learned how to run PowerPoint using the Start menu and the search box. The following steps, which assume Windows is running, use File Explorer to run PowerPoint based on a typical installation. *Why? Another way to run an Office app is to open an existing file from File Explorer, which causes the app in which the file was created to run and then open the selected file.* You may need to ask your instructor how to run PowerPoint for your computer.

- If necessary, display the file to open in the folder window in File Explorer (shown in Figure 82).
- Right-click the file icon or file name you want to open (Recommended Travel Agents, in this case) to display a shortcut menu (Figure 83).

Figure 83

2

- Click Open on the shortcut menu to open the selected file in the app used to create the file, PowerPoint in this case.
- If the window is not maximized, click the Maximize button on the title bar to maximize the window.

Other Ways

1. Double-click file name in file list

To Enter Text in a Slide

The next step is to enter text in the blank PowerPoint slide. The following step enters a line of text.

1 Click anywhere in the rectangle labeled, 'Click to add first slide', and then type `Recommended Travel Agents` in the title text placeholder.

2 Type `Customized birding and nature tours` in the subtitle text placeholder (shown in Figure 84).

To Save an Existing Office File with the Same File Name

1 SIGN IN | 2 USE WINDOWS | 3 USE APPS | 4 FILE MANAGEMENT | 5 SWITCH APPS | 6 SAVE FILES
7 CHANGE SCREEN RESOLUTION | 8 EXIT APPS | 9 USE ADDITIONAL APP FEATURES | 10 USE HELP

Saving frequently cannot be overemphasized. **Why?** *You have made modifications to the file (presentation) since you created it. Thus, you should save again. Similarly, you should continue saving files frequently so that you do not lose the changes you have made since the time you last saved the file.* You can use the same file name, such as Recommended Travel Agents, to save the changes made to the presentation. The following step saves a file again with the same file name.

1

- Click the Save button on the Quick Access Toolbar to overwrite the previously saved file (Recommended Travel Agents, in this case) in the PowerPoint folder (Figure 84).

Figure 84

Other Ways

1. Press CTRL+S   2. Press SHIFT+F12

To Save a File with a New File Name

You might want to save a file with a different file name or to a different location. For example, you might start a homework assignment with a data file and then save it with a final file name for submission to your instructor, saving it to a location designated by your instructor. The following steps save a file with a different file name.

1 Click the File tab to open the Backstage view.

2 Click the Save As tab to display the Save As gallery.

3 If necessary, click This PC to display options in the right pane related to saving on your computer.

4 Click the Browse button in the left pane to display the Save As dialog box.

5 Type `Travel Agents` in the File name box (Save As dialog box) to change the file name. Do not press the ENTER key after typing the file name because you do not want to close the dialog box at this time.

6 If necessary, navigate to the desired save location (in this case, the PowerPoint folder in the CIS 101 folder [or your class folder] in the Documents folder). For specific instructions, perform the tasks in Steps 4a and 4b in the previous section titled To Save a File in a Folder.

7 Click the Save button (Save As dialog box) to save the presentation in the selected folder on the selected drive with the entered file name.

To Exit an Office App

You are finished using PowerPoint. The following steps exit PowerPoint.

1 Because you have multiple PowerPoint documents open, right-click the PowerPoint app button on the taskbar and then click 'Close all windows' on the shortcut menu to close all open documents and exit PowerPoint.

2 If a dialog box appears, click the Save button to save any changes made to the file since the last save.

Renaming, Moving, and Deleting Files

Earlier in this module, you learned how to organize files in folders, which is part of a process known as **file management**. The following sections cover additional file management topics including renaming, moving, and deleting files.

To Rename a File

1 SIGN IN | 2 USE WINDOWS | 3 USE APPS | **4 FILE MANAGEMENT** | 5 SWITCH APPS | 6 SAVE FILES
7 CHANGE SCREEN RESOLUTION | 8 EXIT APPS | 9 USE ADDITIONAL APP FEATURES | 10 USE HELP

In some circumstances, you may want to change the name of, or rename, a file or a folder. *Why? You may want to distinguish a file in one folder or drive from a copy of a similar file, or you may decide to rename a file to better identify its contents.* The following steps change the name of the Birding Apps file in the PowerPoint folder to Birding Apps Presentation.

1

- If necessary, click the File Explorer button on the taskbar to make the folder window the active window.
- Navigate to the location of the file to be renamed (in this case, the PowerPoint folder in the CIS 101 [or your class folder] folder in the Documents folder) to display the file(s) it contains in the file list.
- Click the file to be renamed, the Birding Apps icon or file name in the file list in this case, to select it.
- Right-click the selected file to display a shortcut menu that presents a list of commands related to files (Figure 85).

Figure 85

2

- Click Rename on the shortcut menu to place the current file name in a text box.
- Type **Birding Apps Presentation** in the text box and then press the ENTER key (Figure 86).

Q&A

Are any risks involved in renaming files that are located on a hard drive?

If you inadvertently rename a file that is associated with certain apps, the apps may not be able to find the file and, therefore, may not run properly. Always use caution when renaming files.

Can I rename a file when it is open?

No, a file must be closed to change the file name.

Figure 86

Other Ways

1. Select file, press F2, type new file name, press ENTER

2. Select file, click Rename (Home tab | Organize group), type new file name, press ENTER

To Move a File

1 SIGN IN | 2 USE WINDOWS | 3 USE APPS | **4 FILE MANAGEMENT** | 5 SWITCH APPS | 6 SAVE FILES
7 CHANGE SCREEN RESOLUTION | 8 EXIT APPS | 9 USE ADDITIONAL APP FEATURES | **10 USE HELP**

Why? At some time, you may want to move a file from one folder, called the source folder, to another, called the destination folder. When you move a file, it no longer appears in the original folder. If the destination and the source folders are on the same media, you can move a file by dragging it. If the folders are on different media, you will need to right-drag the file and then click Move here on the shortcut menu. The following step moves the Recommended Travel Agents file from the PowerPoint folder to the CIS 101 folder.

1

- If necessary, in File Explorer, navigate to the location of the file to be moved (in this case, the PowerPoint folder in the CIS 101 folder [or your class folder] in the Documents folder).
- If necessary, click the PowerPoint folder in the navigation pane to display the files it contains in the right pane.
- Drag the file to be moved, the Recommended Travel Agents file in the right pane in this case, to the CIS 101 folder in the navigation pane (Figure 87).

Experiment

- Click the CIS 101 folder in the navigation pane to verify that the file was moved.

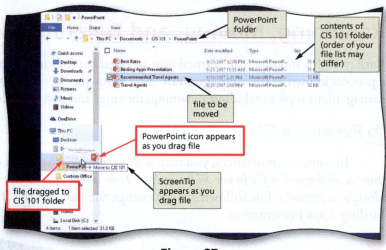

Figure 87

Other Ways

1. Right-click file to move, click Cut on shortcut menu, right-click destination folder, click Paste on shortcut menu

2. Select file to move, press CTRL+X, select destination folder, press CTRL+V

1 SIGN IN | 2 USE WINDOWS | 3 USE APPS | **4 FILE MANAGEMENT** | 5 SWITCH APPS | 6 SAVE FILES
7 CHANGE SCREEN RESOLUTION | 8 EXIT APPS | 9 USE ADDITIONAL APP FEATURES | **10 USE HELP**

To Delete a File

A final task you may want to perform is to delete a file. Exercise extreme caution when deleting a file or files. When you delete a file from a hard drive, the deleted file is stored in the Recycle Bin where you can recover it until you empty the Recycle Bin. If you delete a file from removable media, such as a USB flash drive, the file is deleted permanently. The next steps delete the Recommended Travel Agents file from the CIS 101 folder. *Why? When a file no longer is needed, you can delete it to conserve space on your storage location.*

1

- If necessary, in File Explorer, navigate to the location of the file to be deleted (in this case, the CIS 101 folder [or your class folder] in the Documents folder).
- Click the file to be deleted, the Recommended Travel Agents icon or file name in the right pane in this case, to select the file.
- Right-click the selected file to display a shortcut menu (Figure 88).

2

- Click Delete on the shortcut menu to delete the file.
- If a dialog box appears, click the Yes button to delete the file.

Q&A Can I use this same technique to delete a folder?

Yes. Right-click the folder and then click Delete on the shortcut menu. When you delete a folder, all of the files and folders contained in the folder you are deleting, together with any files and folders on lower hierarchical levels, are deleted as well. For example, if you delete the CIS 101 folder, you will delete all folders and files inside the CIS 101 folder.

Figure 88

Other Ways

1. Select file, press DELETE key

Microsoft Office and Windows Help

At any time while you are using one of the Office apps, such as PowerPoint, you can use Office Help to display information about all topics associated with the app. Help in other Office apps operates in a similar fashion.

In Office, Help is presented in a window that has browser-style navigation buttons. Each Office app has its own Help home page, which is the starting Help page that is displayed in the Help window. If your computer is connected to the Internet, the contents of the Help page reflect both the local help files installed on the computer and material from Microsoft's website.

To Open the Help Window in an Office App

1 SIGN IN | 2 USE WINDOWS | 3 USE APPS | 4 FILE MANAGEMENT | 5 SWITCH APPS | 6 SAVE FILES
7 CHANGE SCREEN RESOLUTION | 8 EXIT APPS | 9 USE ADDITIONAL APP FEATURES | 10 USE HELP

The following step opens the PowerPoint Help window. *Why? You might not understand how certain commands or operations work in PowerPoint, so you can obtain the necessary information using help.*

1

- Run PowerPoint.
- Click the Blank Presentation thumbnail to display a blank presentation.
- Press F1 to open the PowerPoint Help window (Figure 89).

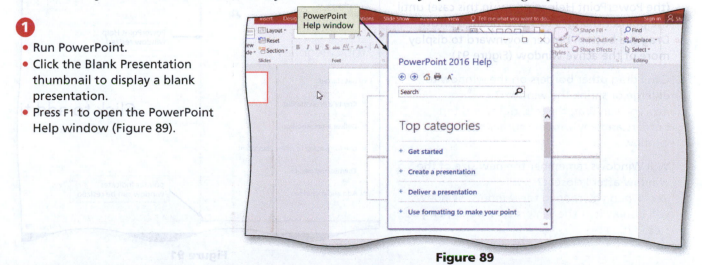

Figure 89

Moving and Resizing Windows

At times, it is useful, or even necessary, to have more than one window open and visible on the screen at the same time. You can resize and move these open windows so that you can view different areas of and elements in the window. In the case of the Help window, for example, it could be covering text in the PowerPoint window that you need to see.

To Move a Window by Dragging

1 SIGN IN | 2 USE WINDOWS | 3 USE APPS | 4 FILE MANAGEMENT | 5 SWITCH APPS | 6 SAVE FILES
7 CHANGE SCREEN RESOLUTION | 8 EXIT APPS | 9 USE ADDITIONAL APP FEATURES | 10 USE HELP

You can move any open window that is not maximized to another location on the desktop by dragging the title bar of the window. **Why?** *You might want to have a better view of what is behind the window or just want to move the window so that you can see it better.* The following step drags the PowerPoint Help window to the upper-left corner of the desktop.

1

- Drag the window title bar (the PowerPoint Help window title bar, in this case) so that the window moves to the upper-left corner of the desktop, as shown in Figure 90.

Figure 90

To Resize a Window by Dragging

1 SIGN IN | 2 USE WINDOWS | 3 USE APPS | 4 FILE MANAGEMENT | 5 SWITCH APPS | 6 SAVE FILES
7 CHANGE SCREEN RESOLUTION | 8 EXIT APPS | 9 USE ADDITIONAL APP FEATURES | 10 USE HELP

A method used to change the size of a window is to drag the window borders. The following step changes the size of the PowerPoint Help window by dragging its borders. **Why?** *Sometimes, information is not visible completely in a window, and you want to increase the size of the window.*

1

- Point to the lower-right corner of the window (the PowerPoint Help window, in this case) until the pointer changes to a two-headed arrow.
- Drag the bottom border downward to display more of the active window (Figure 91).

Q&A

Can I drag other borders on the window to enlarge or shrink the window?
Yes, you can drag the left, right, and top borders and any window corner to resize a window.

Will Windows remember the new size of the window after I close it?
Yes. When you reopen the window, Windows will display it at the same size it was when you closed it.

Figure 91

Using Office Help

Once an Office app's Help window is open, several methods exist for navigating Help. You can search for help by using any of the three following methods from the Help window:

1. Enter search text in the Search text box.
2. Click the links in the Help window.
3. Use the Table of Contents.

To Obtain Help Using the Search Text Box

1 SIGN IN | 2 USE WINDOWS | 3 USE APPS | 4 FILE MANAGEMENT | 5 SWITCH APPS | 6 SAVE FILES
7 CHANGE SCREEN RESOLUTION | 8 EXIT APPS | 9 USE ADDITIONAL APP FEATURES | 10 USE HELP

Assume for the following example that you want to know more about fonts. The following steps use the Search text box to obtain useful information about fonts by entering the word, fonts, as search text. *Why? You may not know the exact help topic you are looking to find, so using keywords can help narrow your search.*

1

- Type **fonts** in the Search text box at the top of the PowerPoint Help window to enter the search text.
- Press the ENTER key to display the search results (Figure 92).

Q&A

Why do my search results differ?
If you do not have an Internet connection, your results will reflect only the content of the Help files on your computer. When searching for help online, results also can change as content is added, deleted, and updated on the online Help webpages maintained by Microsoft.

Why were my search results not very helpful?
When initiating a search, be sure to check the spelling of the search text; also, keep your search specific to return the most accurate results.

Figure 92

2

- Click the 'Change the fonts', or a similar, link to display the Help information associated with the selected topic (Figure 93).

Figure 93

3

- Click the Home button in the Help window to clear the search results and redisplay the Help home page (Figure 94).
- Click the Close button in the PowerPoint 2016 Help window to close the window.

Figure 94

BTW
Customizing the Ribbon
In addition to customizing the Quick Access Toolbar, you can add items to and remove items from the ribbon. To customize the ribbon, click File on the ribbon to open the Backstage view, click the Options tab in the Backstage view, and then click Customize Ribbon in the left pane of the Options dialog box. More information about customizing the ribbon is presented in a later module.

Obtaining Help while Working in an Office App

Help in the Office apps, such as PowerPoint, provides you with the ability to obtain help directly, without opening the Help window and initiating a search. For example, you may be unsure about how a particular command works, or you may be presented with a dialog box that you are not sure how to use.

Figure 95 shows one option for obtaining help while working in an Office app. If you want to learn more about a command, point to its button and wait for the ScreenTip to appear. If the Help icon and 'Tell me more' link appear in the ScreenTip, click the 'Tell me more' link or press the F1 key while pointing to the button to open the Help window associated with that command.

Figure 95

Figure 96 shows a dialog box that contains a Help button. Clicking the Help button or pressing the F1 key while the dialog box is displayed opens a Help window. The Help window contains help about that dialog box, if available. If no help file is available for that particular dialog box, then the main Help window opens.

Figure 96

As mentioned previously, the Tell Me box is available in most Office apps and can perform a variety of functions. One of these functions is to provide easy access to commands by typing a description of the command.

To Obtain Help Using the Tell Me Box

1 SIGN IN | 2 USE WINDOWS | 3 USE APPS | 4 FILE MANAGEMENT | 5 SWITCH APPS | 6 SAVE FILES
7 CHANGE SCREEN RESOLUTION | 8 EXIT APPS | 9 USE ADDITIONAL APP FEATURES | 10 USE HELP

If you are having trouble finding a command in an Office app, you can use the Tell Me box to search for the function you are trying to perform. As you type, the Tell Me box will suggest commands that match the search text you are entering. *Why? You can use the Tell Me box to access commands quickly that you otherwise may be unable to find on the ribbon.* The following steps find information about margins.

1
- Type **border** in the Tell Me box and watch the search results appear.
- Point to Border Style to display a submenu displaying the various border designs (Figure 97).
- Click an empty area of the presentation window to close the search results.

2
- Exit Microsoft PowerPoint.

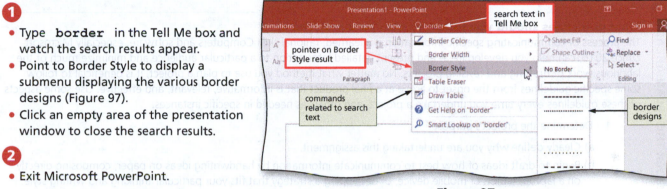

Figure 97

Using the Windows Search Box

One of the more powerful Windows features is the Windows search box. The search box is a central location from where you can type search text and quickly access related Windows commands or web search results. In addition, **Cortana** is a new search tool in Windows that you can access using the search box. It can act as a personal assistant by performing functions such as providing ideas; searching for apps, files, and folders; and setting reminders. In addition to typing search text in the search box, you also can use your computer or mobile device's microphone to give verbal commands.

To Use the Windows Search Box

1 SIGN IN | 2 USE WINDOWS | 3 USE APPS | 4 FILE MANAGEMENT | 5 SWITCH APPS | 6 SAVE FILES
7 CHANGE SCREEN RESOLUTION | 8 EXIT APPS | 9 USE ADDITIONAL APP FEATURES | 10 USE HELP

The following step uses the Windows search box to search for a Windows command. *Why? Using the search box to locate apps, settings, folders, and files can be faster than navigating windows and dialog boxes to search for the desired content.*

1
- Type **notification** in the search box to display the search results. The search results include related Windows settings, Windows Store apps, and web search results (Figure 98).
- Click an empty area of the desktop to close the search results.

Figure 98

Summary

In this module, you learned how to use the Windows interface, several touch screen and mouse operations, and file and folder management. You also learned some basic features of PowerPoint and discovered the common elements that exist among Microsoft Office apps. Topics covered included signing in, using Windows, using apps, file management, switching between apps, saving files, changing screen resolution, exiting apps, using additional app features, and using Help.

CONSIDER THIS: PLAN AHEAD

What guidelines should you follow to plan your projects?

The process of communicating specific information is a learned, rational skill. Computers and software, especially Microsoft Office 2016, can help you develop ideas and present detailed information to a particular audience and minimize much of the laborious work of drafting and revising projects. No matter what method you use to plan a project, it is beneficial to follow some specific guidelines from the onset to arrive at a final product that is informative, relevant, and effective. Use some aspects of these guidelines every time you undertake a project, and others as needed in specific instances.

1. Determine the project's purpose.

    a) Clearly define why you are undertaking this assignment.

    b) Begin to draft ideas of how best to communicate information by handwriting ideas on paper; composing directly on a laptop, tablet, or mobile device; or developing a strategy that fits your particular thinking and writing style.

2. Analyze your audience.

    a) Learn about the people who will read, analyze, or view your work.

    b) Determine their interests and needs so that you can present the information they need to know and omit the information they already possess.

    c) Form a mental picture of these people or find photos of people who fit this profile so that you can develop a project with the audience in mind.

3. Gather possible content.

    a) Locate existing information that may reside in spreadsheets, databases, or other files.

    b) Conduct a web search to find relevant websites.

    c) Read pamphlets, magazine and newspaper articles, and books to gain insights of how others have approached your topic.

    d) Conduct personal interviews to obtain perspectives not available by any other means.

    e) Consider video and audio clips as potential sources for material that might complement or support the factual data you uncover.

4. Determine what content to present to your audience.

    a) Write three or four major ideas you want an audience member to remember after reading or viewing your project.

    b) Envision your project's endpoint, the key fact you wish to emphasize, so that all project elements lead to this final element.

    c) Determine relevant time factors, such as the length of time to develop the project, how long readers will spend reviewing your project, or the amount of time allocated for your speaking engagement.

    d) Decide whether a graph, photo, or artistic element can express or enhance a particular concept.

    e) Be mindful of the order in which you plan to present the content, and place the most important material at the beginning or end of the presentation, because readers and audience members generally remember the first and last pieces of information they see and hear.

How should you submit solutions to questions in the assignments identified with a ✻ symbol?

Every assignment in this book contains one or more questions with a ✻ symbol. These questions require you to think beyond the assigned file. Present your solutions to the question in the format required by your instructor. Possible formats may include one or more of these options: write the answer; create a presentation that contains the answer; present your answer to the class; discuss your answer in a group; record the answer as audio or video using a webcam, smartphone, or portable media player; or post answers on a blog, wiki, or website.

Apply Your Knowledge

Reinforce the skills and apply the concepts you learned in this module.

Creating a Folder and a Presentation

Instructions: You will create a PowerPoint Assignments folder and then create a PowerPoint presentation and save it in the folder.

Perform the following tasks:

1. Open the File Explorer window and then double-click to open the Documents folder.
2. Click the New folder button on the Quick Access Toolbar to display a new folder icon and text box for the folder name.
3. Type **PowerPoint Assignments** in the text box to name the folder. Press the ENTER key to create the folder in the Documents folder.
4. Run PowerPoint and create a new blank presentation.
5. Type **Contact Information** in the title text placeholder (Figure 99).

Figure 99

6. If requested by your instructor, enter your name, phone number, and email address in the subtitle placeholder.
7. Click the Save button on the Quick Access Toolbar. Navigate to the PowerPoint Assignments folder in the Documents folder and then save the presentation using the file name, Apply 1 Document (Figure 99).
8. If your Quick Access Toolbar does not show the Quick Print button, add the Quick Print button to the Quick Access Toolbar. Print the presentation using the Quick Print button on the Quick Access Toolbar. When you are finished printing, remove the Quick Print button from the Quick Access Toolbar.
9. Submit the printout to your instructor.
10. Exit PowerPoint.
11. ✻ What other commands might you find useful to include on the Quick Access Toolbar?

Extend Your Knowledge

Extend the skills you learned in this module and experiment with new skills. You will use Help to complete the assignment.

Using Help

Instructions: Use PowerPoint Help to perform the following tasks.

Perform the following tasks:

1. Run PowerPoint.

2. Press F1 to open the PowerPoint Help window (shown in Figure 89).

3. Search PowerPoint Help to answer the following questions.

   a. What are three new features of PowerPoint 2016?

   b. What type of training is available through PowerPoint Help for PowerPoint 2016?

   c. What are the steps to customize the ribbon?

   d. What is the purpose of the Office Clipboard?

   e. What is the purpose of Slide Sorter view?

   f. How do you change a slide layout?

   g. How do you insert pictures?

   h. How do you change the size of text?

   i. What are the steps to zoom in and out of a slide?

   j. What is the purpose of the Insights pane? How do you display it?

4. Type the answers from your searches in a new blank PowerPoint presentation. Save the presentation with a new file name and then submit it in the format specified by your instructor.

5. If requested by your instructor, enter your name in the PowerPoint slide.

6. Exit PowerPoint.

7. ✷ What search text did you use to perform the searches above? Did it take multiple attempts to search and locate the exact information for which you were searching?

Expand Your World

Create a solution that uses cloud or web technologies by learning and investigating on your own from general guidance.

Creating Folders on OneDrive and Using the PowerPoint Online App

Instructions: You will create the folders shown in Figure 100 on OneDrive. Then, you will use the PowerPoint Online app to create a small file and save it in a folder on OneDrive.

Figure 100

Perform the following tasks:

1. Sign in to OneDrive in your browser.

2. Use the New button to create the folder structure shown in Figure 100.

3. In the Upcoming Events folder, use the New button to create a PowerPoint presentation with the file name, Expand 1 Task List, that contains the text, Prepare agenda for Tuesday's meeting.

4. If requested by your instructor, add your name to the PowerPoint slide.

5. Save the presentation in the Upcoming Events folder and then exit the app.

6. Submit the assignment in the format specified by your instructor.

7. ☀ Based on your current knowledge of OneDrive, do you think you will use it? What about the PowerPoint Online app?

In the Labs

Design, create, modify, and/or use files following the guidelines, concepts, and skills presented in this module. Labs 1 and 2, which increase in difficulty, require you to create solutions based on what you learned in the module; Lab 3 requires you to apply your creative thinking and problem-solving skills to design and implement a solution.

Lab 1: **Creating Folders for a Bookstore**

Problem: Your friend works for a local bookstore. He would like to organize his files in relation to the types of books available in the store. He has seven main categories: fiction, biography, children, humor, social science, nonfiction, and medical. You are to create a folder structure similar to Figure 101.

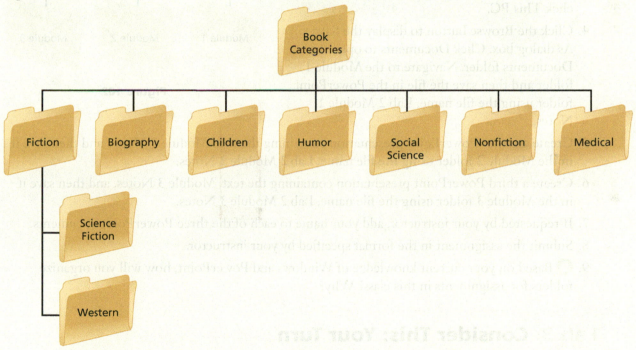

Figure 101

Perform the following tasks:

1. Click the File Explorer button on the taskbar and display the contents of the Documents folder.

2. In the Documents folder, create the main folder and name it Book Categories.

3. Navigate to the Book Categories folder.

4. Within the Book Categories folder, create a folder for each of the following: Fiction, Biography, Children, Humor, Social Science, Nonfiction, and Medical.

5. Within the Fiction folder, create two additional folders, one for Science Fiction and the second for Western.

Continued >

In the Labs continued

6. If requested by your instructor, add another folder using your last name as the folder name.

7. Submit the assignment in the format specified by your instructor.

8. ✸ Think about how you use your computer for various tasks (consider personal, professional, and academic reasons). What folders will be required to store the files you save?

Lab 2: Creating PowerPoint Presentations and Saving Them in Appropriate Folders

Problem: You are taking a class that requires you to complete three PowerPoint modules. You will save the work completed in each module in a different folder (Figure 102).

Perform the following tasks:

1. Create the folders shown in Figure 102.

2. Create a PowerPoint presentation containing the text, Module 1 Notes.

3. In the Backstage view, click Save As and then click This PC.

4. Click the Browse button to display the Save As dialog box. Click Documents to open the Documents folder. Navigate to the Module 1 folder and then save the file in the PowerPoint folder using the file name, Lab 2 Module 1 Notes.

Figure 102

5. Create another PowerPoint presentation containing the text, Module 2 Notes, and then save it in the Module 2 folder using the file name, Lab 2 Module 2 Notes.

6. Create a third PowerPoint presentation containing the text, Module 3 Notes, and then save it in the Module 3 folder using the file name, Lab 2 Module 3 Notes.

7. If requested by your instructor, add your name to each of the three PowerPoint documents.

8. Submit the assignment in the format specified by your instructor.

9. ✸ Based on your current knowledge of Windows and PowerPoint, how will you organize folders for assignments in this class? Why?

Lab 3: Consider This: Your Turn

Performing Research about Malware

Problem: You have just installed a new computer with the Windows operating system. Because you want to be sure that it is protected from the threat of malware, you decide to research malware, malware protection, and removing malware.

Perform the following tasks:

Part 1:   Research the following three topics: malware, malware protection, and removing malware. Use the concepts and techniques presented in this module to use the search box to find information regarding these topics. Create a PowerPoint presentation that contains steps to safeguard a computer properly from malware, ways to prevent malware, as well as the different ways to remove malware or a virus should your computer become infected. Submit your assignment and the answers to the following critical thinking questions in the format specified by your instructor.

Part 2:   ✸ You made several decisions while searching for this assignment. What decisions did you make? What was the rationale behind them? How did you locate the information about malware?

1 | Creating and Editing a Presentation with Pictures

Objectives

You will have mastered the material in this module when you can:

- Select and change a document theme and variant
- Create a title slide and a text slide with a multilevel bulleted list
- Add new slides and change slide layouts
- Insert pictures into slides with and without content placeholders
- Move and resize pictures
- Change font size and color
- Bold and italicize text
- Duplicate a slide
- Arrange slides
- Select slide transitions
- View a presentation in Slide Show view

Introduction

A PowerPoint **presentation**, also called a **slide show**, can help you deliver a dynamic, professional-looking message to an audience. PowerPoint allows you to produce slides to use in an academic, business, or other environment. The collection of slides in a presentation is called a **deck**, resembling a deck of cards that are stacked on top of each other. A common use of slide decks is to enhance an oral presentation. A speaker might desire to convey information, such as urging students to volunteer at a fund-raising event, explaining changes in employee compensation packages, or describing a new laboratory procedure. The PowerPoint slides should reinforce the speaker's message and help the audience retain the information presented. Custom slides can fit your specific needs and contain diagrams, charts, tables, pictures, shapes, video, sound, and animation effects to make your presentation more effective. An accompanying handout gives audience members reference notes and review material for your presentation.

Project — Presentation with a Bulleted List and Pictures

In this module's project, you will follow proper design guidelines and learn to use PowerPoint to create, save, and view the slides shown in Figures 1–1a through 1–1e. The objective is to produce a presentation, titled Tall Oaks, to promote three programs at the nature center. This slide show has a variety of pictures and visual elements to add interest and give facts about the events. Some of the text has formatting and color enhancements. Transitions help one slide flow gracefully into the next during a slide show.

font color changed

picture inserted and sized

text italicized

(a) Slide 1 (Title Slide with Picture)

picture inserted and sized

text bolded and size increased

(b) Slide 2 (Multilevel Bulleted List with Picture)

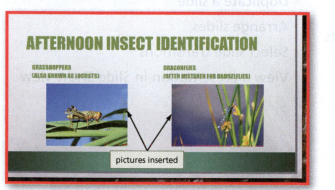

pictures inserted

(c) Slide 3 (Comparison Layout and Pictures)

illustration inserted and sized

(d) Slide 4 (Title and Illustration)

text edited

(e) Slide 5 (Closing Slide)

Figure 1–1

In this module, you will learn how to perform basic tasks using PowerPoint. The following roadmap identifies general activities you will perform as you progress through this module:

1. INSERT the four PRESENTATION SLIDES, using various layouts.
2. ENTER the TEXT for the slides.
3. FORMAT the TEXT on each slide.
4. INSERT GRAPHICAL ELEMENTS, including pictures.
5. SIZE AND POSITION the graphical elements.
6. ENHANCE the SLIDE SHOW by adding a closing slide and transition.
7. DISPLAY the SLIDES.

For an introduction to Office and instructions about how to perform basic tasks in Office apps, read the Office and Windows module at the beginning of this book, where you can learn how to run an application, use the ribbon, save a file, open a file, print a file, exit an application, use Help, and much more.

Choosing a Document Theme and Variant

You easily can give the slides in a presentation a professional and integrated appearance by using a theme. A document **theme** is a specific design with coordinating colors, fonts, and special effects such as shadows and reflections. Several themes are available when you run PowerPoint, each with a specific name. Using one of the formatted themes makes creating a professional-looking presentation easier and quicker than using the Blank Presentation template, where you would need to make all design decisions.

Each theme has a set of four alternate designs, called **variants**. Each variant has the same overall composition, but the colors, fonts, and design elements differ. Once you select a theme, you then can select a variation that best fits your overall design needs. If you later decide that another theme or variant would better fit the presentation's general theme, you can change these elements while you are developing slides.

For an introduction to Windows and instructions about how to perform basic Windows tasks, read the Office and Windows module at the beginning of this book, where you can learn how to resize windows, change screen resolution, create folders, move and rename files, use Windows Help, and much more.

To Choose a Document Theme and Variant

1 INSERT PRESENTATION SLIDES | 2 ENTER TEXT | 3 FORMAT TEXT | 4 INSERT GRAPHICAL ELEMENTS
5 SIZE & POSITION | 6 ENHANCE SLIDE SHOW | 7 DISPLAY SLIDES

When you begin creating a new PowerPoint presentation, you need to select a theme. You either can start with no design elements by using the Blank Presentation, or you can select one of the available professionally designed themes. The following steps apply the Berlin theme and then change the variant. *Why? The title slide will have text and a picture, so you want to select a theme, like Berlin, with an uncluttered background. The presentation discusses three events occurring at the nature center, and green is the color commonly associated with nature's forests and grasslands. The default Berlin theme is predominantly orange and black, but one of its variants is green and is an appropriate choice to relate to the nature concept.*

BTW

The PowerPoint Window
The modules in this book begin with the PowerPoint window appearing as it did at the initial installation of the software. Your PowerPoint window may look different depending on your screen resolution and other PowerPoint settings.

1

- Run PowerPoint and point to the Berlin theme on the Recent screen (Figure 1–2).

Q&A I do not see the Berlin theme. What should I do?
Your list of available templates may differ from those shown in the figure. You may need to scroll down to locate the Berlin theme or enter "Berlin" in the Search box.

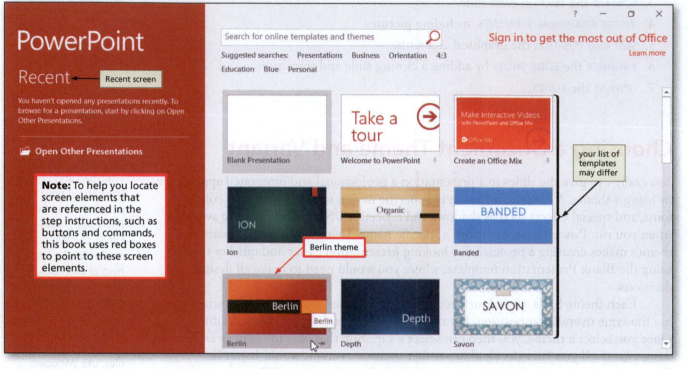

Figure 1–2

2

- Click the Berlin theme to display a theme preview dialog box with a thumbnail view of the theme and its variants (Figure 1–3).

Q&A Can I see previews of other themes?
Yes. Click the right or left arrows on the sides of the theme preview dialog box.

Figure 1–3

3

- Click the lower-left (green) variant to view a preview of that style applied to the thumbnail.

Q&A Can I see previews of the Berlin theme and green variant applied to layouts other than the title slide?
Yes. Click the right or left arrows beside the words, More Images, below the thumbnail. Three other layouts will be displayed: Title and Content, Two Content, and Photo.

- Click the Create button to apply the Berlin theme and green variant to the presentation and to display Slide 1 (Figure 1–4).

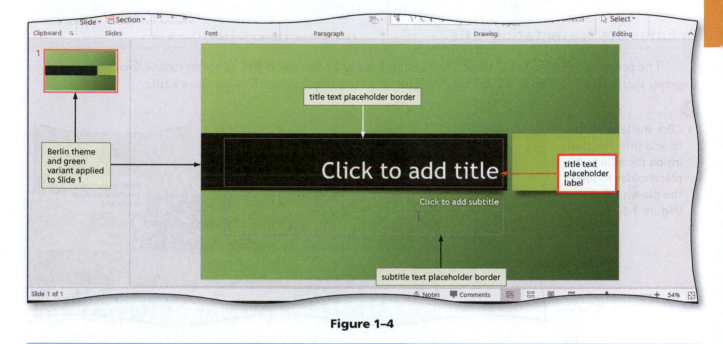

Figure 1–4

Creating a Title Slide

When you open a new presentation, the default **Title Slide** layout appears. The purpose of this layout is to introduce the presentation to the audience. PowerPoint includes other standard layouts for each of the themes. The slide layouts are set up in **landscape orientation**, where the slide width is greater than its height. In landscape orientation, the slide size is preset to 10 inches wide and 7.5 inches high when printed on a standard sheet of paper measuring 11 inches wide and 8.5 inches high.

Placeholders are boxes with dotted or hatch-marked borders that are displayed when you create a new slide. Most layouts have both a title text placeholder and at least one content placeholder. Depending on the particular slide layout selected, title and subtitle placeholders are displayed for the slide title and subtitle; a content text placeholder is displayed for text, art, or a table, chart, picture, graphic, or movie. The title slide has two text placeholders where you can type the main heading, or title, of a new slide and the subtitle.

With the exception of the Blank slide layout, PowerPoint assumes every new slide has a title. To make creating a presentation easier, any text you type after a new slide appears becomes title text in the title text placeholder. The following steps create the title slide for this presentation.

BTW

PowerPoint Screen Resolution
If you are using a computer or mobile device to step through the project in this module and you want your screens to match the figures in this book, you should change your screen's resolution to 1366 x 768. For information about how to change a computer's resolution, refer to the Office and Windows module at the beginning of this book.

How do I choose the words for the slide?

All presentations should follow the 7 × 7 rule, which states that each slide should have a maximum of seven lines, and each line should have a maximum of seven words. PowerPoint designers must choose their words carefully and, in turn, help viewers read the slides easily.

Avoid line wraps. Your audience's eyes want to stop at the end of a line. Thus, you must plan your words carefully or adjust the font size so that each point displays on only one line.

To Enter the Presentation Title

1 INSERT PRESENTATION SLIDES | 2 ENTER TEXT | 3 FORMAT TEXT | 4 INSERT GRAPHICAL ELEMENTS
5 SIZE & POSITION | 6 ENHANCE SLIDE SHOW | 7 DISPLAY SLIDES

The presentation title for Project 1 is Autumn Family Programs. *Why? The presentation discusses three programs that will be held during the fall months.* The following steps create the slide show's title.

1

- Click the label, 'Click to add title', located inside the title text placeholder to select the placeholder (Figure 1–5).

Figure 1–5

2

- Type **Autumn Family Programs** in the title text placeholder. Do not press the ENTER key (Figure 1–6).

Figure 1–6

Correcting a Mistake When Typing

If you type the wrong letter, press the BACKSPACE key to erase all the characters back to and including the one that is incorrect. If you mistakenly press the ENTER key after typing the title and the insertion point is on the new line, simply press the BACKSPACE key to return the insertion point to the right of the last letter in the word, Programs.

By default, PowerPoint allows you to reverse up to the last 20 changes by clicking the Undo button on the Quick Access Toolbar. The ScreenTip that appears when you point to the Undo button changes to indicate the type of change just made. For example, if you type text in the title text placeholder and then point to the Undo button, the ScreenTip that appears is Undo Typing. For clarity, when referencing the Undo button in this project, the name displaying in the ScreenTip is used. You can reapply a change that you reversed with the Undo button by clicking the Redo button on the Quick Access Toolbar. Clicking the Redo button reverses the last undo action. The ScreenTip name reflects the type of reversal last performed.

Paragraphs

Text in the subtitle text placeholder supports the title text. It can appear on one or more lines in the placeholder. To create more than one subtitle line, you press the ENTER key after typing some words. PowerPoint creates a new line, which is the second paragraph in the placeholder. A **paragraph** is a segment of text with the same format that begins when you press the ENTER key and ends when you press the ENTER key again. This new paragraph is the same level as the previous paragraph. A **level** is a position within a structure, such as an outline, that indicates the magnitude of importance. PowerPoint allows for five paragraph levels.

How do you use the touch keyboard with a touch screen?

To display the on-screen keyboard, tap the Touch Keyboard button on the Windows taskbar. When finished using the touch keyboard, tap the X button on the touch keyboard to close the keyboard.

CONSIDER THIS

To Enter the Presentation Subtitle Paragraph

1 INSERT PRESENTATION SLIDES | **2 ENTER TEXT** | 3 FORMAT TEXT | 4 INSERT GRAPHICAL ELEMENTS
5 SIZE & POSITION | 6 ENHANCE SLIDE SHOW | 7 DISPLAY SLIDES

The first subtitle paragraph is related to the title. **Why?** *The subtitle gives an additional detail, the nature center's name.* The following steps enter the presentation subtitle.

1
- Click the label, 'Click to add subtitle', located inside the subtitle text placeholder to select the placeholder (Figure 1–7).

Autumn Family Programs

label disappears when placeholder is selected

sizing handles and dashed lines around border indicate placeholder is selected

Figure 1–7

②

- Type **Tall Oaks Nature Center** but do not press the ENTER key (Figure 1–8).

subtitle text entered in placeholder

Figure 1–8

1 INSERT PRESENTATION SLIDES | **2 ENTER TEXT** | 3 FORMAT TEXT | 4 INSERT GRAPHICAL ELEMENTS
5 SIZE & POSITION | 6 ENHANCE SLIDE SHOW | 7 DISPLAY SLIDES

To Zoom a Slide

You can **zoom** the view of the slide on the screen so that the text or other content is enlarged or shrunk. When you zoom in, you get a close-up view of your slide; when you zoom out, you see more of the slide at a reduced size. You will be modifying the text and other slide components as you create the presentation, so you can enlarge the slide on the screen. *Why? Zooming the slide can help you see slide elements more clearly so that you can position them precisely where desired.* The following step changes the zoom to 70 percent.

①

🔍 **Experiment**

- Repeatedly click the Zoom In and Zoom Out buttons on the status bar and watch the size of the slide change in the Slide pane.

- Click the Zoom In or Zoom Out button as many times as necessary until the Zoom button on the status bar displays 70% on its face (Figure 1–9).

Q&A

If I change the zoom percentage, will the slide display differently when I run the presentation?

No. Changing the zoom helps you develop the slide content and does not affect the slide show.

slide shown at 70% zoom

Zoom Out button

Zoom In button

Zoom slider

clicking Zoom button would display Zoom dialog box

Figure 1–9

Other Ways

1. Drag Zoom slider on status bar	2. Click Zoom level button on status bar, select desired zoom percent or type (Zoom dialog box), click OK button	3. Click Zoom button (View tab | Zoom group), select desired zoom percent or type (Zoom dialog box), click OK button	4. For touch screens: Pinch two fingers together in Slide pane (zoom out) or stretch two fingers apart (zoom in)

Formatting Characters in a Presentation

Recall that each document theme determines the color scheme, font set, and layout of a presentation. You can use a specific document theme and then change the characters' formats any time before, during, or after you type the text.

Fonts and Font Styles

Characters that appear on the screen are a specific shape and size. Examples of how you can modify the appearance, or **format**, of these typed characters on the screen and in print include changing the font, style, size, and color. The **font**, or typeface, defines the appearance and shape of the letters, numbers, punctuation marks, and symbols. **Style** indicates how the characters are formatted. PowerPoint's text font styles include regular, italic, bold, and bold italic. **Size** specifies the height of the characters and is gauged by a measurement system that uses points. A **point** is 1/72 of an inch in height. Thus, a character with a font size of 36 is 36/72 (or 1/2) of an inch in height. **Color** defines the hue of the characters.

This presentation uses the Berlin document theme, which has particular font styles and font sizes. The Berlin document theme default title text font is named Trebuchet MS. It has no special effects, and its size is 54 point. The Berlin default subtitle text font also is Trebuchet MS with a font size of 20 point.

To Select a Paragraph

1 INSERT PRESENTATION SLIDES | 2 ENTER TEXT | 3 FORMAT TEXT | 4 INSERT GRAPHICAL ELEMENTS
5 SIZE & POSITION | 6 ENHANCE SLIDE SHOW | 7 DISPLAY SLIDES

You can use many techniques to format characters. When you want to apply the same formats to multiple words or paragraphs, it is helpful to select these words. *Why? It is efficient to select the desired text and then make the desired changes to all the characters simultaneously.* The first formatting change you will make will apply to the title slide subtitle. The following step selects this paragraph.

1
- Triple-click the paragraph, Tall Oaks Nature Center, in the subtitle text placeholder to select the paragraph (Figure 1–10).

mini toolbar appears whenever you select text

subtitle text paragraph to be formatted is selected

Figure 1–10

Other Ways

1. Position pointer to left of first paragraph and drag to end of line

To Italicize Text

Different font styles often are used on slides. *Why? These style changes make the words more appealing to the reader and emphasize particular text.* **Italic** text has a slanted appearance. Used sparingly, it draws the readers' eyes to these characters. The following step adds emphasis to the line of the subtitle text by changing regular text to italic text.

1

- With the subtitle text still selected, click the Italic button on the mini toolbar to italicize that text on the slide (Figure 1–11).

Q&A If I change my mind and decide not to italicize the text, how can I remove this style?
Immediately click the Undo button on the Quick Access Toolbar, click the Italic button a second time, or press CTRL+Z.

Figure 1–11

Other Ways

1. Right-click selected text, click Italic button in mini toolbar near shortcut menu	2. Select text, click Italic button (Home tab | Font group)	3. Click Font dialog box launcher (Home tab | Font group), click Font tab (Font dialog box), click Italic in Font style list, click OK button	4. Select text, press CTRL+I

To Increase Font Size

Why? To add emphasis, you increase the font size for the subtitle text. The 'Increase Font Size' button on the mini toolbar increases the font size in preset increments. The following step uses this button to increase the font size.

1

- With the text, Tall Oaks Nature Center, selected, click the 'Increase Font Size' button on the mini toolbar four times to increase the font size of the selected text from 20 to 36 point (Figure 1–12).

Figure 1–12

Other Ways

1. Click Font Size arrow on mini toolbar, click desired font size in Font Size gallery	2. Click 'Increase Font Size' button (Home tab | Font group)	3. Click Font Size arrow (Home tab | Font group), click desired font size in Font size gallery	4. Press CTRL+SHIFT+>

To Select a Word

PowerPoint designers use many techniques to emphasize words and characters on a slide. To accentuate the word, Autumn, on your slide, you want to increase the font size and change the font color to orange for this word in the title text. To make these changes, you should begin by selecting the word, Autumn. *Why? You could perform these actions separately, but it is more efficient to select the word and then change the font attributes.* The following step selects a word.

1
- Position the pointer somewhere in the word to be selected (in this case, in the word, Autumn).
- Double-click the word to select it (Figure 1–13).

Figure 1–13

Other Ways

1. Position pointer before first character, press CTRL+SHIFT+RIGHT ARROW   2. Position pointer before first character, drag right to select word

---

To Change the Text Color

PowerPoint allows you to use one or more text colors in a presentation. You decide to change the color of the word you selected, Autumn. *Why? The color, orange, is associated with that season, and you want to add more emphasis, subtly, to this word in your title slide text.* The following steps add emphasis to this word by changing the font color from white to orange.

1
- With the word, Autumn, selected, click the Font Color arrow on the mini toolbar to display the Font Color gallery, which includes Theme Colors and Standard Colors (Figure 1–14).

Q&A
If the mini toolbar disappears from the screen, how can I display it once again?
Right-click the text, and the mini toolbar should appear.

Experiment
- Point to various colors in the gallery and watch the word's font color change.

Figure 1–14

2

- Click Orange in the Standard Colors row on the mini toolbar (third color from left) to change the font color to Orange (Figure 1–15).

Q&A

Why did I select the color Orange?
Orange is one of the 10 standard colors associated with every document theme, and it is a universal color representing the fall colors. The new color will emphasize the fact that the presentation focuses on programs suited for this time of year.

What is the difference between the colors shown in the Theme Colors area and the Standard Colors?
The 10 colors in the top row of the Theme Colors area are two text, two background, and six accent colors in the Berlin theme; the five colors in each column under the top row display different transparencies. The Standard Colors are available in every document theme.

Figure 1–15

3

- Click outside the selected area to deselect the word.

4

- Save the presentation on your hard disk, OneDrive, or other storage location using Tall Oaks as the file name.

Q&A

Why should I save the presentation at this time?
You have performed many tasks while creating this presentation and do not want to risk losing work completed thus far.

Other Ways

1. Right-click selected text, click Font on shortcut menu, click Font Color button, click desired color

2. Click Font Color arrow (Home tab | Font group), click desired color

---

BTW

Organizing Files and Folders
You should organize and store files in folders so that you easily can find the files later. For example, if you are taking an introductory technology class called CIS 101, a good practice would be to save all PowerPoint files in a PowerPoint folder in a CIS 101 folder. For a discussion of folders and detailed examples of creating folders, refer to the Office and Windows module at the beginning of this book.

Adding a New Slide to a Presentation

With the text for the title slide for the presentation created, the next step is to add the first text slide immediately after the title slide. Usually, when you create a presentation, you add slides with text, pictures, graphics, or charts. Some placeholders allow you to double-click the placeholder and then access other objects, such as videos, charts, diagrams, and organization charts. You can change the layout for a slide at any time during the creation of a presentation.

To Add a New Text Slide with a Bulleted List

1 INSERT PRESENTATION SLIDES | 2 ENTER TEXT | 3 FORMAT TEXT | **4 INSERT GRAPHICAL ELEMENTS**
5 SIZE & POSITION | 6 ENHANCE SLIDE SHOW | 7 DISPLAY SLIDES

When you add a new slide, PowerPoint uses the Title and Content slide layout. This layout provides a title placeholder and a content area for text, art, charts, and other graphics. A vertical scroll bar appears in the Slide pane when you add the second slide. *Why?* *The scroll bar allows you to move from slide to slide easily.* A small image of this slide also appears in the Slides tab. The following step adds a new slide with the Title and Content slide layout.

1

- Click the New Slide button (Home tab | Slides group) to insert a new slide with the Title and Content layout (Figure 1–16).

Q&A

Why does the bullet character display a white dot?
The Berlin document theme determines the bullet characters. Each paragraph level has an associated bullet character.

I clicked the New Slide arrow instead of the New Slide button. What should I do?
Click the Title and Content slide thumbnail in the Berlin layout gallery.

How do I know which slide number I am viewing?
The left edge of the status bar shows the current slide number followed by the total number of slides in the document. In addition, the slide number is displayed to the left of the slide thumbnail.

What are those six icons grouped in the middle of the Slide pane?
You can click one of the icons to insert a specific type of content: table, chart, SmartArt graphic, pictures, online pictures, or video.

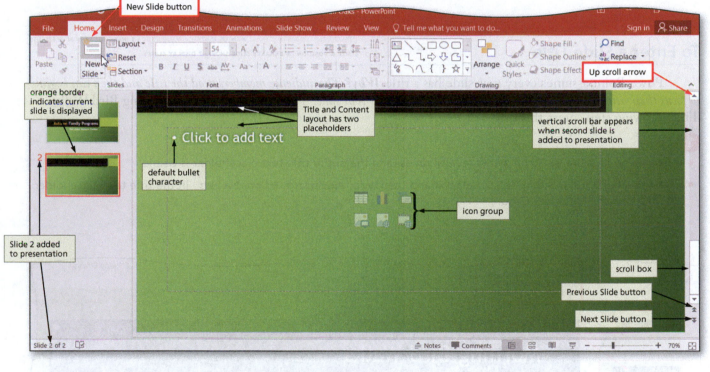

Figure 1–16

Other Ways

1. Click New Slide button (Insert tab | Slides group)   2. Press CTRL+M

Creating a Text Slide with a Multilevel Bulleted List

The information in the Slide 2 text placeholder is presented in a bulleted list with three levels. A **bulleted list** is a list of paragraphs, each of which may be preceded by a bullet character, such as a dot, arrow, or checkmark. Most themes display a bullet character at the start of a paragraph by default. A slide that consists of more than one

BTW

The Ribbon and Screen Resolution
PowerPoint may change how the groups and buttons within the groups appear on the ribbon, depending on the computer or mobile device's screen resolution. Thus, your ribbon may look different from the ones in this book if you are using a screen resolution other than 1366 x 768.

level of bulleted text is called a **multilevel bulleted list slide**. In a multilevel bulleted list, a lower-level paragraph is a subset of a higher-level paragraph. It usually contains information that supports the topic in the paragraph immediately above it.

As you can see in Figure 1–1b, two of the Slide 2 paragraphs appear at the same level, called the first level: Enjoy a hike on natural surface trails, and 9 a.m. every Saturday. Beginning with the second level, each paragraph indents to the right of the preceding level and is pushed down to a lower level. For example, if you increase the indent of a first-level paragraph, it becomes a second-level paragraph. The second and fourth paragraphs on Slide 2 are second-level paragraphs. The last paragraph, Extra supplies will be available, is a third-level paragraph.

Creating a text slide with a multilevel bulleted list requires several steps. Initially, you enter a slide title in the title text placeholder. Next, you select the content text placeholder. Then, you type the text for the multilevel bulleted list, increasing and decreasing the indents as needed. The next several sections add a slide with a multilevel bulleted list.

BTW

File Type
Depending on your Windows settings, the file type .pptx may be displayed on the title bar immediately to the right of the file name after you save the file. The file type .pptx identifies a PowerPoint document.

To Enter a Slide Title

1 INSERT PRESENTATION SLIDES | **2 ENTER TEXT** | 3 FORMAT TEXT | **4 INSERT GRAPHICAL ELEMENTS**
5 SIZE & POSITION | 6 ENHANCE SLIDE SHOW | 7 DISPLAY SLIDES

PowerPoint assumes every new slide has a title. *Why? The audience members read the title and then can begin to focus their attention on the information being presented on that slide.* The title for Slide 2 is Morning Bird Walks. The following step enters this title.

1
- If necessary, click the Up scroll arrow several times until the entire title text placeholder is visible.
- Click the label 'Click to add title', to select it and then type **Morning Bird Walks** in the title text placeholder. Do not press the ENTER key (Figure 1–17).

Figure 1–17

To Select a Text Placeholder

Why? Before you can type text into a content placeholder, you first must select it. The following step selects the text placeholder on Slide 2.

1

- Click the label, 'Click to add text', to select the content placeholder (Figure 1–18).

Q&A Why does my pointer have a different shape?
If you move the pointer away from the bullet, it will change shape.

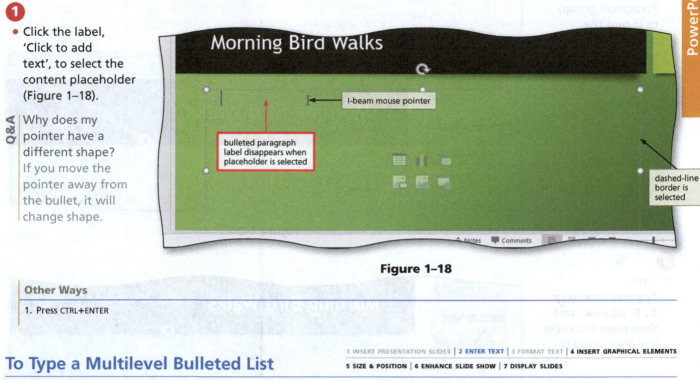

Figure 1–18

Other Ways
1. Press CTRL+ENTER

To Type a Multilevel Bulleted List

The content placeholder provides an area for the text characters. When you click inside a placeholder, you then can type or paste text. As discussed previously, a bulleted list is a list of paragraphs, each of which is preceded by a bullet. A paragraph is a segment of text ended by pressing the ENTER key. The theme determines the bullets for each level. *Why? The bullet variations are determined by the specific paragraph levels, and they generally vary in size, shape, and color.*

The content text placeholder is selected, so the next step is to type the multilevel bulleted list that consists of six paragraphs, as shown in Figure 1–1b. Creating a lower-level paragraph is called **demoting** text; creating a higher-level paragraph is called **promoting** text. The following steps create a multilevel bulleted list consisting of three levels.

1

- Type **Enjoy a hike on natural surface trails** and then press the ENTER key (Figure 1–19).

Figure 1–19

2

• Click the 'Increase List Level' button (Home tab | Paragraph group) to indent the second paragraph below the first and create a second-level paragraph (Figure 1–20).

Q&A
Why does the bullet for this paragraph have a different size?
A different bullet is assigned to each paragraph level.

Figure 1–20

3

• Type **Approximately 1.5 miles** and then press the ENTER key (Figure 1–21).

Figure 1–21

4

• Click the 'Decrease List Level' button (Home tab | Paragraph group) so that the second-level paragraph becomes a first-level paragraph (Figure 1–22).

Q&A
Can I delete bullets on a slide?
Yes. If you do not want bullets to display in a particular paragraph, click the Bullets button (Home tab | Paragraph group) or right-click the paragraph and then click the Bullets button on the shortcut menu.

Figure 1–22

Other Ways

1. Press TAB to promote paragraph; press SHIFT+TAB to demote paragraph

To Type the Remaining Text for Slide 2

The following steps complete the text for Slide 2.

1 Type `9 a.m. every Saturday` and then press the ENTER key.

2 Click the 'Increase List Level' button (Home tab | Paragraph group) to demote the paragraph to the second level.

3 Type `Bring binoculars and a field guide` and then press the ENTER key to add a new paragraph at the same level as the previous paragraph.

4 Click the 'Increase List Level' button (Home tab | Paragraph group) to demote the paragraph to the third level.

5 Type `Extra supplies will be available` but do not press the ENTER key (Figure 1–23).

Q&A I pressed the ENTER key in error, and now a new bullet appears after the last entry on this slide. How can I remove this extra bullet?
Press the BACKSPACE key twice.

Figure 1–23

To Select a Group of Words

1 INSERT PRESENTATION SLIDES | 2 ENTER TEXT | **3 FORMAT TEXT** | 4 INSERT GRAPHICAL ELEMENTS
5 SIZE & POSITION | 6 ENHANCE SLIDE SHOW | 7 DISPLAY SLIDES

PowerPoint designers use many techniques to emphasize words and characters on a slide. To highlight the day of the week when the walks are held, you want to bold and increase the font size of the words, every Saturday, in the body text. The following steps select two words. *Why? You could perform these actions separately, but it is more efficient to select the words and then change the font attributes.*

1
• Position the pointer immediately to the left of the first character of the text to be selected (in this case, the e in the word, every) (Figure 1–24).

Figure 1–24

②

- Drag the pointer through the last character of the text to be selected (in this case, the y in the word, Saturday) (Figure 1–25).

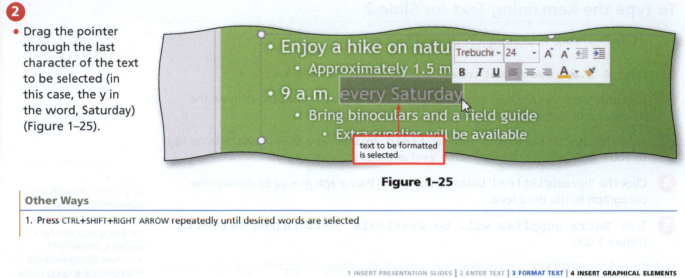

text to be formatted is selected

Figure 1–25

Other Ways

1. Press CTRL+SHIFT+RIGHT ARROW repeatedly until desired words are selected

1 INSERT PRESENTATION SLIDES | 2 ENTER TEXT | **3 FORMAT TEXT** | 4 INSERT GRAPHICAL ELEMENTS
5 SIZE & POSITION | 6 ENHANCE SLIDE SHOW | 7 DISPLAY SLIDES

To Bold Text

Why? Bold characters display somewhat thicker and darker than those that display in a regular font style. Clicking the Bold button on the mini toolbar is an efficient method of bolding text. To add more emphasis to the fact that the body needs nature for cooling purposes, you want to bold the words, every Saturday. The following step bolds this text.

①

- With the words, every Saturday, selected, click the Bold button on the mini toolbar to bold the two words (Figure 1–26).

default font size is 24 point

Bold button selected

selected words are bolded

Figure 1–26

Other Ways

1. Right-click selected text, click Font on shortcut menu, click Font tab (Font dialog box), click Bold in Font style list, click OK button

2. Select text, click Bold button (Home tab | Font group)

3. Click Font dialog box launcher (Home tab | Font group), click Font tab (Font dialog box), click Bold in Font style list, click OK button

4. Select text, press CTRL+B

To Increase Font Size

The following steps increase the font size from 24 to 28 point. *Why? To add emphasis, you increase the font size for the words, every Saturday.*

① With the words, every Saturday, still selected, click the 'Increase Font Size' button on the mini toolbar once (Figure 1–27).

② Click outside the selected area to deselect the two words.

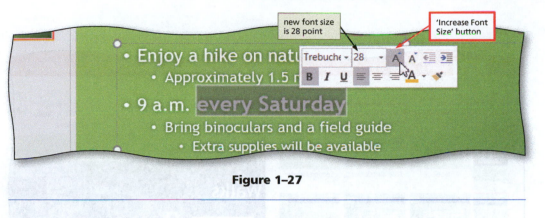

Figure 1–27

Adding New Slides, Changing Slide Layouts, and Changing the Theme

Slide 3 in Figure 1–1c contains two pictures: a grasshopper and a dragonfly. Slide 4 in Figure 1–1d contains an illustration of a firefly and does not contain a bulleted list. When you add a new slide, PowerPoint applies the Title and Content layout. This layout and the Title Slide layout for Slide 1 are the default styles. A **layout** specifies the arrangement of placeholders on a slide. These placeholders are arranged in various configurations and can contain text, such as the slide title or a bulleted list, or they can contain content, such as SmartArt graphics, pictures, charts, tables, and shapes. The placement of the text, in relationship to content, depends on the slide layout. You can specify a particular slide layout when you add a new slide to a presentation or after you have created the slide.

Using the **layout gallery**, you can choose a slide layout. The nine layouts in this gallery have a variety of placeholders to define text and content positioning and formatting. Three layouts are for text: Title Slide, Section Header, and Title Only. Five are for text and content: Title and Content, Two Content, Comparison, Content with Caption, and Picture with Caption. The Blank layout has no placeholders. If none of these standard layouts meets your design needs, you can create a **custom layout**. A custom layout specifies the number, size, and location of placeholders, background content, and optional slide and placeholder-level properties.

When you change the layout of a slide, PowerPoint retains the text and objects and repositions them into the appropriate placeholders. Using slide layouts eliminates the need to resize objects and the font size because PowerPoint automatically sizes the objects and text to fit the placeholders. At any time when creating the slide content, you can change the theme and variant to give the presentation a different look and feel.

BTW
Customizing a Slide Layout
PowerPoint provides a wide variety of slide layouts for each theme, but you can customize the layouts to make your deck unique. Display the View tab, click Slide Master (View tab | Master Views group), select the thumbnail below the slide master in the left pane that you would like to customize, and then make the desired modifications.

To Add a New Slide and Enter a Slide Title and Headings

1 INSERT PRESENTATION SLIDES | 2 ENTER TEXT | 3 FORMAT TEXT | 4 INSERT GRAPHICAL ELEMENTS
5 SIZE & POSITION | 6 ENHANCE SLIDE SHOW | 7 DISPLAY SLIDES

The text on Slide 3 in Figure 1–1c consists of a title and two headings. The appropriate layout for this slide is named Comparison. *Why? The Comparison layout has two headings and two text placeholders adjacent to each other, so an audience member easily can compare and contrast the items shown side by side.* The following steps add Slide 3 to the presentation with the Comparison layout and then enter the title and heading text for this slide.

1
- Click the New Slide arrow in the Slides group to display the Berlin layout gallery (Figure 1–28).

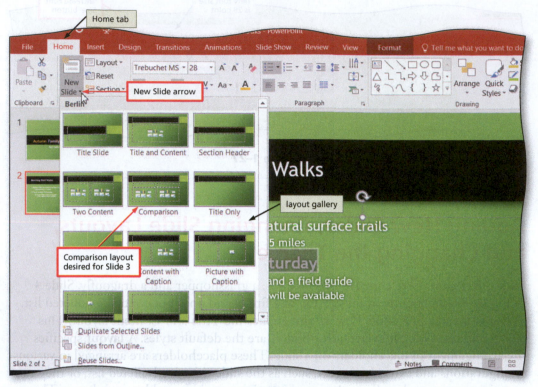

Figure 1–28

2
- Click Comparison to add Slide 3 and apply that layout (Figure 1–29).

Figure 1–29

3

- Type **Afternoon Insect Identification** in the title text placeholder.

- Click the left heading placeholder with the label, 'Click to add text', to select this placeholder (Figure 1–30).

Figure 1–30

4

- Type **Grasshoppers** and then press the ENTER key.

- Type **(also known as locusts)** but do not press the ENTER key.

- Select the right heading placeholder and then type **Dragonflies** and press the ENTER key.

Figure 1–31

- Type **(often mistaken for damselflies)** but do not press the ENTER key (Figure 1–31).

Q&A What is the white box with the arrow between the placeholders?
The text is too large to fit in the placeholder using the default font and paragraph attributes, so PowerPoint adjusts the text so it displays properly. That icon informs you that the font was altered.

To Add a Slide with the Title Only Layout

1 INSERT PRESENTATION SLIDES | 2 ENTER TEXT | 3 FORMAT TEXT | **4 INSERT GRAPHICAL ELEMENTS**
5 SIZE & POSITION | **6 ENHANCE SLIDE SHOW** | **7 DISPLAY SLIDES**

The following steps add Slide 4 to the presentation with the Title Only slide layout style. *Why? The only text on the slide is the title, and the majority of the slide content is the illustration.*

1

- If necessary, click Home on the ribbon to display the Home tab.

- Click the New Slide arrow (Home tab | Slides group) to display the Berlin layout gallery (Figure 1–32).

Figure 1–32

2

- Click Title Only to add a new slide and apply that layout to Slide 4 (Figure 1–33).

Figure 1–33

To Enter a Slide Title

The only text on Slide 4 is the title. The following step enters the title text for this slide.

1 Type **Twilight Firefly Hikes** as the title text but do not press the ENTER key (Figure 1–34).

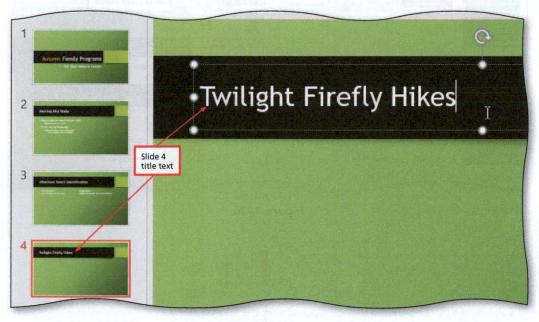

Slide 4 title text

Figure 1–34

To Change the Theme

1 INSERT PRESENTATION SLIDES | 2 ENTER TEXT | **3 FORMAT TEXT** | 4 INSERT GRAPHICAL ELEMENTS
5 SIZE & POSITION | 6 ENHANCE SLIDE SHOW | 7 DISPLAY SLIDES

A theme provides consistency in design and color throughout the entire presentation by setting the color scheme, font set, and layout of a presentation. This collection of formatting choices includes a set of colors (the Theme Colors group), a set of heading and content text fonts (the Theme Fonts group), and a set of lines and fill effects (the Theme Effects group). These groups allow you to choose and change the appearance of all the slides or individual slides in your presentation. *Why? At any time while creating the slide deck, you may decide to switch the theme so that the slides have a totally different appearance.* The following steps change the theme for this presentation from Berlin to Main Event.

1

• Click Design on the ribbon to display the Design tab (Figure 1–35).

Design tab

clicking More button in Themes group will show more design themes

Themes

Themes group

Variants

Figure 1–35

2

- Click the More button (Design tab | Themes group) to expand the gallery, which shows more theme gallery options. If necessary, scroll down to the bottom of the gallery to view the Main Event thumbnail (Figure 1–36).

Experiment

- Point to various document themes in the Themes gallery and watch the colors and fonts change on the title slide.

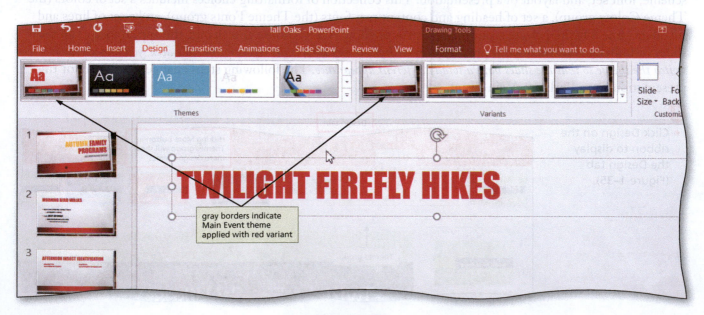

Figure 1–36

Q&A | Are the themes displayed in a specific order?
No. Your themes might be in a different order than shown here.

How can I determine the theme names?
If you point to a theme, a ScreenTip with the theme's name appears on the screen.

3

- Click the Main Event theme to apply this theme to all four slides (Figure 1–37).

Q&A | If I decide at some future time that this design does not fit the theme of my presentation, can I apply a different design?
Yes. You can repeat these steps at any time while creating your presentation.

Figure 1–37

Creating and Editing a Presentation with Pictures **PowerPoint Module 1** PPT 25

1 INSERT PRESENTATION SLIDES | 2 ENTER TEXT | 3 FORMAT TEXT | 4 INSERT GRAPHICAL ELEMENTS
5 SIZE & POSITION | 6 ENHANCE SLIDE SHOW | 7 DISPLAY SLIDES

PowerPoint Module 1

To Change the Variant

When you began creating this presentation, you selected the Berlin theme and then chose a green variant. You can change the color variation at any time for any theme. *Why? The new Main Event theme has a default red color, but you want to emphasize the green color associated with nature, just like you initially did when you chose the green variant for the Berlin theme.* The following steps change the variant from red to green.

1

- Point to the green variant (Design tab | Variants group) to see a preview of the green variant on Slide 4 (Figure 1–38).

🔍 **Experiment**

- Point to the orange, green, and blue variants and watch the colors change on the slide.

Figure 1–38

2

- Click the green variant to apply this color to all four slides (Figure 1–39).

Q&A If I decide at some future time that this color variation does not fit the theme of my presentation, can I apply a different variant?
Yes. You can repeat these steps at any time.

Figure 1–39

3

- Save the presentation again on the same storage location with the same file name.

Q&A Why should I save the presentation again?
You have made several modifications to the presentation since you last saved it. Thus, you should save it again.

Break Point: If you wish to take a break, this is a good place to do so. You can exit PowerPoint now. To resume at a later time, run PowerPoint, open the file called Tall Oaks, and continue following the steps from this location forward. For a detailed example of exiting PowerPoint, running PowerPoint, and opening a file, refer to the Office and Windows module at the beginning of the book.

PowerPoint Views

BTW
Welcome Back!
If you are designing a slide in your deck other than Slide 1 and then save and close the document, PowerPoint's Welcome back! feature allows you to continue where you left off at the last save when you open the document. You may need to adjust the zoom if you are working at a different level than the default setting.

The PowerPoint window display varies depending on the view. A **view** is the mode in which the presentation appears on the screen. You will use some views when you are developing slides and others when you are delivering your presentation. When creating a presentation, you most likely will use Normal, Slide Sorter, Notes Pane, and Outline views. When presenting your slides to an audience, you most likely will use Slide Sorter, Presenter, and Reading views.

The default view is **Normal view**, which is composed of three areas that allow you to work on various aspects of a presentation simultaneously. The large area in the middle, called the **Slide pane**, displays the slide you currently are developing and allows you to enter text, tables, charts, graphics, pictures, video, and other elements. As you create the slides, miniature views of the individual slides, called thumbnails, are displayed in the **Slides tab** on the left of the screen. You can rearrange the thumbnails in this pane. The **Notes pane**, by default, is hidden at the bottom of the window. If you want to type notes to yourself or remarks to share with your audience, you can click the Notes button in the status bar to open the Notes pane. After you have created at least two slides, a **scroll bar** containing **scroll arrows** and **scroll boxes** will appear on the right edge of the window.

To Move to Another Slide in Normal View

1 INSERT PRESENTATION SLIDES | 2 ENTER TEXT | 3 FORMAT TEXT | 4 INSERT GRAPHICAL ELEMENTS
5 SIZE & POSITION | 6 ENHANCE SLIDE SHOW | 7 DISPLAY SLIDES

Why? When creating or editing a presentation in Normal view (the view you are currently using), you often want to display a slide other than the current one. Before continuing with developing this project, you want to display the title slide. You can click the desired slide in the Slides tab or drag the scroll box on the vertical scroll bar; if you are using a touch screen, you can tap the desired slide in the Slides tab. When you drag the scroll box, the **slide indicator** shows the number and title of the slide you are about to display. Releasing shows the slide. The following steps move from Slide 4 to Slide 1 using the scroll box in the Slide pane.

1

- Position the pointer on the scroll box.

- Press and hold down the mouse button so that Slide: 4 of 4 Twilight Firefly Hikes appears in the slide indicator (Figure 1–40).

Figure 1–40

2

- Drag the scroll box up the vertical scroll bar until Slide: 1 of 4 Autumn Family Programs appears in the slide indicator (Figure 1–41).

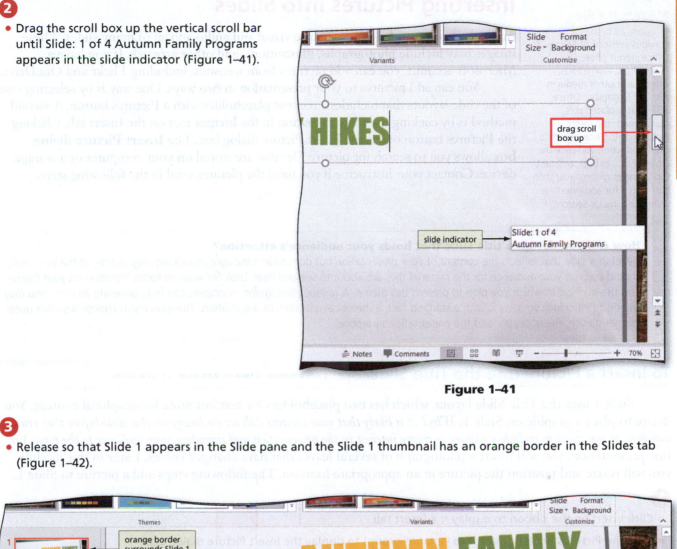

Figure 1–41

3

- Release so that Slide 1 appears in the Slide pane and the Slide 1 thumbnail has an orange border in the Slides tab (Figure 1–42).

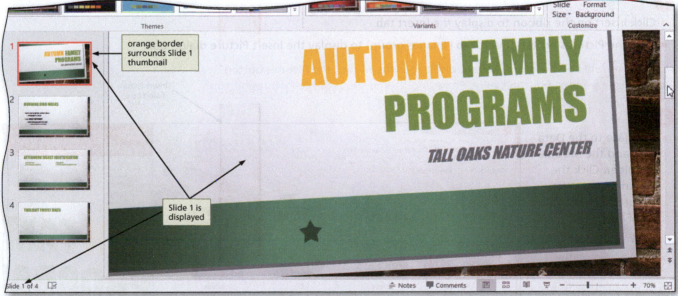

Figure 1–42

Other Ways

1. Click Next Slide button or Previous Slide button to move forward or back one slide

2. Click slide in Slides tab

3. Press PAGE DOWN or PAGE UP to move forward or back one slide

BTW

Microsoft Clip Organizer
Previous versions of Microsoft Office stored photos, illustrations, animations, videos, and other media in the Clip Organizer. Office 2016 has replaced this feature with the Insert Pictures dialog box, which is displayed when you click the Online Pictures button (Insert tab | Images group). You then can search for and insert files using Bing Image Search.

Inserting Pictures into Slides

Adding pictures can help increase the visual and audio appeal of many slides. These images may include photographs, illustrations, and other artwork. If you have a Microsoft account, you can add pictures from websites, including Flickr and OneDrive.

You can add pictures to your presentation in two ways. One way is by selecting one of the slide layouts that includes a content placeholder with a Pictures button. A second method is by clicking the Pictures button in the Images area on the Insert tab. Clicking the Pictures button opens the Insert Picture dialog box. The **Insert Picture dialog box** allows you to search for picture files that are stored on your computer or a storage device. Contact your instructor if you need the pictures used in the following steps.

CONSIDER THIS

How can you design a title slide that holds your audience's attention?
Develop a slide that reflects the content of your presentation but does so in a thought-provoking way. A title, at the very least, should prepare your audience for the material they are about to see and hear. Look for ways to focus attention on your theme and the method in which you plan to present this theme. A unique photograph or graphic can help generate interest. You may decide to introduce your topic with a startling fact, a rhetorical question, or a quotation. The device you choose depends upon your audience, the occasion, and the presentation's purpose.

To Insert a Picture into the Title Slide

1 INSERT PRESENTATION SLIDES | 2 ENTER TEXT | 3 FORMAT TEXT | **4 INSERT GRAPHICAL ELEMENTS**
5 SIZE & POSITION | 6 ENHANCE SLIDE SHOW | 7 DISPLAY SLIDES

Slide 1 uses the Title Slide layout, which has two placeholders for text but none for graphical content. You desire to place a graphic on Slide 1. *Why? It is likely that your viewers will see an image on this slide before they read any text, so you want to include a picture to create interest in the presentation and introduce your audience to the topic.* For this presentation, you will insert a photograph of several leaves that have changed colors. Later in this module, you will resize and position the picture in an appropriate location. The following steps add a picture to Slide 1.

1

• Click Insert on the ribbon to display the Insert tab.

• Click the Pictures button (Insert tab | Images group) to display the Insert Picture dialog box.

Q&A What should I do if no pictures are displayed when I click the Pictures button?
You may need to click the Online Pictures button instead of the Pictures button.

2

• Navigate to the Data Files and the Module 01 folder. Click the Autumn Leaves picture to select that file (Figure 1–43).

Q&A Why do I see only a list of file names and not thumbnails of the pictures in my folder?
Your view is different from the view shown in Figure 1–43.

Figure 1–43

3

- Click the Insert button (Insert Picture dialog box) to insert the picture into Slide 1 (Figure 1–44).

Q&A Can I double-click the picture or file name instead of selecting it and clicking the Insert button?
Yes. Either method inserts the picture.

Why is this picture displayed in this location on the slide?
The slide layout does not have a content placeholder, so PowerPoint inserts the file in an area of the slide. You will move and resize the picture later in this module.

Figure 1–44

To Insert a Picture into a Slide without a Content Placeholder

The next step is to add an owl picture to Slide 2. This slide has a bulleted list in the text placeholder, so the icon group does not display in the center of the placeholder. Later in this module, you will resize the inserted picture. The following steps add one picture to Slide 2.

1 Click the Slide 2 thumbnail in the Slides tab to display Slide 2.

2 Click Insert on the ribbon to display the Insert tab and then click the Pictures button (Insert tab | Images group) to display the Insert Picture dialog box.

3 If necessary, scroll down the list of files, click Owl to select the file, and then click the Insert button to insert the picture into Slide 2 (Figure 1–45).

Q&A Why is my picture a different size from the one shown in Figure1-1b?
The clip was inserted into the slide and not into a content placeholder. You will resize the picture later in this module.

BTW

Wrapping Text around a Photo
PowerPoint does not allow you to wrap text around a picture or other graphics, such as tables, shapes, and charts. This feature, however, is available in Word.

Figure 1–45

To Insert a Picture
into a Content Placeholder

Slide 3 uses the Comparison layout, which has a content placeholder below each of the two headings. You desire to insert pictures into both content placeholders. *Why? You want to display two insects that participants likely will identify during the program at the nature center.* The following steps insert a picture of a grasshopper into the left content placeholder and a dragonfly into the right content placeholder on Slide 3.

1

- Click the Slide 3 thumbnail in the Slides tab to display Slide 3 (Figure 1–46).

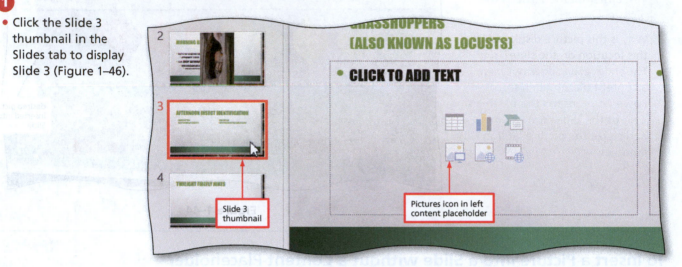

Figure 1–46

2

- Click the Pictures icon in the left content placeholder to select that placeholder and to open the Insert Picture dialog box.

- If necessary, scroll down the list of files, click Grasshopper to select the file, and then double-click to insert the picture into the left content placeholder (Figure 1–47).

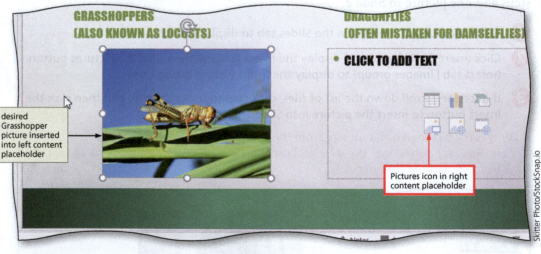

Skitter Photo/StockSnap.io

Figure 1–47

Q&A

Do I need to select the file name before double-clicking to insert the picture?
No. You just can double-click the file name.

3
- Click the Pictures icon in the right content placeholder to select that placeholder and to open the Insert Picture dialog box.
- If necessary, scroll down the list to display the Dragonfly file name and then insert this picture into the right content placeholder (Figure 1–48).

desired Dragonfly picture inserted into right content placeholder

Skitter Photo/StockSnap.io

Figure 1–48

To Insert a Picture into a Slide without a Content Placeholder

Next, you will add a picture to Slide 4. This picture is an illustration, not an actual photograph, of a firefly. You will not insert this file into a content placeholder, so it will display in the center of the slide. Later in this module, you will resize this picture. You locate and insert illustrations in the same manner you used to insert photos. The following steps add an illustration picture to Slide 4.

1 Click the Slide 4 thumbnail in the Slides tab.

2 Display the Insert tab, click the Pictures button, and then insert the Firefly file into Slide 4 (Figure 1–49).

desired Firefly illustration inserted into Slide 4

Figure 1–49

Break Point: If you wish to take a break, this is a good place to do so. You can save your presentation and then exit PowerPoint now. To resume at a later time, run PowerPoint, open the file called Tall Oaks, and continue following the steps from this location forward.

Resizing Photos and Illustrations

Sometimes it is necessary to change the size of pictures and illustrations. **Resizing** includes enlarging or reducing the size of a graphic. You can resize these images using a variety of techniques. One method involves changing the size of a picture by specifying exact dimensions in a dialog box. Another method involves sliding or dragging one of the graphic's sizing handles to the desired location. A selected graphic appears surrounded by a **selection rectangle**, which has small circles, called **sizing handles** or move handles, at each corner and middle location.

To Proportionally Resize Pictures

1 INSERT PRESENTATION SLIDES | 2 ENTER TEXT | 3 FORMAT TEXT | 4 INSERT GRAPHICAL ELEMENTS
5 SIZE & POSITION | 6 ENHANCE SLIDE SHOW | 7 DISPLAY SLIDES

Why? On Slides 1, 2, and 4, the picture and illustration sizes are too large to display aesthetically on the slides. At times it is important to maintain the proportions of a picture, such as when a person is featured prominently. To change the size of a picture and keep the width and height in proportion to each other, drag the corner sizing handles to view how the image will look on the slide. Using these corner handles maintains the graphic's original proportions. If, however, the proportions do not need to be maintained precisely, as with the owl picture on Slide 2, drag the side sizing handles to alter the proportions so that the graphic's height and width become larger or smaller. The following steps proportionally decrease the size of the Slide 1 picture using a corner sizing handle.

1

- Click the Slide 1 thumbnail in the Slides tab to display Slide 1.

- Click the leaves picture to select it and display the selection rectangle.

- Point to the lower-right corner sizing handle on the picture so that the pointer changes to a two-headed arrow (Figure 1–50).

Q&A I am using a touch screen and do not see a two-headed arrow when I press and hold the lower-right sizing handle. Why?
Touch screens may not display pointers; you can just press and slide sizing handles to resize.

Figure 1–50

2

- Drag the sizing handle diagonally toward the upper-left corner of the slide until the lower-right sizing handle or the crosshair is positioned approximately as shown in Figure 1–51.

Q&A What if the picture is not the same size as the one shown in Figure 1–51?
Repeat Steps 1 and 2.

Can I drag any corner sizing handle diagonally inward toward the opposite corner to resize the picture?
Yes.

3

- Release to resize the picture.

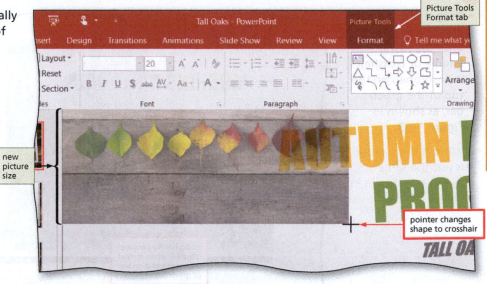

Figure 1–51

To Nonproportionally Resize the Photograph on Slide 2

1 INSERT PRESENTATION SLIDES | 2 ENTER TEXT | 3 FORMAT TEXT | 4 INSERT GRAPHICAL ELEMENTS

5 SIZE & POSITION | 6 ENHANCE SLIDE SHOW | 7 DISPLAY SLIDES

Why? *The height of the owl picture in Slide 2 extends from the top to the bottom of the slide. The width, however, will cover some of the text when the picture is positioned on the right side of the slide.* The width of this picture can be decreased slightly without negatively distorting the original image. You can decrease the width of a picture by sliding or dragging one of the sizing handles on the sides of the image. The following steps resize the width of the nature bottle picture using a sizing handle along the side of the image.

1

- Display Slide 2 and then click the owl picture to select it and display the selection rectangle.

- Click the Zoom Out button as many times as necessary until the Zoom level is 50%.

- Point to the middle sizing handle on the bottom edge of the picture so that the pointer changes to a two-headed arrow (Figure 1–52).

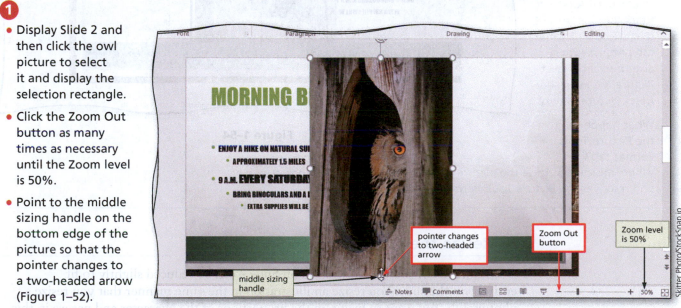

Figure 1–52

2

- Drag the sizing handle upward until the sizing handle or crosshair is positioned on the top of the green bar, as shown in Figure 1–53.

Q&A What if the picture is not the same size as the one shown in Figure 1–53?
Repeat Steps 1 and 2.

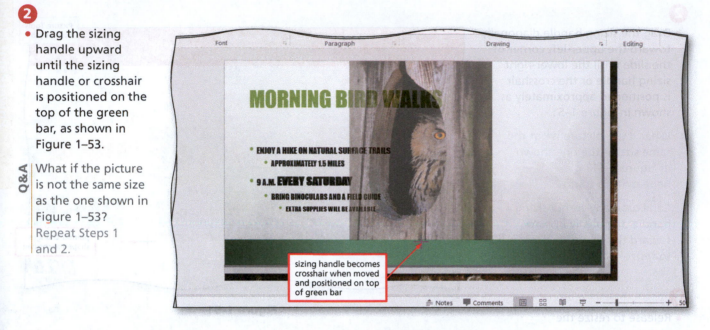

sizing handle becomes crosshair when moved and positioned on top of green bar

Figure 1–53

3

- Release to resize the picture.

- Click outside the picture to deselect it (Figure 1–54).

Q&A What if I want to return the picture to its original size and start again?
With the picture selected, click the Reset Picture arrow (Picture Tools Format tab | Adjust group) and then click Reset Picture & Size in the Reset Picture gallery.

What happened to the Picture Tools Format tab?
When you click outside the picture, PowerPoint deselects the object and removes the Picture Tools Format tab from the screen.

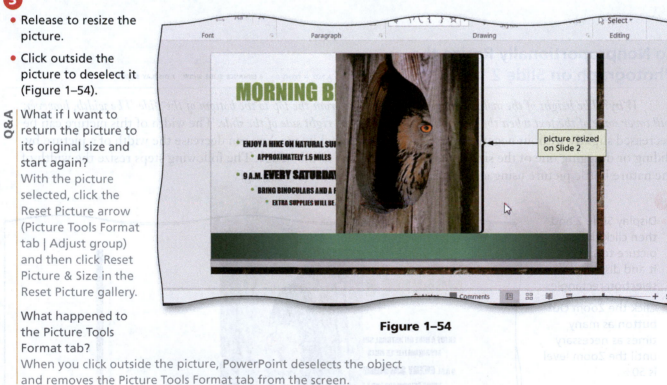

picture resized on Slide 2

Figure 1–54

To Resize the Illustration on Slide 4

The firefly picture illustration on Slide 4 can be reduced slightly to fit entirely on the slide. You resize an illustration in the same manner that you resize a photograph. You want to maintain the proportions of the character and nature in this illustration, so you will drag one of the corner sizing handles. The following steps resize this illustration using a corner sizing handle.

1 Display Slide 4 and then click the firefly illustration to select it.

2 Drag any corner sizing handle on the illustration diagonally inward until the illustration is positioned and resized approximately as shown in Figure 1–55.

Figure 1–55

To Move Pictures

Why? After you insert a photo or an illustration on a slide, you might want to reposition it. The leaves picture on Slide 1 could be moved to the lower-left side of the slide, the owl on Slide 2 could be moved to the right side of the slide, and the illustration on Slide 4 could be positioned in the center of the slide. PowerPoint displays **Smart Guides** automatically when a picture, shape, or other object is moved and is close to lining up with another slide element. These layout guides, which display as dashed lines, help you align slide elements vertically and horizontally. They display when aligning to the left, right, top, bottom, and middle of placeholders and other objects on a slide. For example, a Smart Guide will display to help you align the right or left edge of a picture in relation to a text placeholder or to another picture. The following steps center the illustration on Slide 4 and move the pictures on Slides 2 and 1.

1

- If necessary, click the firefly illustration on Slide 4 to select it.

- With the four-headed arrow displaying, drag the illustration downward and toward the left until the horizontal Smart Guide is displayed under the title text placeholder and the vertical Smart Guide is displayed through the center of the slide, as shown in Figure 1–56, and then release.

- If necessary, select the illustration and then use the ARROW keys to position it precisely as shown in Figure 1–56.

Q&A The firefly still is not located exactly where I want it to display. What can I do to align the image?
Press the CTRL key while you press the ARROW keys. This key combination moves the illustration in smaller increments than when you press only an ARROW key.

Figure 1–56

2

- Display Slide 2 and then click the owl picture to select it.

- Drag the picture downward and to the right until the horizontal Smart Guide is displayed above the title text placeholder and the right edge is aligned with the vertical gray bar on the right side of the slide (Figure 1–57).

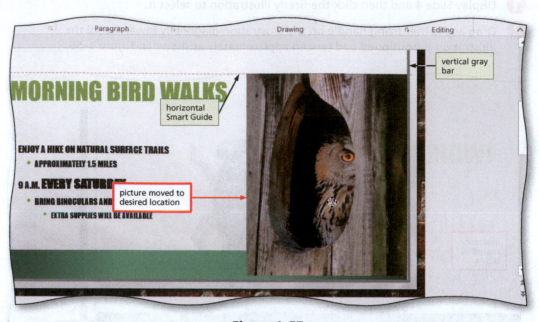

Figure 1–57

3

- Display Slide 1 and then click the leaves picture to select it.

- Drag the picture downward until the horizontal Smart Guide is displayed under the title text placeholder and the vertical Smart Guide is displayed near the left side of the slide, as shown in Figure 1–58, and then release.

 Q&A

Can I move the picture in small increments?
Yes. To move or nudge the picture in very small increments, hold down the CTRL key with the picture selected while pressing the ARROW keys. You cannot perform this action using a touch screen.

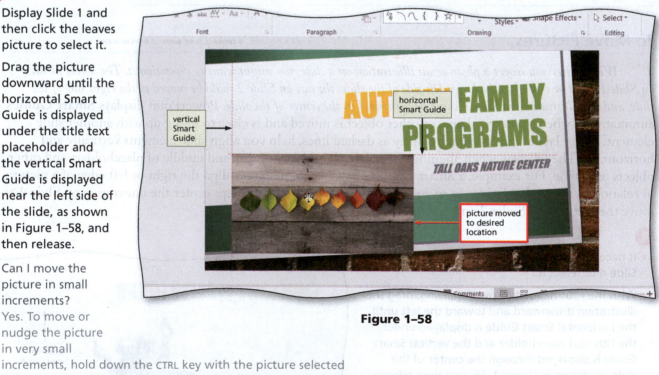

Figure 1–58

To Rotate a Picture

1 INSERT PRESENTATION SLIDES | 2 ENTER TEXT | 3 FORMAT TEXT | 4 INSERT GRAPHICAL ELEMENTS
5 SIZE & POSITION | 6 ENHANCE SLIDE SHOW | 7 DISPLAY SLIDES

Why? *The Main Event Title Slide layout is angled, so the picture would complement the design by being angled, too.* Dragging the **rotation handle** above a selected object allows you to rotate an object in any direction. The following steps rotate the leaves picture.

1

• With the leaves picture selected, position the mouse pointer over the rotation handle so that it changes to a Free Rotate pointer (Figure 1–59).

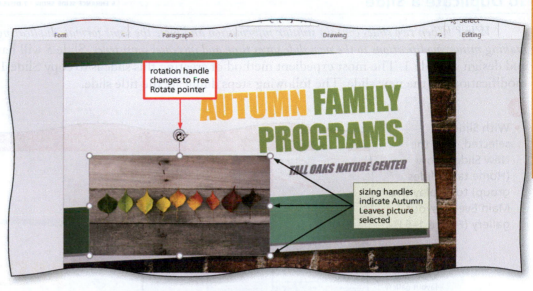

Figure 1–59

2

• Drag the rotation handle counterclockwise and then move the picture so that it is displayed as shown in Figure 1–60.

Figure 1–60

Ending a Slide Show with a Closing Slide

All the text for the slides in the Tall Oaks slide show has been entered. This presentation thus far consists of a title slide, one text slide with a multilevel bulleted list, a third slide with a Comparison layout, and a fourth slide for an illustration. A closing slide that resembles the title slide is the final slide to create.

What factors should you consider when developing a closing slide for the presentation?
After the last slide appears during a slide show, the default PowerPoint setting is to end the presentation with a **black slide**. This black slide appears only when the slide show is running and concludes the slide show, so your audience never sees the PowerPoint window. It is a good idea, however, to end your presentation with a final closing slide to display at the end of the presentation. This slide ends the presentation gracefully and should be an exact copy, or a very similar copy, of your title slide. The audience will recognize that the presentation is drawing to a close when this slide appears. It can remain on the screen when the audience asks questions, approaches the speaker for further information, or exits the room.

CONSIDER THIS

To Duplicate a Slide

Why? *When two slides contain similar information and have the same format, duplicating one slide and then making minor modifications to the new slide saves time and increases consistency.* Slide 5 will have the same layout and design as Slide 1. The most expedient method of creating this slide is to copy Slide 1 and then make minor modifications to the new slide. The following steps duplicate the title slide.

1

- With Slide 1 selected, click the New Slide arrow (Home tab | Slides group) to display the Main Event layout gallery (Figure 1–61).

Figure 1–61

2

- Click 'Duplicate Selected Slides' in the Main Event layout gallery to create a new Slide 2, which is a duplicate of Slide 1 (Figure 1–62).

Figure 1–62

To Arrange a Slide

The new Slide 2 was inserted directly below Slide 1 because Slide 1 was the selected slide. This duplicate slide needs to display at the end of the presentation directly after the final title and content slide. *Why? It is a closing slide that reinforces the concept presented in Slide 1 and indicates to your audiences that your presentation is ending.*

Changing slide order is an easy process and is best performed in the Slides tab. When you click the thumbnail and begin to drag it to a new location, the remaining thumbnails realign to show the new sequence. When you release, the slide drops into the desired location. Hence, this process of sliding or dragging and then dropping the thumbnail in a new location is called **drag and drop.** You can use the drag-and-drop method to move any selected item, including text and graphics. The following step moves the new Slide 2 to the end of the presentation so that it becomes a closing slide.

1

- With Slide 2 selected, drag the Slide 2 slide thumbnail below the last slide in the Slides tab so that it becomes the new Slide 5 (Figure 1–63).

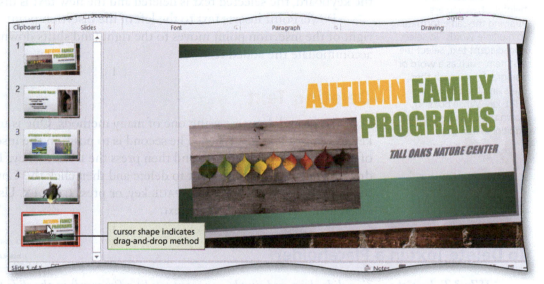

cursor shape indicates drag-and-drop method

Figure 1–63

Other Ways

1. Click Slide Sorter button on status bar, drag thumbnail to new location

2. Click Slide Sorter button (View tab | Presentation Views group), click slide thumbnail, drag thumbnail to new location

Break Point: If you wish to take a break, this is a good place to do so. Be sure to save the Tall Oaks file again and then you can exit PowerPoint. To resume at a later time, run PowerPoint, open the file called Tall Oaks, and continue following the steps from this location forward.

Making Changes to Slide Text Content

After creating slides in a presentation, you may find that you want to make changes to the text. Changes may be required because a slide contains an error, the scope of the presentation shifts, or the style is inconsistent. This section explains the types of changes that commonly occur when creating a presentation.

You generally make three types of changes to text in a presentation: additions, replacements, and deletions.

- Additions are necessary when you omit text from a slide and need to add it later. You may need to insert text in the form of a sentence, word, or single character. For example, you may want to add the presenter's middle name on the title slide.

- Replacements are needed when you want to revise the text in a presentation. For example, you may want to substitute the word, *their*, for the word, *there*.

- Deletions are required when text on a slide is incorrect or no longer is relevant to the presentation. For example, a slide may look cluttered. Therefore, you may want to remove one of the bulleted paragraphs to add more space.

Editing text in PowerPoint basically is the same as editing text in a word processing program. The following sections illustrate the most common changes made to text in a presentation.

Replacing Text in an Existing Slide

When you need to correct a word or phrase, you can replace the text by selecting the text to be replaced and then typing the new text. As soon as you press any key on the keyboard, the selected text is deleted and the new text is displayed.

PowerPoint inserts text to the left of the insertion point. The text to the right of the insertion point moves to the right (and shifts downward if necessary) to accommodate the added text.

Deleting Text

You can delete text using one of many methods. One is to use the BACKSPACE key to remove text just typed. The second is to position the insertion point to the left of the text you want to delete and then press the DELETE key. The third method is to drag through the text you want to delete and then click the Cut button on the mini toolbar, press DELETE or BACKSPACE key, or press CTRL+X. Use the third method when deleting large sections of text.

To Delete Text in a Placeholder

1 INSERT PRESENTATION SLIDES | 2 ENTER TEXT | **3 FORMAT TEXT** | 4 INSERT GRAPHICAL ELEMENTS

5 SIZE & POSITION | 6 ENHANCE SLIDE SHOW | **7 DISPLAY SLIDES**

Why? *To keep the ending slide clean and simple, you want to edit a few words in the slide title and subtitle text.* The following steps change Autumn to Register For and then change Tall Oaks Nature Center to Call 555-8928 today! in the placeholders.

1

- With Slide 5 selected, position the pointer immediately to the left of the first character of the text to be selected in the title text placeholder (in this case, the A in the word, Autumn).

- Drag the pointer through the last character of the text to be selected (in this case, the n in the word, Autumn) (Figure 1–64).

Q&A Can I drag from left to right or right to left?
Yes. Either direction will select the letters.

Could I also have selected the word, Autumn, by double-clicking it?
Yes. Either method works to select a word.

Figure 1–64

2

- Press the DELETE key to delete the selected text.
- Type **Register for** as the first words in the title text placeholder (Figure 1–65).

Q&A Could I have typed these words while the word, Autumn, was selected without cutting the text first?
Yes. Either method works to replace words. You will use this alternate method in the next step.

Why does the text display with all capital letters despite the fact that I am typing uppercase and lowercase letters?
The Main Event theme uses the All Caps effect for the title and subtitle text. This effect converts lowercase letters to uppercase letters.

Figure 1–65

3

- Position the pointer anywhere in the subtitle text placeholder other than on the picture and then triple-click to select all the text, Tall Oaks Nature Center (Figure 1–66).

Figure 1–66

4

- Type **Call 816-555-8928 today!** as the new subtitle text (Figure 1-67).
- If requested by your instructor, change the last four digits of the phone number in the subtitle text placeholder, 8928, to the last four digits of your phone number.

Figure 1–67

Other Ways

1. Right-click selected text, click Cut on shortcut menu   2. Select text, press DELETE or BACKSPACE key   3. Select text, press CTRL+X

Adding a Transition

PowerPoint includes a wide variety of visual and sound effects that can be applied to text or content. A **slide transition** is a special effect used to progress from one slide to the next in a slide show. You can control the speed of the transition effect and add a sound.

To Add a Transition between Slides

1 INSERT PRESENTATION SLIDES | 2 ENTER TEXT | 3 FORMAT TEXT | 4 INSERT GRAPHICAL ELEMENTS

5 SIZE & POSITION | **6 ENHANCE SLIDE SHOW** | 7 DISPLAY SLIDES

Why? Transitions add interest when you advance the slides in a presentation and make a slide show presentation look professional. In this presentation, you apply the Wind transition in the Exciting category to all slides and change the transition speed from 2 seconds to 3 seconds. The following steps apply this transition to the presentation.

1

• Click the Transitions tab on the ribbon and then point to the More button (Transitions tab | Transition to This Slide group) in the Transition to This Slide gallery (Figure 1–68).

Q&A Is a transition applied now?
No. None, the first slide icon in the Transition to This Slide group, is selected, which indicates no transition has been applied.

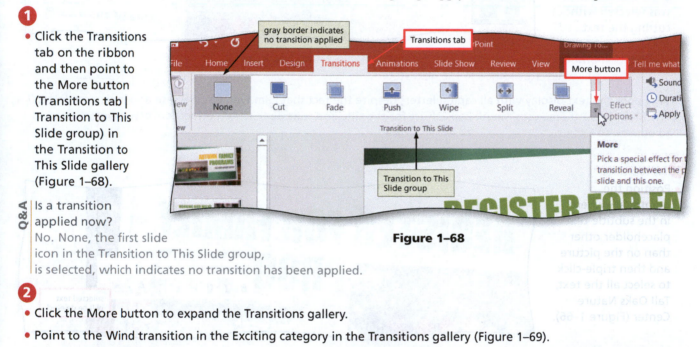

Figure 1–68

2

• Click the More button to expand the Transitions gallery.

• Point to the Wind transition in the Exciting category in the Transitions gallery (Figure 1–69).

Figure 1–69

3

- Click Wind in the Exciting category in the Transitions gallery to view a preview of this transition and to apply this transition to the closing slide.

Q&A Why does a star appear next to Slide 5 in the Slides tab? The star indicates that a transition animation effect is applied to that slide.

- Click the Duration up arrow (Transitions tab | Timing group) four times to change the transition speed from 02.00 seconds to 03.00 seconds (Figure 1–70).

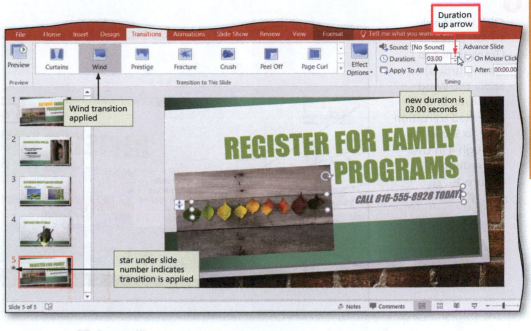

Figure 1–70

Q&A Why did the time change from the default 02.00 to 03.00?
Each transition has a default duration time. The default Wind transition time is 02.00 seconds.

4

- Click the Preview Transitions button (Transitions tab | Preview area) to view the transition and the new transition time (Figure 1–71).

Q&A Can I adjust the duration time I just set?
Yes. Click the Duration up or down arrows or type a speed in the Duration box and preview the transition until you find the time that best fits your presentation.

Figure 1–71

5

● Click the 'Apply To All' button (Transitions tab | Timing group) to apply the Wind transition and the increased transition time to Slides 1 through 4 in the presentation (Figure 1–72).

Q&A What if I want to apply a different transition and duration to each slide in the presentation? Repeat Steps 2 and 3 for each slide individually.

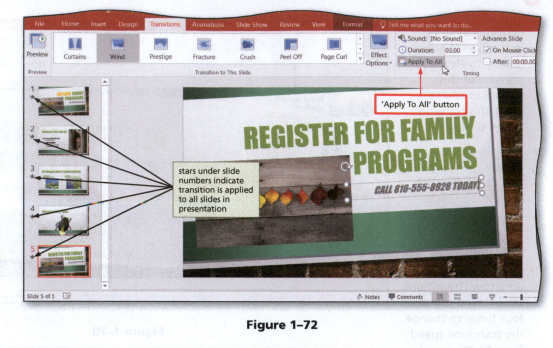

Figure 1–72

Document Properties

PowerPoint helps you organize and identify your files by using **document properties**, which are the details about a file such as the project author, title, and subject. For example, a class name or presentation topic can describe the file's purpose or content.

CONSIDER THIS

Why would you want to assign document properties to a presentation?

Document properties are valuable for a variety of reasons:

- Users can save time locating a particular file because they can view a file's document properties without opening the presentation.
- By creating consistent properties for files having similar content, users can better organize their presentations.
- Some organizations require PowerPoint users to add document properties so that other employees can view details about these files.

The more common document properties are standard and automatically updated properties. **Standard properties** are associated with all Microsoft Office files and include author, title, and subject. **Automatically updated properties** include file system properties, such as the date you create or change a file, and statistics, such as the file size.

TO CHANGE DOCUMENT PROPERTIES

To change document properties, you would follow these steps.

1. Click File on the ribbon to open the Backstage view and then, if necessary, click the Info tab in the Backstage view to display the Info gallery.

2. If the property you wish to change is displayed in the Properties list in the right pane of the Info gallery, try to click that property. If a text box with that property is displayed, type the text for the property in the box, and then click the Back button in the upper-left corner of the Backstage view to return to the PowerPoint window. Skip the remaining steps.

BTW

Printing Document Properties

PowerPoint 2016 does not allow you to print document properties. This feature, however, is available in other Office 2016 apps, including Word and Excel.

3. If the property you wish to change is not displayed in the Properties list in the right pane of the Info gallery or you cannot change it in the Info gallery, click the Properties button in the right pane to display the Properties menu, and then click Advanced Properties on the Properties menu to display the Summary tab in the Properties dialog box.

Q&A Why are some of the document properties in my Document Information Panel already filled in?
The person who installed Office 2016 on your computer or network may have set or customized the properties.

4. Type the desired text in the appropriate property boxes.

5. Click the OK button (Properties dialog box) to close the dialog box

6. Click the Back button in the upper-left corner of the Backstage view to return to the PowerPoint presentation window.

Viewing the Presentation in Slide Show View

The 'Start From Beginning' button, located in the Quick Access Toolbar, allows you to show a presentation using a computer. As the name implies, the first slide to be displayed always will be Slide 1. You also can run a presentation starting with the slide currently displaying when you click the Slide Show button on the status bar. In either case, PowerPoint displays the slides on the full screen without any of the PowerPoint window objects, such as the ribbon. The full-screen slide hides the toolbars, menus, and other PowerPoint window elements.

To Start Slide Show View

1 INSERT PRESENTATION SLIDES | 2 ENTER TEXT | 3 FORMAT TEXT | 4 INSERT GRAPHICAL ELEMENTS
5 SIZE & POSITION | 6 ENHANCE SLIDE SHOW | **7 DISPLAY SLIDES**

Why? *You run a presentation for your audience so they can see the slides in their entirety and view any transitions or other effects added to the slides.* When making a presentation, you use **Slide Show view**. You can start Slide Show view from Normal view or Slide Sorter view. Slide Show view begins when you click the 'Start From Beginning' button or the Slide Show button. The following steps start Slide Show view starting with Slide 1.

1
● Point to the 'Start From Beginning' button (Figure 1–73).

Q&A What would have displayed if I had clicked the Slide Show button instead of the 'Start From Beginning' button?
When you click the Slide Show button to start the presentation, PowerPoint begins the show with the currently displayed slide, which in this case is Slide 5. Only Slide 5 would display during the slide show.

Figure 1–73

2

- Click the 'Start From Beginning' button to display the transition and the title slide (Figure 1–74).

Q&A Where is the PowerPoint window? When you run a slide show, the PowerPoint window is hidden. It will reappear once you end your slide show.

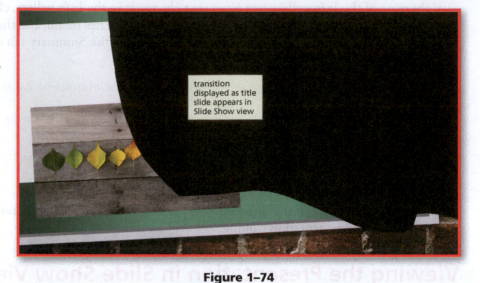

transition displayed as title slide appears in Slide Show view

Figure 1–74

Other Ways

1. Display Slide 1, click Slide Show button on status bar

2. Click 'Start From Beginning' button (Slide Show tab | Start Slide Show group)

3. Press F5

To Move Manually through Slides in a Slide Show

1 INSERT PRESENTATION SLIDES | 2 ENTER TEXT | 3 FORMAT TEXT | 4 INSERT GRAPHICAL ELEMENTS
5 SIZE & POSITION | 6 ENHANCE SLIDE SHOW | **7 DISPLAY SLIDES**

After you begin Slide Show view, you can move forward or backward through the slides. PowerPoint allows you to advance through the slides manually or automatically. During a slide show, each slide in the presentation shows on the screen, one slide at a time. Each time you click, the next slide appears. The following steps move manually through the slides. ***Why?*** *You can control the length of time each slide is displayed and change the preset order if you need to review a slide already shown or jump ahead to another slide designed to display later in the presentation.*

1

- Click each slide until Slide 5 (Register for Family Programs) is displayed (Figure 1–75).

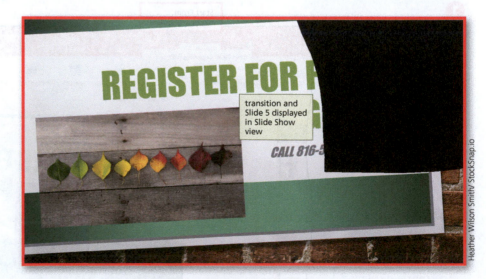

transition and Slide 5 displayed in Slide Show view

Figure 1–75

2

- Click Slide 5 so that the black slide appears with a message announcing the end of the slide show (Figure 1–76).

Q&A I see a small toolbar in the lower-left corner of my slide. What is this toolbar?

You may see the Slide Show toolbar when you begin running a slide show and then click a slide or move the pointer. The buttons on this toolbar allow you to navigate to the next slide or the previous slide, to mark up the current slide, or to change the current display. If you do not see the toolbar, hover the mouse near the lower-left corner of the screen.

Figure 1–76

3

- Click the black slide to return to Normal view in the PowerPoint window.

Other Ways

1. Press PAGE DOWN to advance one slide at a time, or press PAGE UP to go back one slide at a time

2. Press RIGHT ARROW or DOWN ARROW to advance one slide at a time, or press LEFT ARROW or UP ARROW to go back one slide at a time

3. If Slide Show toolbar is displayed, click Next Slide or Previous Slide button on toolbar

---

To Save and Print the Presentation

It is a good practice to save a presentation before printing it, in the event you experience difficulties printing. For a detailed example of the procedure summarized below for saving and printing a presentation, refer to the Office and Windows module at the beginning of this book.

1 Save the presentation again on the same storage location with the same file name.

2 Print the presentation.

Q&A Do I have to wait until my presentation is complete to print it?

No, you can print a presentation at any time while you are creating it.

3 Because the project now is complete, you can exit PowerPoint.

BTW

Conserving Ink and Toner
If you want to conserve ink or toner, you can instruct PowerPoint to print draft quality documents by clicking File on the ribbon to open the Backstage view, clicking the Options tab in the Backstage view to display the PowerPoint Options dialog box, clicking Advanced in the left pane (PowerPoint Options dialog box), scrolling to the Print area in the right pane, not placing a check mark in the High quality check box, and then clicking the OK button. Then, use the Backstage view to print the document as usual.

BTW

Distributing a Document
Instead of printing and distributing a hard copy of a document, you can distribute the document electronically. Options include sending the document via email; posting it on cloud storage (such as OneDrive) and sharing the file with others; posting it on social media, a blog, or other website; and sharing a link associated with an online location of the document. You also can create and share a PDF or XPS image of the document, so that users can view the file in Acrobat Reader or XPS Viewer instead of in PowerPoint.

Summary

In this module, you learned how to use PowerPoint to create and enhance a presentation. Topics covered included applying and changing a document theme and variant, creating a title slide and text slides with a bulleted list, inserting pictures and then resizing and moving them on a slide, formatting and editing text, adding a slide transition, and viewing the presentation in Slide Show view.

CONSIDER THIS: PLAN AHEAD

What decisions will you need to make when creating your next presentation?
Use these guidelines as you complete the assignments in this module and create your own slide show decks outside of this class.

1. Determine the content you want to include on your slides.

2. Determine which theme and variant are appropriate.

3. Identify the slide layouts that best communicate your message.

4. Format various text elements to emphasize important points.

    a) Select appropriate font sizes.

    b) Emphasize important words with bold or italic type and color.

5. Locate graphical elements, such as pictures, that reinforce your message.

    a) Size and position them aesthetically on slides.

6. Determine a storage location for the presentation.

7. Determine the best method for distributing the presentation.

Apply Your Knowledge

Reinforce the skills and apply the concepts you learned in this module.

Modifying Character Formats and Paragraph Levels and Moving an Illustration

Note: To complete this assignment, you will be required to use the Data Files. Please contact your instructor for information about accessing the Data Files.

Instructions: Run PowerPoint. Open the presentation called Apply 1-1 Email Fraud, which is located in the Data Files.

The two slides in the presentation discuss phishing, which is a scam in which a perpetrator attempts to obtain an individual's personal and/or financial information. The document you open is an unformatted presentation. You are to modify the document theme, indent the paragraphs, resize and move the image, and format the text so the slides look like Figure 1–77.

Perform the following tasks:

1. Change the document theme to Droplet. Select the blue (third) variant.

2. On the title slide, use your name in place of Student Name and bold and italicize your name.

3. If requested by your instructor, change your first name to your grandmother's first name on the title slide.

4. Increase the title text font size to 60 point and then bold this text. Resize and position the illustration using the Smart Guides to align the image with the bottom of the subtitle placeholder and the right edge of the placeholders, as shown in Figure 1–77a.

5. On Slide 2, increase the indent of the second, third, and fourth paragraphs to second-level paragraphs. Then combine paragraphs six and seven (Work related and Personal) to read, **Work and personal messages can contain threats**, as shown in Figure 1–77b. Increase the indent of this paragraph to second level.

(a) Slide 1 (Title Slide with a Picture)   (b) Slide 2 (Multilevel Bulleted List)

Figure 1–77

6. Apply the Ripple transition in the Exciting category to both slides. Change the duration to 3.00 seconds. Click the 'Start From Beginning' button to start the show from the first slide. Then click to display each slide and again to end the presentation.

Continued >

7. Save the presentation using the file name, Apply 1-1 Phishing.

8. Submit the revised document in the format specified by your instructor.

9. ✳ In Step 5 you combined two paragraphs and added text. How did this action improve the slide content?

Extend Your Knowledge

Extend the skills you learned in this module and experiment with new skills. You may need to use Help to complete the assignment.

Changing Slide Theme, Layout, and Text

Note: To complete this assignment, you will be required to use the Data Files. Please contact your instructor for information about accessing the Data Files.

Instructions: Run PowerPoint. Open the presentation called Extend 1-1 Waterfalls, which is located in the Data Files. Slide 1 is shown in Figure 1-78. You are aware that geologists have classified many types of waterfalls, including cascade and cataract, and the three slides in this file are part of a presentation you are developing for your geology class on this topic. Choose a theme, format the slides, and create a closing slide.

Perform the following tasks:

1. Change the document theme to Slice and the variant to green.

2. On Slide 1, format the text using techniques you learned in this module, such as changing the font size and color and bolding and italicizing words.

3. Replace the text, Student Name, with your name. In addition, delete the bullet preceding your name because, in most cases, a bullet is displayed as the first character in a list consisting of several paragraphs, not just one line of text. To delete the bullet, position the insertion point in the paragraph and then click the Bullets button (Home tab | Paragraph group).

4. Resize the picture and move it to an appropriate area on the slide.

5. On Slide 2, add bullets to the three paragraphs. To add bullets, select the paragraphs and then click the Bullets button (Home tab | Paragraph group). Insert the picture called Cascade, which is located in the Data Files, resize it, and then move it to an appropriate area on the slide.

6. On Slide 3, add bullets to the two paragraphs. Insert the picture called Cataract, which is located in the Data Files, resize it, and then move it to an appropriate area on the slide.

7. Create a closing slide using the title slide as a guide. Change the subtitle text to Natural Wonders and then underline this text. Insert the two waterfall pictures, Cascade and Cataract, and then size and move all three pictures to appropriate places on the slide.

Figure 1–78

8. Apply the Drape transition in the Exciting category to all slides and then change the duration for Slide 1 to 3.50 seconds. Click the 'Start From Beginning' button to start the show from the first slide. Then click to display each slide and again to end the presentation.

9. Save the presentation using the file name, Extend 1-1 Natural Wonders.

10. Submit the revised document in the format specified by your instructor.

11. If requested by your instructor, replace your last name on Slide 1 with the name of your hometown.

12. ✳ How did you determine the appropriate size and location of the three pictures on the closing slide?

Expand Your World

Create a solution that uses cloud and web technologies by learning and investigating on your own from general guidance.

Modifying and Exporting a Presentation

Note: To complete this assignment, you will be required to use the Data Files. Please contact your instructor for information about accessing the Data Files.

Instructions: Run PowerPoint. Open the presentation called Expand 1-1 Youth Group, which is located in the Data Files. The local youth group in your community is sponsoring a talent show, and you are part of a committee to publicize the event. You want to share the one slide you developed with some of the participants, so you have decided to store the file on OneDrive. You are going to modify the slide you have created, shown in Figure 1–79, and save it to OneDrive.

Perform the following tasks:

1. Insert the pictures called Musician and Singers, which are located in the Data Files. Size and then move them to the areas indicated in Figure 1–79. Use the guides to help you position the pictures.

2. If requested to do so by your instructor, change the words, Phoenix, AZ, to the town and state where you were born.

3. Save the presentation using the file name, Expand 1-1 Talent Show.

4. Export the file to your OneDrive account.

5. Submit the assignment in the format specified by your instructor.

6. ✳ When would you save one of your files for school or your job to OneDrive? Do you think using OneDrive enhances collaboration efforts? Why?

Anthony Delanoix/StockSnap.io; Morgan Sessions/StockSnap.io; Jay Wennington/StockSnap.io

Figure 1–79

In the Labs

Design, create, modify, and/or use a presentation following the guidelines, concepts, and skills presented in this module. Labs 1 and 2, which increase in difficulty, require you to create solutions based on what you learned in the module; Lab 3 requires you to apply your creative thinking and problem-solving skills to design and implement a solution.

Lab 1: Creating a Presentation with Pictures

Note: To complete this assignment, you will be required to use the Data Files. Please contact your instructor for information about accessing the Data Files.

Problem: Your friend, Bobby, has expanded her Bake Shoppe and wants to publicize new offerings. She has asked you to help her create a presentation that showcases pastries and breads. You prepare the PowerPoint presentation shown in Figure 1–80.

Perform the following tasks:

1. Run PowerPoint. Create a new presentation using the Retrospect document theme. Do not change the variant.
2. Using Figure 1–80a, create the title slide. Type the title text and subtitle text shown in the figure. Decrease the font size of the title text to 60 point and bold this text. Change the font color to Orange, Accent 1 (in Theme Colors row).

(a) Slide 1 (Title Slide)   (b) Slide 2

(c) Slide 3   (d) Slide 4 (Closing Slide)

Figure 1–80

3. On Slide 1, insert the illustration called Bakery, which is located in the Data Files. Move the illustration up to the top of the slide and then use the Smart Guides to align its left and right edges with the sides of the text placeholders. Use the lower-center sizing handle to resize this illustration so that it fits above the title text.

skip 4. Replace the words, Anytown, USA, with your hometown city and state.

5. Create Slide 2 using the Title Only layout. Type the title text, Fresh Daily, bold this text, and then change the font color to Orange, Accent 1 (in Theme Colors row). Insert the picture called Doughnut, which is located in the Data Files, resize it as shown in Figure 1–80b, and then move it to the left side of the slide. Insert the picture called Muffin, which is located in the Data Files, and then resize and move it to the right side of the slide, as shown in the figure.

6. Using Figure 1–80c as a guide, create Slide 3 using the Picture with Caption layout. Insert the picture called Bread, which is located in the Data Files. Type the title text, Artisan Breads, increase the font size to 48 point, and then bold this text. Type `All natural ingredients` as the subtitle text, press the Tab key four times, and then type `No preservatives` in the placeholder. Increase this subtitle text size to 28 point.

7. Create a closing slide by duplicating Slide 1. Change the subtitle text using Figure 1–80d as a guide.

8. Apply the Clock transition in the Exciting category to all slides. Change the duration to 2.00 seconds.

9. Click the 'Start From Beginning' button to start the show from the first slide. Then click to display each slide and again to end the presentation.

10. Save the presentation using the file name, Lab 1-1 Bake. Submit the document in the format specified by your instructor.

skip 11. ✴ What is the significance of changing the font color on Slides 1 and 2 but not Slide 3?

Lab 2: **Creating a Presentation with Bulleted Lists and Pictures**

Note: To complete this assignment, you will be required to use the Data Files. Please contact your instructor for information about accessing the Data Files.

Problem: The history museum in your town is a popular destination for residents, tourists, and researchers. Among the more popular exhibits are the dinosaurs, mummies, and antiques. You want to highlight these three attractions, so you create the presentation shown in Figure 1–81.

Perform the following tasks:

1. Run PowerPoint. Create a new presentation using the Quotable document theme.

2. Using Figure 1–81, create the title slide. Use your name in place of Student Name.

skip 3. If requested by your instructor, substitute the name of your hometown in place of your last name.

4. On Slide 1 (Figure 1–81a), italicize the text, History Museum. Increase the font size of the subtitle text, Popular Exhibits, to 32 point and the font size of your name to 24 point. Change the font color of the title text to Dark Blue (in Standard Colors row).

5. Create the three slides shown in Figures 1-81b, 1-81c, and 1-81d. Use the Comparison layout for Slide 2, the Section Header layout for Slide 3, and the Two Content layout for Slide 4. Change the color of the title text on these three text slides to Dark Blue. Increase the font size of the subtitle text on Slides 2 and 3 to 24 point.

Continued >

In the Labs *continued*

(a) Slide 1 (Title Slide)

(b) Slide 2

(c) Slide 3

(d) Slide 4

Sergey Zolkin/Unsplash.com,
Gabe Rodriguez/Unsplash.com

Figure 1–81

6. Add the pictures shown in Figures 1-81a through 1-81d using the guides on Slides 1 and 3 to help align them. The pictures to be inserted are called Museum Icon, Girls in Museum, T-rex Skeleton, T-rex 3D, Pharaoh, Car, and Typewriter, and they are located in the Data Files. Zoom the slides and then resize the pictures when necessary.

7. Apply the Gallery transition in the Exciting category to all slides. Change the duration to 2.25 seconds.

8. Click the 'Start From Beginning' button to start the show from the first slide. Then click to display each slide and again to end the presentation.

9. Save the presentation using the file name, Lab 1-2 History Museum.

10. Submit the revised document in the format specified by your instructor.

11. ✳ How does changing the title text font color to Dark Blue complement the theme color?

Lab 3: Consider This: Your Turn

Design and Create a Presentation about the Building Construction Technology Program

Note: To complete this assignment, you will be required to use the Data Files. Please contact your instructor for information about accessing the Data Files.

Part 1: Your school is expanding the courses offered in the Building Construction Technology Program, and the department chair has asked you to help promote the program. He informs you that students obtain hands-on experience using the latest methods of construction, and they receive instruction in the classroom and in the lab. The capstone courses are held in the field, where students build an actual energy-efficient home from the ground up. The skills learned and experience gained prepare students for careers in carpentry, masonry, plumbing, electrical, project supervision, cost estimating, and drafting. Use the concepts and techniques presented in this module to prepare a presentation with a minimum of four slides that showcase the Building Construction Technology program. Select a suitable theme, and include a title slide, bulleted list, closing slide, and transition. The presentation should contain pictures and illustrations resized appropriately. Several pictures are available in the Data Files: Backhoe, Concrete, Hammer, Hard Hat, Measuring Tape, Nail, and Tool Belt. Review and revise your presentation as needed. Submit your assignment in the format specified by your instructor.

Part 2: You made several decisions while creating the presentation in this assignment: what theme to use, where to place text, how to format the text (font, font size, paragraph alignment, bulleted paragraphs, italics, bold, color). You decided which images to use and where to position them. You also chose a transition. What was the rationale behind each of these decisions? When you reviewed the slides, what further revisions did you make and why? Where would you recommend showing this slide show?

2 Enhancing a Presentation with Pictures, Shapes, and WordArt

Objectives

You will have mastered the material in this module when you can:

- Search for and download an online theme
- Insert and format pictures
- Insert and size a shape
- Apply effects to a shape
- Add text to a shape

- Change the text font
- Insert a picture to create a background
- Insert and format WordArt
- Format slide backgrounds
- Find and replace text and check spelling
- Add and print speaker notes

Introduction

In our visually oriented culture, audience members enjoy viewing effective graphics. Whether reading a document or viewing a PowerPoint presentation, people increasingly want to see photographs, artwork, graphics, and a variety of typefaces. Researchers have known for decades that documents with visual elements are more effective than those that consist of only text because the illustrations motivate audiences to study the material. People remember at least one-third more information when the document they are seeing or reading contains visual elements. These graphics help clarify and emphasize details, so they appeal to audience members with differing backgrounds, reading levels, attention spans, and motivations.

Project — Presentation with Pictures, Shapes, and WordArt

The project in this module focuses on publicizing a basketball camp held each summer for children living in the park district. Professionals teach boys and girls a variety of offensive and defensive skills during this fun and educational event. The presentation shown in Figure 2–1 follows graphical guidelines and has a variety of illustrations and visual elements that are colorful and appealing to child athletes and their parents. For example, the pictures have particular shapes and effects. The enhanced type has a style that blends well with the formatted background and illustrations. Pictures and type are formatted using picture styles and WordArt, which give the presentation a professional look. You plan to present the material during winter and spring sports tournaments, so you want to add notes explaining concepts you will be discussing during these events.

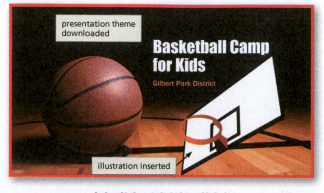

(a) Slide 1 (Title Slide)

(b) Slide 2 (Formatted Picture)

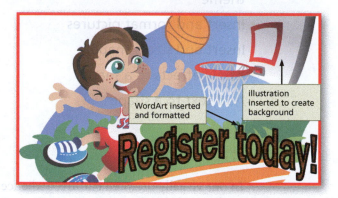

(c) Slide 3 (Shapes Inserted and Formatted)

(d) Slide 4 (Picture Background)

Figure 2–1

For an introduction to Windows and instructions about how to perform basic Windows tasks, read the Office and Windows module at the beginning of this book, where you can learn how to resize windows, change screen resolution, create folders, move and rename files, use Windows Help, and much more.

In this module, you will learn how to create the slides shown in Figure 2–1. The following roadmap identifies general activities you will perform as you progress through this module:

1. **DOWNLOAD** a theme and **SELECT SLIDES** for the presentation.
2. **INSERT** and **FORMAT PICTURES** for the slides.
3. **INSERT** and **FORMAT SHAPES** on one slide.
4. **FORMAT SLIDE BACKGROUNDS** with a gradient, texture, and picture fill.
5. **INSERT** and **FORMAT WORDART** by changing the shape, fill, and outline.
6. **REVIEW, REVISE,** and **PRINT SLIDES** by finding a synonym, checking spelling, and adding speaker notes.

Downloading a Theme and Editing Slides

In Module 1, you selected a theme and then typed the content for the title and text slides. In this module, you will type the slide content for the title and text slides, select a background, insert and format pictures and shapes, and then insert and format WordArt. To begin creating the four slides in this presentation, you will download a theme, delete unneeded slides in this downloaded presentation, and then enter text in three of the four slides.

To Search for and Download an Online Theme

1 DOWNLOAD & SELECT SLIDES | 2 INSERT & FORMAT PICTURES | 3 INSERT & FORMAT SHAPES
4 FORMAT SLIDE BACKGROUNDS | 5 INSERT & FORMAT WORDART | 6 REVIEW, REVISE, & PRINT SLIDES

PowerPoint displays many themes that are varied and appealing and give you an excellent start at designing a presentation. At times, however, you may have a specific topic and design concept and could use some assistance in starting to develop the presentation. Microsoft offers hundreds of predesigned themes and templates that could provide you with an excellent starting point. *Why? You can search for one of these ready-made presentations, or you can browse one of the predefined categories, such as business and education. The themes and templates can save you time and help you develop content.* The following steps search for a theme with a basketball concept.

1

• Run PowerPoint and then type **basketball** in the 'Search for online templates and themes' box (Figure 2–2).

Q&A
Why are my theme thumbnails displaying in a different order?
The order changes as you choose themes for presentations. In addition, Microsoft occasionally adds and modifies the themes, so the order may change.

Can I choose one of the keywords listed below the 'Search for online templates and themes' box?
Yes. Click one of the terms in the Suggested searches list to display a variety of templates and themes relating to those topics.

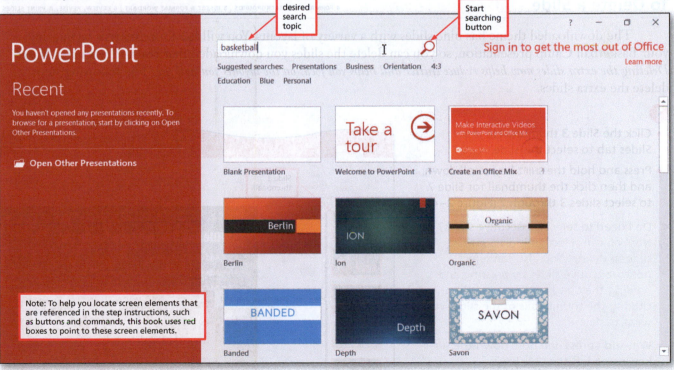

Figure 2–2

2

- Click the Start searching button (the magnifying glass) or press the ENTER key to search for and display all themes with the keyword, basketball.

- Click the 'Basketball presentation (widescreen)' theme to display a theme preview dialog box with a thumbnail view of the theme (Figure 2–3).

Figure 2–3

Q&A Can I see previews of the slides in this theme?
Yes. Click the right or left arrows beside the words, More Images, below the thumbnail. On some devices, a preview of all slides starts automatically after you tap the theme.

3

- Click the Create button to download the theme and open a presentation with that theme in PowerPoint.

To Delete a Slide

1 DOWNLOAD & SELECT SLIDES | 2 INSERT & FORMAT PICTURES | 3 INSERT & FORMAT SHAPES
4 FORMAT SLIDE BACKGROUNDS | 5 INSERT & FORMAT WORDART | 6 REVIEW, REVISE, & PRINT SLIDES

The downloaded theme has nine slides with a variety of layouts. You will use four different layouts in your Basketball Camp presentation, so you can delete the slides you downloaded that you will not need. *Why? Deleting the extra slides now helps reduce clutter and helps you focus on the layouts you will use.* The following steps delete the extra slides.

1

- Click the Slide 3 thumbnail in the Slides tab to select this slide.

- Press and hold the SHIFT key, scroll down, and then click the thumbnail for Slide 7 to select slides 3 through 7 (Figure 2–4).

Q&A Do I need to select consecutive slides?
No. You can select an individual slide to delete. You also can select nonconsecutive slides by pressing and holding the CTRL key down and then clicking the thumbnails of the slides you want to delete.

Why did I press and hold down the SHIFT key instead of the CTRL key?
Holding down the SHIFT key selects consecutive slides between the first and last selected slides, whereas holding the CTRL key selects only the slides you click.

Figure 2–4

2

- Right-click any selected slide to display the shortcut menu (Figure 2–5).

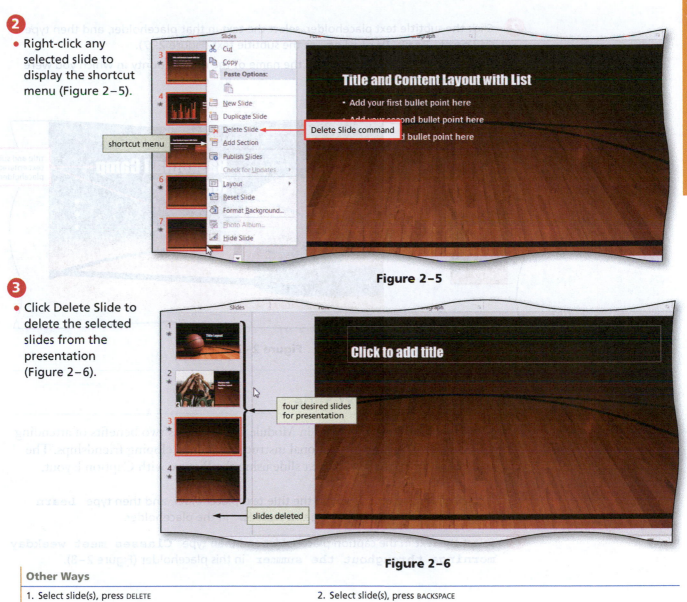

Figure 2–5

3

- Click Delete Slide to delete the selected slides from the presentation (Figure 2–6).

Figure 2–6

Other Ways

1. Select slide(s), press DELETE

2. Select slide(s), press BACKSPACE

To Create a Title Slide

Recall from Module 1 that the title slide introduces the presentation to the audience. In addition to introducing the presentation, this project uses the title slide to capture the audience's attention by using title text and an illustration. *Why? The presentation focuses on basketball, so the picture of a ball and court on the title slide can be supplemented with a backboard illustration that you will insert later on this slide.* The following steps create the slide show's title slide.

1 Display Slide 1, select the text in the title text placeholder, and then type **Basketball Camp for Kids** as the title text.

Q&A Why do I have to select the text in the placeholder before typing?
This downloaded template includes text in some of the placeholders that must be replaced with your own text.

BTW

PowerPoint Screen Resolution
If you are using a computer or mobile device to step through the project in this module and you want your screens to match the figures in this book, you should change your screen's resolution to 1366 x 768. For information about how to change a computer's resolution, refer to the Office and Windows module at the beginning of this book.

For an introduction to Office and instructions about how to perform basic tasks in Office apps, read the Office and Windows module at the beginning of this book, where you can learn how to run an application, use the ribbon, save a file, open a file, print a file, exit an application, use Help, and much more.

2 Click the subtitle text placeholder, select the text in that placeholder, and then type **Gilbert Park District** as the subtitle text (Figure 2–7).

- If requested by your instructor, type the name of the city or county in which you were born instead of the word, Gilbert.

Figure 2–7

To Create the First Text Slide

The first text slide you create in Module 2 emphasizes two benefits of attending the weekly camp: receiving professional instruction and developing friendships. The following steps create the Slide 2 text slide using the Picture with Caption layout.

1 Display Slide 2, select the text in the title text placeholder, and then type **Learn from pros and make acquaintances** in the placeholder.

2 Select the text in the caption placeholder and then type **Classes meet weekday mornings throughout the summer** in this placeholder (Figure 2–8).

Figure 2–8

To Create the Second Text Slide

The second text slide you create shows three skills that will be taught: ball handling, offensive moves, and defensive strategies. The following steps add a title to Slide 3, which uses the Title Only layout, and save the presentation.

1 Display Slide 3 and then type **You will lern…** in the title text placeholder. The word, lern, is misspelled intentionally; the red wavy line indicates the misspelling (Figure 2-9).

2 Save the presentation using **Basketball Camp** as the file name.

Figure 2–9

Inserting and Formatting Pictures in a Presentation

With the text entered in three of the four slides, the next step is to insert pictures into Slides 1 and 2 and then format the pictures. These graphical images draw the viewers' eyes to the slides and help them retain the information presented.

In the following pages, you will perform these tasks:

1. Insert an illustration into Slide 1.
2. Resize the illustration.
3. Change the Slide 2 photo.
4. Change the photo's brightness and contrast.
5. Change the photo's style and effect.
6. Add and modify the photo's border.

To Insert a Picture into a Slide without a Content Placeholder

1 DOWNLOAD & SELECT SLIDES | 2 INSERT & FORMAT PICTURES | 3 INSERT & FORMAT SHAPES
4 FORMAT SLIDE BACKGROUNDS | 5 INSERT & FORMAT WORDART | 6 REVIEW, REVISE, & PRINT SLIDES

In Module 1, you inserted photos and an illustration into slides without a content placeholder. *Why? Some slide layouts do not have a content placeholder, so you must insert and move the pictures to appropriate locations on the slide.* The illustration for Slide 1 is available in the Data Files. Contact your instructor if you need the pictures used in the following steps. The instructions in this module show the required files in the Module 02 folder in the Data Files folder. The following steps insert an illustration into the title slide.

BTW

Organizing Files and Folders

You should organize and store files in folders so that you easily can find the files later. For example, if you are taking an introductory technology class called CIS 101, a good practice would be to save all PowerPoint files in a PowerPoint folder in a CIS 101 folder. For a discussion of folders and detailed examples of creating folders, refer to the Office and Windows module at the beginning of this book.

1

- Display Slide 1 and then click Insert on the ribbon to display the Insert tab.
- Click the Pictures button (Insert tab | Images group) to display the Insert Picture dialog box.

2

- If necessary, navigate to the PowerPoint Module 02 folder and then click Backboard to select the file name (Figure 2–10).

Q&A What if Backboard is not displayed in the navigation pane?
Drag the navigation pane scroll bar (Insert Picture dialog box) until Backboard appears. If this file is not in the list, see your instructor.

Why do I see just file names and not thumbnails of the pictures in my folder?
Your view is different from the view shown in Figure 2–10.

Figure 2–10

3

- Click the Insert button (Insert Picture dialog box) to insert the illustration into Slide 1.
- Drag the upper-left sizing handle diagonally toward the lower-right corner of the slide until the crosshair is positioned approximately as shown in Figure 2–11.

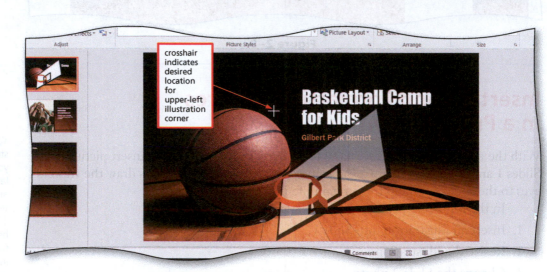

Figure 2–11

4

- Release to resize the illustration.
- Drag the illustration to the right until the vertical Smart Guide is displayed near the right side of the slide, as shown in Figure 2–12, and then release.

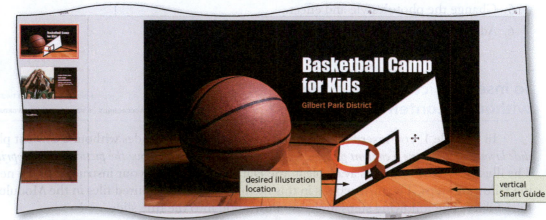

Figure 2–12

To Change a Picture

Why? The downloaded theme included the photo of several team members on Slide 2. You need to change the photo because those players are wearing green uniforms, which are not the clothes your camp participants will wear. The next task in the presentation is to change the default picture on Slide 2 to one of the pictures in the Data Files. The following steps change the Slide 2 photo to the Teamwork photo, which, in this example, is located in the Module 02 folder in the Data Files folder.

1

- Display Slide 2 and then right-click the picture to display the shortcut menu (Figure 2–13).

Q&A Why are the Style and Crop buttons displayed near the shortcut menu on my screen? These two buttons display either above or below the shortcut menu depending upon where you right-click on the screen.

2

- Click Change Picture to display the Insert Pictures dialog box (Figure 2–14).

3

- Click the Browse button in the 'From a file' area to display the Insert Picture dialog box.
- If necessary, navigate to the PowerPoint Module 02 folder, scroll down, and then click Teamwork to select the file (Figure 2–15).

Figure 2–13

Figure 2–14

Figure 2–15

4

- Click the Insert button (Insert Picture dialog box) to insert the photo into the Slide 2 picture placeholder.
- Click the gray text box on the right side of the slide to select this object (Figure 2–16).

Q&A Why should I select and then delete this gray text box?
When you delete the box, the slide will expand to the right to fill that space and you will be able to view a larger slide image.

Figure 2–16

5

- Press the DELETE key to delete this text box.

Q&A Could I have followed the directions in the gray box on the right to change the image?
Yes, either method works. You also could have selected the gray box and then clicked the Cut button (Home tab | Clipboard group) button to delete the text box.

Other Ways

1. Click Change Picture button (Picture Tools Format tab | Adjust group)

---

1 DOWNLOAD & SELECT SLIDES | 2 INSERT & FORMAT PICTURES | 3 INSERT & FORMAT SHAPES
4 FORMAT SLIDE BACKGROUNDS | 5 INSERT & FORMAT WORDART | 6 REVIEW, REVISE, & PRINT SLIDES

To Correct a Picture

A photo's color intensity can be modified by changing the brightness and contrast. **Brightness** determines the overall lightness or darkness of the entire image, whereas **contrast** is the difference between the darkest and lightest areas of the image. The brightness and contrast are changed in predefined percentage increments. The following step decreases the brightness and increases the contrast. *Why? Altering the photo's brightness will coordinate with the dark colors on the basketball court while increasing the contrast will sharpen the image. It is important for the audience to recognize the basketball and the players' overlapping hands but not focus on each aspect of this photo.*

1

- Select the Teamwork photo on Slide 2 and then click Format on the ribbon to display the Picture Tools Format tab.

- Click the Corrections button (Picture Tools Format tab | Adjust group) to display the Corrections gallery.

- Scroll down to display the last row of images in the Corrections gallery and then

Figure 2–17

point to Brightness: −20% Contrast: +40% (second picture in last Brightness/Contrast row) to display a live preview of these corrections on the picture (Figure 2–17).

Q&A Can I use live preview on a touch screen?
Live preview is not available on a touch screen.

Why is a gray border surrounding the pictures in the center of the Sharpen/Soften and Brightness/Contrast areas of the gallery?
The image on Slide 2 currently has normal sharpness, brightness, and contrast (0%), which is represented by these center images in the gallery.

🔎 **Experiment**

- Point to various pictures in the Brightness/Contrast area and watch the brightness and contrast change on the picture in Slide 2.

- Click Brightness: −20% Contrast: +40% to apply this correction to the Teamwork photo.

Q&A How can I remove all effects from the picture?
Click the Reset Picture button (Picture Tools Format tab | Adjust group).

Other Ways

1. Click Picture Corrections Options (Corrections gallery), move Brightness or Contrast sliders or enter number in box next to slider (Format Picture pane)

To Apply a Picture Style

1 DOWNLOAD & SELECT SLIDES | **2 INSERT & FORMAT PICTURES** | 3 INSERT & FORMAT SHAPES
4 FORMAT SLIDE BACKGROUNDS | 5 INSERT & FORMAT WORDART | 6 REVIEW, REVISE, & PRINT SLIDES

A **style** is a named group of formatting characteristics. The picture on Slide 2 emphasizes the concept of teamwork in this sport, and you can increase its visual appeal by applying a style. *Why? PowerPoint provides more than 25 picture styles that enable you easily to change a picture's look to a more visually appealing style, including a variety of shapes, angles, borders, and reflections.* You want to use a style that applies a shadow to the Teamwork photo. The following steps apply a picture style to the Slide 2 photo.

1

- With the Slide 2 picture selected and the Picture Tools Format tab displaying, click the More button in the Picture Styles gallery (Picture Tools Format tab | Picture Styles group) (shown in Figure 2–17) to expand the gallery.
- Point to Bevel Rectangle in the Picture Styles gallery (last style in third row) to display a live preview of that style applied to the picture in the document (Figure 2–18).

Figure 2–18

Experiment

- Point to various picture styles in the Picture Styles gallery and watch the style of the picture change in the document window.

2

- Click Bevel Rectangle in the Picture Styles gallery to apply the style to the selected picture.

To Add a Picture Border

1 DOWNLOAD & SELECT SLIDES | **2 INSERT & FORMAT PICTURES** | 3 INSERT & FORMAT SHAPES
4 FORMAT SLIDE BACKGROUNDS | 5 INSERT & FORMAT WORDART | 6 REVIEW, REVISE, & PRINT SLIDES

The next step is to add a border to the Slide 2 picture. *Why? Some picture styles do not have a border; others, such as the Bevel Rectangle style you applied to this picture, do have this edging. This border is small, and you want a larger edge around the photo to draw attention to the graphic.* The following steps add a border to the Teamwork picture.

1

- With the Slide 2 picture still selected, click the Picture Border arrow (Picture Tools Format tab | Picture Styles group) to display the Picture Border gallery.

Q&A What if the Picture Tools Format tab no longer is displayed on my ribbon?
Click the picture to display the Picture Tools Format tab.

2

- Point to Weight on the Picture Border gallery to display the Weight gallery.

- Point to 6 pt to display a live preview of this line weight on the picture (Figure 2–19).

Q&A Can I make the line width more than 6 pt?
Yes. Click More Lines, Click Solid line in the Line section of the Format Picture pane, and then increase the amount in the Width box.

Figure 2–19

Experiment

- Point to various line weights in the Weight gallery and watch the line thickness change.

3

- Click 6 pt to add this line weight to the picture.

1 DOWNLOAD & SELECT SLIDES | 2 INSERT & FORMAT PICTURES | 3 INSERT & FORMAT SHAPES
4 FORMAT SLIDE BACKGROUNDS | 5 INSERT & FORMAT WORDART | 6 REVIEW, REVISE, & PRINT SLIDES

To Change a Picture Border Color

The default color for the border you added to the Slide 2 picture is white, but you will change the border color to black. *Why? The black color coordinates with other elements on the slide, especially the lines on the basketball and the court.* The following steps change the Slide 2 picture border color.

1

- With the Slide 2 photo still selected, click the Picture Border arrow (Picture Tools Format tab | Picture Styles group) to display the Picture Border gallery again.

2

- Point to Black, Background 1 (first color in first row) in the Picture Border gallery to display a live preview of that border color on the picture (Figure 2–20).

Figure 2–20

🅟 **Experiment**

• Point to various colors in the Picture Border gallery and watch the border on the picture change in the slide.

3

• Click Black, Background 1 in the Picture Border gallery to change the picture border color.

To Apply Picture Effects

1 DOWNLOAD & SELECT SLIDES | **2 INSERT & FORMAT PICTURES** | 3 INSERT & FORMAT SHAPES
4 FORMAT SLIDE BACKGROUNDS | 5 INSERT & FORMAT WORDART | 6 REVIEW, REVISE, & PRINT SLIDES

Why? Picture effects allow you to further customize a picture. PowerPoint provides a variety of picture effects, including shadows, reflections, glow, soft edges, bevel, and 3-D rotation. The difference between the effects and the styles is that each effect has several options, providing you with more control over the exact look of the image.

In this presentation, the photo on Slide 2 has a brown glow effect and a bevel applied to its edges. The following steps apply picture effects to the selected picture.

1

• With the Slide 2 picture still selected, click the Picture Effects button (Picture Tools Format tab | Picture Styles group) to display the Picture Effects menu.

◁
Q&A | What if the Picture Tools Format tab no longer is displayed on my ribbon?
| Click the picture to display the Picture Tools Format tab.

• Point to Glow on the Picture Effects menu to display the Glow gallery.

• Point to Brown, 18 pt glow, Accent color 3 in the Glow Variations area (third glow in last row) to display a live preview of the selected glow effect applied to the picture in the document window (Figure 2–21).

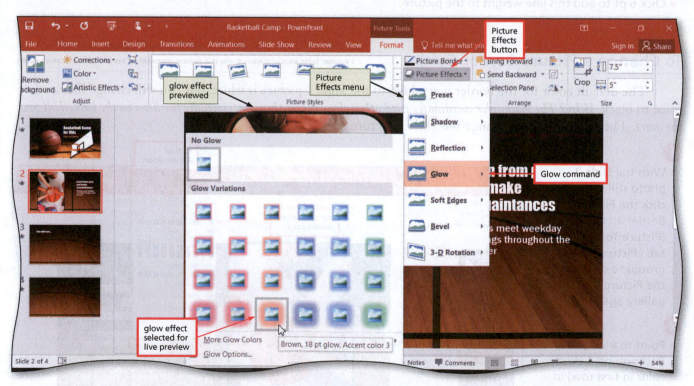

Figure 2–21

🅟 **Experiment**

• Point to various glow effects in the Glow gallery and watch the picture change in the document window.

2
- Click Brown, 18 pt glow, Accent color 3 in the Glow gallery to apply the selected picture effect.

3
- Click the Picture Effects button (Picture Tools Format tab | Picture Styles group) to display the Picture Effects menu again.
- Point to Bevel on the Picture Effects menu to display the Bevel gallery.
- Point to Angle (first bevel in second Bevel row) to display a live preview of the selected bevel effect applied to the Slide 2 picture (Figure 2–22).

Figure 2–22

Experiment
- Point to various bevel effects in the Bevel gallery and watch the picture change in the slide.

4
- Click Angle in the Bevel gallery to apply the selected picture effect.

Other Ways

1. Right-click picture, click Format Picture on shortcut menu, select desired options (Format Picture pane), click Close button

2. Click Format Shape pane launcher (Picture Tools Format tab | Picture Styles group), select desired options (Format Picture pane), click Close button

Break Point: If you wish to take a break, this is a good place to do so. Be sure to save the Basketball Camp file again and then you can exit PowerPoint. To resume at a later time, run PowerPoint, open the file called Basketball Camp, and continue following the steps from this location forward.

Inserting and Formatting a Shape

One method of getting the audience's attention and reinforcing the major concepts being presented is to have graphical elements on the slide. PowerPoint provides a wide variety of predefined shapes that can add visual interest to a slide. Shape elements include lines, basic geometrical shapes, arrows, equation shapes, flowchart symbols, stars, banners, and callouts. After adding a shape to a slide, you can change its default characteristics by adding text, bullets, numbers, and styles. You also can combine multiple shapes to create a more complex graphic.

The predefined shapes are found in the Shapes gallery. This collection is found on the Home tab | Drawing group and the Insert tab | Illustrations group. Once you have inserted and selected a shape, the Drawing Tools Format tab is displayed, and the Shapes gallery also is displayed in the Insert Shapes group.

BTW

Inserting Special Characters
Along with adding shapes to a slide, you can insert characters not found on your keyboard, such as the section sign (§), the copyright sign (©), and Greek capital letters (e.g., Δ, Ω, and ß). To insert these characters, click the Insert tab and then click the Symbol button (Insert tab | Symbols group). When the Symbol dialog box is displayed, you can use the same font you currently are using in your presentation, or you can select another font. The Webdings, Wingdings, Wingdings 2, and Wingdings 3 fonts have a variety of symbols.

Slide 3 in this presentation is enhanced in a variety of ways. First, an oval, an arrow, and a pentagon shape are inserted on the slide and formatted. Then, text is added to the oval and pentagon and formatted. The pentagon is copied, and the text is modified in this new shape. Finally, the arrow shape is duplicated twice and moved into position.

To Add a Shape

1 DOWNLOAD & SELECT SLIDES | 2 INSERT & FORMAT PICTURES | 3 INSERT & FORMAT SHAPES
4 FORMAT SLIDE BACKGROUNDS | 5 INSERT & FORMAT WORDART | 6 REVIEW, REVISE, & PRINT SLIDES

Many of the shapes included in the Shapes gallery can direct the viewer to important aspects of the presentation. The following steps add an oval shape, which displays as a circle, to Slide 3. *Why? A circle shape complements the basketball photo on Slide 1 and helps reinforce the presentation's basketball theme.*

1
- Display Slide 3 and then, if necessary, click the Home tab (Figure 2–23).

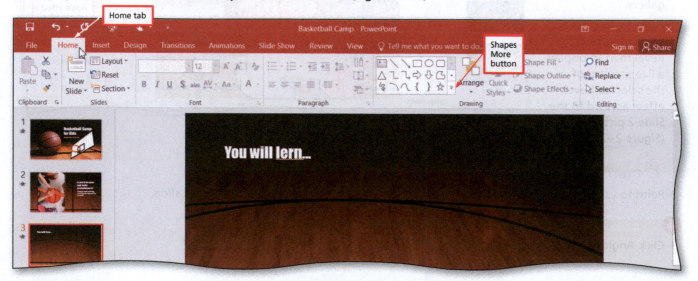

Figure 2–23

2
- Click the Shapes More button (Home tab | Drawing group) shown in Figure 2–23 to display the Shapes gallery (Figure 2–24).

Q&A I do not see a Shapes More button and the three rows of the shapes shown in Figure 2–24. Instead, I have a Shapes button. Why?
Monitor dimensions and resolution affect how buttons display on the ribbon. Click the Shapes button to display the entire Shapes gallery.

Figure 2–24

3

- Click the Oval shape in the Basic Shapes area of the Shapes gallery.

Q&A

Why did my pointer change shape?

The pointer changed to a plus shape to indicate the Oval shape has been added to the Clipboard.

- Position the pointer (a crosshair) near the center of the slide, as shown in Figure 2–25.

4

- Click Slide 3 to insert the Oval shape.

Other Ways

1. Click Shapes button (Insert tab | Illustrations group)

Figure 2–25

To Resize a Shape

1 DOWNLOAD & SELECT SLIDES | 2 INSERT & FORMAT PICTURES | 3 INSERT & FORMAT SHAPES

4 FORMAT SLIDE BACKGROUNDS | 5 INSERT & FORMAT WORDART | 6 REVIEW, REVISE, & PRINT SLIDES

The next step is to resize the Oval shape. **Why?** *The oval should be enlarged so that it is a focal point in the middle area of the slide.* The following steps resize the selected shape.

1

- Press and hold down the SHIFT key and then drag the upper-left corner sizing handle until the shape is resized approximately as shown in Figure 2–26 and the top is aligned with a horizontal Smart Guide.

Q&A

Why did I need to press the SHIFT key while enlarging the shape?

Holding down the SHIFT key while dragging keeps the proportions of the original shape.

What if my shape is not selected?

To select a shape, click it.

If I am using a touch screen, how can I maintain the shape's original proportion?

If you drag one of the corner sizing handles, the object should stay in proportion.

Figure 2–26

2

- Release to resize the shape.
- Drag the shape until the vertical Smart Guide is displayed in the middle of the oval and the horizontal Smart Guide is displayed at the top of the oval, as shown in Figure 2–27, and then release.

Q&A What if I want to move the shape to a precise location on the slide?
With the shape selected, press the ARROW keys or the CTRL+ARROW keys to move the shape to the desired location.

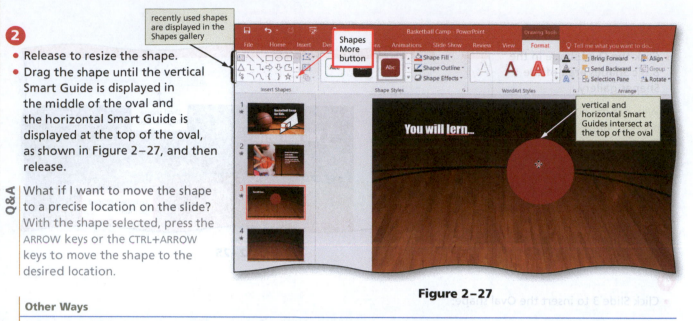

Figure 2–27

Other Ways

1. Enter shape height and width in Height and Width boxes (Drawing Tools Format tab | Size group)
2. Click Size and Position pane launcher (Drawing Tools Format tab | Size group), click Size tab, enter desired height and width values in boxes, click Close button

To Add Other Shapes

1 DOWNLOAD & SELECT SLIDES | 2 INSERT & FORMAT PICTURES | **3 INSERT & FORMAT SHAPES**
4 FORMAT SLIDE BACKGROUNDS | 5 INSERT & FORMAT WORDART | 6 REVIEW, REVISE, & PRINT SLIDES

Ovals, squares, arrows, stars, and equation shapes are among the items included in the Shapes gallery. These shapes can be combined to show relationships among the elements, and they can help illustrate the basic concepts presented in your slide show. **Why?** *Arrows are especially useful in showing the relationship among slide elements and guiding the viewer's eyes to move from one shape to the next.* More than two dozen arrow shapes are displayed in the Block Arrows section of the Shapes gallery. The following steps add one of these arrows and the pentagon shapes to Slide 3.

1

- Click the Shapes More button (Drawing Tools Format tab | Insert Shapes group) shown in Figure 2–27 to display the Shapes gallery (Figure 2–28).

Q&A When I inserted the Oval shape, I selected it on the Home tab. Is the same Shapes gallery also displayed on the Drawing Tools Format tab?
Yes. The Shapes gallery is displayed on this tab once an object is inserted and selected on the slide.

Figure 2–28

2
- Click the Curved Left Arrow shape in the Block Arrows area of the Shapes gallery.
- Position the pointer to the right of the oval shape in Slide 3 and then click to insert the Curved Left Arrow shape.

3
- Press and hold down the SHIFT key and then drag a corner sizing handle until the arrow shape is approximately the size shown in Figure 2–29.

Q&A If I am using a touch screen, how can I maintain the Oval shape's original proportion?
The object should stay in proportion when you drag one of the corner sizing handles.

- If necessary, drag the Curved Left Arrow shape to the right side of the oval, as shown in Figure 2–29, and then release.

Figure 2–29

4
- Display the Shapes gallery and then click the Regular Pentagon shape in the Basic Shapes area of the gallery (shown in Figure 2–28).
- Position the pointer toward the lower-left side of the Curved Left Arrow shape and then click to insert the Regular Pentagon shape.

5
- Press and hold down the SHIFT key and then drag a corner sizing handle to resize the pentagon shape so that it is the size shown in Figure 2–30.
- Drag the pentagon shape so that its tip is placed at the intersection of the horizontal Smart Guide above the pentagon and the vertical Smart Guide in the middle of the shape, as shown in Figure 2–30, and then release.

Figure 2–30

To Apply a Shape Style

1 DOWNLOAD & SELECT SLIDES | 2 INSERT & FORMAT PICTURES | **3 INSERT & FORMAT SHAPES**
4 FORMAT SLIDE BACKGROUNDS | 5 INSERT & FORMAT WORDART | 6 REVIEW, REVISE, & PRINT SLIDES

Formatting text in a shape follows the same techniques as formatting text in a placeholder. You can change font, font color and size, and alignment. You later will add information about a skill to the Oval shape, but first you want to apply a shape style. **Why?** *The style will give depth and dimension to the object.* The Quick Styles gallery has a variety of styles that change depending upon the theme applied to the presentation. The following steps apply a style to the oval.

1
- Display the Home tab, click the oval to select it, and then click the Quick Styles button (Home tab | Drawing group) (Figure 2–31).

Figure 2–31

2
- Point to Light 1 Outline, Colored Fill – Black, Dark 1 in the Quick Styles gallery (first shape in third Theme Styles row) to display a live preview of that style applied to the oval in the slide (Figure 2–32).

Figure 2–32

Experiment

- Point to various styles in the Quick Styles gallery and watch the style of the shape change.

3
- Click Light 1 Outline, Colored Fill – Black, Dark 1 in the Quick Styles gallery to apply the selected style to the oval.

Other Ways

1. Click Shape Styles More button (Drawing Tools Format tab | Shape Styles group), select style
2. Right-click shape, click Style button on mini toolbar, select desired style

---

To Apply Another Style

You later will add text to the oval and pentagon about particular skills taught at the camp, but now you want to format the arrow and pentagon shapes. *Why? You can apply shape styles to the arrow and pentagon that will coordinate with the oval's style. A light style color in the arrow shape will help join darker style colors of the oval and rectangle. This formatting will add interest and emphasize the relationship between basketball playing skills.* The following steps apply styles to the arrow and pentagon shapes.

1 Click the arrow shape to select it.

2 Click the Quick Styles button (Home tab | Drawing group) to display the Quick Styles gallery and then apply the Colored Outline – Black, Dark 1 style (first style in first Theme Styles row) to the arrow shape.

3 Click the pentagon shape to select it and then click the Quick Styles button.

4 Click Subtle Effect – Black, Dark 1 (first style in fourth Theme Styles row) to apply that style to the pentagon shape (Figure 2–33).

BTW

Deleting a Shape
If you want to delete a shape you have added to a slide, click that shape to select it and then press the delete key. If you want to DELETE multiple shapes, press the CTRL key while clicking the undesired shapes and then press the DELETE key.

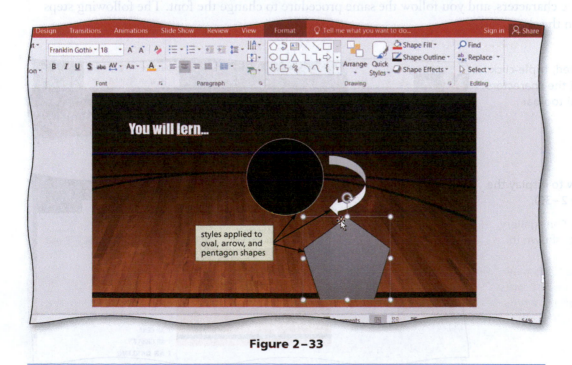

Figure 2–33

To Add Text to a Shape

The three shapes on Slide 3 help call attention to the key aspects of your presentation. *Why? Your goal is to emphasize key skills the campers will learn.* The next step is to add this information to Slide 3. The following steps add text to the oval and pentagon shapes.

1
- With the pentagon selected, type `Offensive moves` to add the text in the shape.

2
- Click the oval to select it and then type `Ball handling skills` to add the text in the shape (Figure 2–34).

Figure 2–34

To Change the Font

The default theme font is Franklin Gothic Medium. To draw more attention to text in the shapes and to help differentiate these slide elements from the title text, you want to change the font to Century Schoolbook. *Why? Century Schoolbook is a serif typeface, meaning the ends of some of the letter are adorned with small decorations, called serifs. These adornments slow down the viewer's reading speed, which might help them retain the information they saw.* To change the font, you must select the letters you want to format. In Module 1, you selected a paragraph and then formatted the characters, and you follow the same procedure to change the font. The following steps change the text font in the shape.

1
- With the oval selected, triple-click the text to select all the characters and display the mini toolbar (Figure 2–35).

2
- Click the Font arrow to display the Font gallery (Figure 2–36).

Q&A | Will the fonts in my Font gallery be the same as those shown in Figure 2–36?
Your list of available fonts may differ, depending on what fonts you have installed and the type of printer you are using.

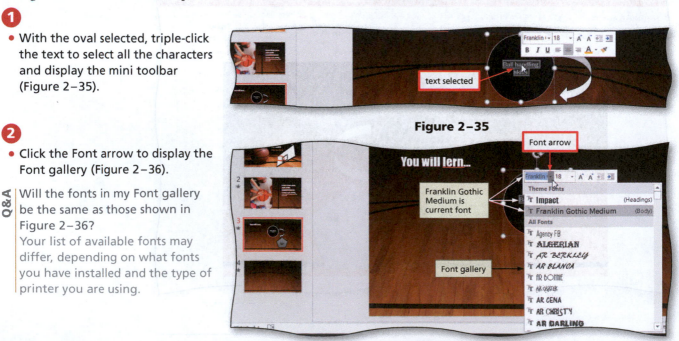

Figure 2–35

Figure 2–36

3

- Drag or scroll through the Font gallery and then point to Century Schoolbook (or a similar font) to display a live preview of the title text in the Century Schoolbook font (Figure 2–37).

🄿 **Experiment**

- Point to various fonts in the Font gallery and watch the subtitle text font change in the slide.

- Click Century Schoolbook (or a similar font) to change the font of the selected text to Century Schoolbook.

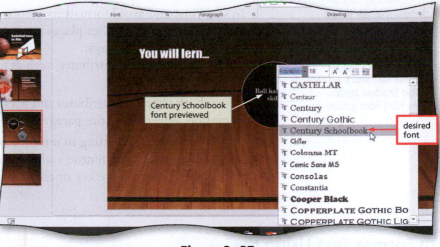

Figure 2–37

Other Ways

1. Click Font arrow (Home tab | Font group), click desired font in Font gallery
2. Right-click selected text, click Font on shortcut menu (Font dialog box), click Font tab, select desired font in Font list, click OK button
3. Click Font dialog box launcher (Home tab | Font group), click Font tab (Font dialog box), select desired font in Font list, click OK button
4. Press CTRL+SHIFT+F, click Font tab (Font dialog box), select desired font in the Font list, click OK button
5. Right-click selected text, click Font arrow on mini toolbar, select desired font

To Format the Text

To increase readability, you can format the oval text by increasing the font size, bolding the characters, and changing the font color to orange. The following steps format the oval text.

1 With the oval text selected, click the Increase Font Size button (Home tab | Font group) two times to increase the font size to 24 pt.

2 Click the Bold button (Home tab | Font group) to bold the text.

3 Click the Font Color arrow and change the color to Orange (third color in Standard Colors row) (Figure 2–38).

Q&A What should I do if one or more letters of the word, handling, wrap to the third line in the shape?
Press and hold down the SHIFT key and then drag a corner sizing handle outward slightly to resize the oval shape.

Could I also add a shadow behind the text to add depth and help the letters display prominently?
Yes. Select the text and then click the Text Shadow button (Home tab | Font group).

BTW

Text in a Shape
When you add text to a shape, it becomes part of the shape. If you rotate or flip the shape, the text also rotates or flips.

Figure 2–38

Other Ways

1. Right-click selected text, click desired text format button on mini toolbar

BTW
Shadowing Text
Adding a shadow to text gives depth and helps the letters display prominently by adding a shadow behind them. To add a shadow, select the text and then click the Text Shadow button (Home tab | Font group).

Format Painter

To save time and avoid formatting errors, you can use the Format Painter to apply custom formatting to other places in your presentation quickly and easily. You can use this feature in three ways:

- To copy only character attributes, such as font and font effects, select text that has these qualities.
- To copy both character attributes and paragraph attributes, such as alignment and indentation, select the entire paragraph.
- To apply the same formatting to multiple words, phrases, or paragraphs, double-click the Format Painter button and then select each item you want to format. You then can press the ESC key or click the Format Painter button to turn off this feature.

To Format Text Using the Format Painter

1 DOWNLOAD & SELECT SLIDES | 2 INSERT & FORMAT PICTURES | **3 INSERT & FORMAT SHAPES**
4 FORMAT SLIDE BACKGROUNDS | 5 INSERT & FORMAT WORDART | 6 REVIEW, REVISE, & PRINT SLIDES

Why? *To save time and duplicated effort, you quickly can use the Format Painter to copy formatting attributes from the oval shape text and apply them to pentagon shape text.* The following steps use the Format Painter to copy formatting features.

1
- With the oval text still selected, double-click the Format Painter button (Home tab | Clipboard group).
- Move the pointer off the ribbon (Figure 2–39).

◄ Q&A | Why does the Format Painter button on my screen display only a paint brush and not the words, Format Painter?
Monitor dimensions and resolution affect how buttons display on the ribbon.

Why did my pointer change shape?
The pointer changed shape by adding a paintbrush to indicate that the Format Painter function is active.

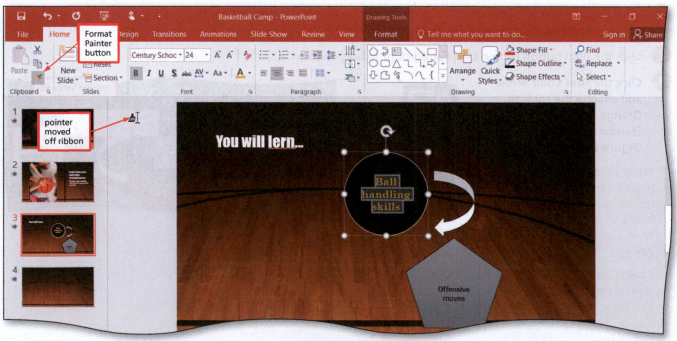

Figure 2–39

2

- Triple-click the pentagon text to apply the format to all characters (Figure 2–40).
- Click the Format Painter button or press the ESC key to turn off the Format Painter feature.

Q&A What should I do if one or more letters of the word, Offensive, wrap to a second line in the shape?
Press and hold down the SHIFT key and then drag a corner sizing handle outward slightly to resize the pentagon shape.

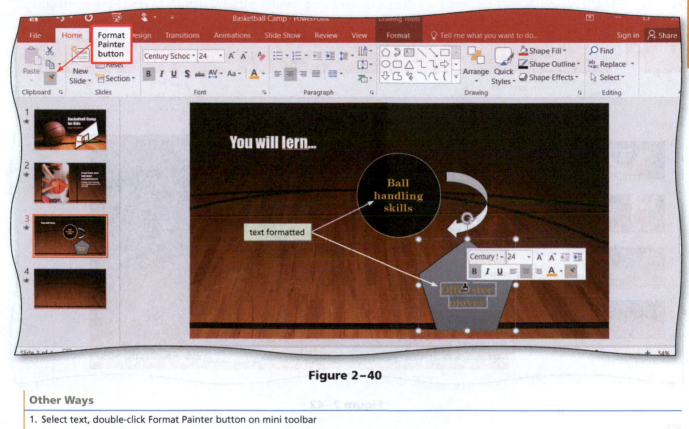

Figure 2–40

Other Ways

1. Select text, double-click Format Painter button on mini toolbar

To Copy and Paste a Shape

1 DOWNLOAD & SELECT SLIDES | 2 INSERT & FORMAT PICTURES | 3 INSERT & FORMAT SHAPES
4 FORMAT SLIDE BACKGROUNDS | 5 INSERT & FORMAT WORDART | 6 REVIEW, REVISE, & PRINT SLIDES

Good basketball players have both offensive and defensive skills. You already have created the shape stating the campers will work on refining their offensive talents. You now need to create a second shape with information about defensive instruction that will be provided at the camp. The following steps copy the pentagon shape and then change the text. *Why? You could repeat all the steps you performed to create the first pentagon, but it is much more efficient to duplicate the shape and then edit the text.*

1

- With the pentagon shape selected, click the Copy button (Home tab | Clipboard group) (Figure 2–41).

Figure 2–41

2

- Click the Paste button (Home tab | Clipboard group) to insert a duplicate Regular Pentagon shape on Slide 3.
- Drag the new pentagon shape to the left of the original pentagon shape, as shown in Figure 2–42.
- In the left pentagon shape, select the text, Offensive moves, and then type **Defensive mindset** as the replacement text (Figure 2–42).

Q&A What should I do if one or more letters of the word, Defensive, wrap to a second line in the shape?
Press and hold down the SHIFT key and then drag a corner sizing handle outward slightly to resize the pentagon shape.

Figure 2–42

3

- Select the arrow shape and then click the Copy button (Home tab | Clipboard group) (Figure 2–43).

Figure 2–43

4

- Click the Paste button (Home tab | Clipboard group) two times to insert two duplicate arrow shapes on Slide 3.
- Drag one of the duplicate arrow shapes between the two pentagon shapes and then drag the other duplicate arrow shape between the left pentagon shape and the oval shape (Figure 2–44).

Figure 2–44

5

- With the left arrow selected, drag its rotation handle clockwise or counterclockwise so that it is displayed as shown in Figure 2–45. Repeat this procedure for the other two arrows, and then adjust the shapes' locations on Slide 3 so that the arrows touch their adjacent shapes (Figure 2–45).
- If the end of an arrow is underneath an oval or a pentagon shape, select the arrow, click the Drawing Tools Format tab, and then click the Bring Forward button (Drawing Tools Format tab | Arrange group) to bring the arrow on top of the shape.

Figure 2–45

Other Ways

1. Right-click selected shape, click Copy on shortcut menu, right-click blank area, click Paste on shortcut menu
2. Select shape, press CTRL+C, press CTRL+V

Break Point: If you wish to take a break, this is a good place to do so. Be sure to save the Basketball Camp file again and then you can exit PowerPoint. To resume at a later time, run PowerPoint, open the file called Basketball Camp, and continue following the steps from this location forward.

Formatting Slide Backgrounds

A slide's background is an integral part of a presentation because it can generate audience interest. Every slide can have the same background, or different backgrounds can be used in a presentation. This background is considered **fill**, which is the content that makes up the interior of a shape, line, or character. Four fills are available: solid, gradient, picture or texture, and pattern. **Solid fill** is one color used throughout the entire slide. **Gradient fill** is one color shade gradually progressing to another shade of the same color or one color progressing to another color. **Picture or texture fill** uses a specific file or an image that simulates a material, such as cork, granite, marble, or canvas. **Pattern fill** adds designs, such as dots or dashes, which repeat in rows across the slide.

Once you add a fill, you can adjust its appearance. For example, you can adjust its **transparency**, which allows you to see through the background, so that any text on the slide is visible. You also can select a color that is part of the theme or a custom color. You can use an **offset**, another background feature, to move the background away from the slide borders in varying distances by percentage. A **tiling option** repeats the background image many times vertically and horizontally on the slide; the smaller the tiling percentage, the greater the number of times the image is repeated.

To Insert a Texture Fill

1 DOWNLOAD & SELECT SLIDES | 2 INSERT & FORMAT PICTURES | 3 INSERT & FORMAT SHAPES
4 FORMAT SLIDE BACKGROUNDS | 5 INSERT & FORMAT WORDART | 6 REVIEW, REVISE, & PRINT SLIDES

Why? Various texture fills are available to give your background a unique look. The 24 pictures in the Texture gallery give the appearance of a physical object, such as water drops, sand, tissue paper, and a paper bag. You also can use your own texture pictures for custom backgrounds. The following steps insert the Brown marble texture fill on Slide 2 in the presentation.

1
• Display Slide 2. Click the Design tab and then click the Format Background button (Design tab | Customize group) to display the Format Background pane (Figure 2–46).

Figure 2–46

2

• With the Fill section displaying (Format Background pane), if necessary, click 'Picture or texture fill' and then click the Texture button to display the Texture gallery (Figure 2–47).

Figure 2–47

3

• Click the Brown marble texture (first texture in third row) to insert this texture fill as the background on Slide 2 (Figure 2–48).

Q&A Is a live preview available to see the various textures on this slide?
No. Live preview is not an option with the background textures and fills.

Could I insert this background on all four slides simultaneously?
Yes. You would click the 'Apply to All' button to insert the Brown marble background on all slides.

Figure 2–48

Other Ways

1. Right-click background, click Format Background on shortcut menu, select desired options (Format Background pane)

To Format the Background Texture Fill Transparency

Why? *The Brown marble texture on Slide 2 is dark, and its pattern may detract from the photo and text.* One method of reducing this darkness is to change the transparency. The **Transparency slider** indicates the amount of opaqueness. The default setting is 0, which is fully opaque. The opposite extreme is 100%, which is fully transparent. To change the transparency, you can move the Transparency slider or enter a number in the box next to the slider. The following step adjusts the texture transparency to 15%.

 1

- Click the Transparency slider (Format Background pane) and drag it to the right until 15% is displayed in the Transparency box (Figure 2–49).

Q&A Can I move the slider in small increments so that I can get a precise percentage easily?
Yes. Click the up or down arrows in the Transparency box to move the slider in 1% increments.

Figure 2–49

To Insert a Gradient Fill

Although you selected Brown marble texture fill on Slide 2 and changed the transparency, you decide that another type of background may be more suitable for Slide 3. *Why?* *The Brown marble texture does not offer sufficient contrast with the oval symbol and may detract from the messages presented in the three symbols.* For each theme, PowerPoint provides 30 preset **gradient fills** with five designs for each of the six major theme colors. Each fill has one dark color shade that gradually lightens to either another shade of the same color or another color. The following steps replace the background on Slide 3 to a preset gradient fill.

1

- Display Slide 3. With the Fill section displaying (Format Background pane), click Gradient fill in the Format Background pane (shown in Figure 2–49) and then click the Preset gradients button to display the Preset gradients gallery (Figure 2–50).

Q&A Are the backgrounds displayed in a specific order?
Yes. The first row has light colors at the top of the background; the middle rows have darker fills at the bottom; the bottom row has overall dark fills on all edges.

Is a live preview available to see the various gradients on this slide?
No. Live preview is not an option with the background textures and fills.

Figure 2–50

2

- Click Bottom Spotlight – Accent 3 (third fill in fourth row) to apply that style to Slide 3 (Figure 2–51).

Q&A
If I decide later that this background gradient does not fit the theme of my presentation, can I apply a different background?
Yes. You can repeat these steps at any time while creating your presentation.

Figure 2–51

Other Ways

1. Click Design tab on ribbon, click Format Background button (Customize group), select desired options (Format Background pane)
2. Right-click background, click Format Background on shortcut menu, select desired options (Format Background pane)

To Insert a Picture to Create a Background

Why? *For variety and interest, you want to use an illustration as the Slide 4 background.* This picture is stored in the Data Files folder. PowerPoint will stretch the height and width of this picture to fill the slide area. The following steps insert the illustration, Basketball Boy, on Slide 4 only.

1

- Display Slide 4. With the Fill section displaying (Format Background pane), if necessary, click 'Picture or texture fill' and then click the File button (Format Background pane) to display the Insert Picture dialog box. If necessary, navigate to the Module 02 folder in the Data Files folder or the location where your data files are located.

- Click Basketball Boy to select the file name (Figure 2–52).

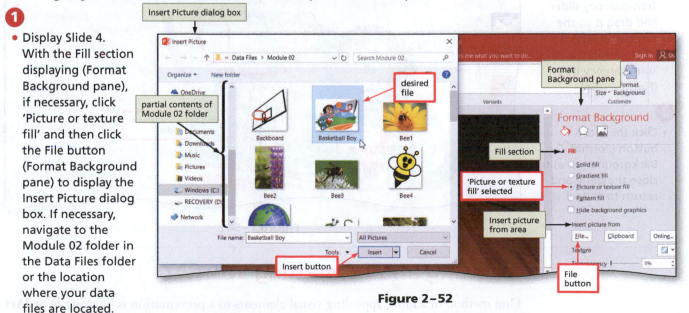

Figure 2–52

2

- Click the Insert button (Insert Picture dialog box) to insert the Basketball Boy illustration as the Slide 4 background (Figure 2–53).

Q&A What if I do not want to use this picture?
Click the Undo button on the Quick Access Toolbar or click the Reset Background button at the bottom of the Format Background pane.

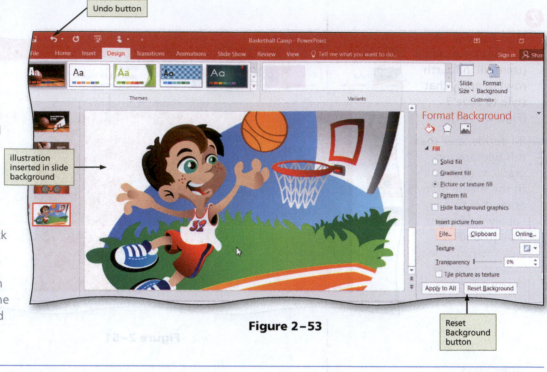

Figure 2–53

To Format the Background Picture Fill Transparency

1 DOWNLOAD & SELECT SLIDES | 2 INSERT & FORMAT PICTURES | 3 INSERT & FORMAT SHAPES
4 FORMAT SLIDE BACKGROUNDS | 5 INSERT & FORMAT WORDART | 6 REVIEW, REVISE, & PRINT SLIDES

Why? *The Basketball Boy illustration on Slide 4 has vibrant colors that will conflict with the WordArt you will add later in this project.* You can adjust the transparency of picture in the same manner that you change the transparency of a slide texture. The following steps adjust the transparency of the background picture to 30% and then close the Format Background pane.

1

- Click the Transparency slider and drag it to the right until 30% is displayed in the Transparency box (Figure 2–54).

2

- Click the Close button (Format Background pane) to close the pane and return to Slide 4.

Figure 2–54

Inserting and Formatting WordArt

One method of adding appealing visual elements to a presentation is by using **WordArt** styles. This feature is found in other Microsoft Office applications, including Word and Excel. This gallery of decorative effects allows you to type new text or convert existing text to WordArt. You then can add elements such as fills, outlines, and effects.

WordArt **fill** in the interior of a letter can consist of a solid color, texture, picture, or gradient. The WordArt **outline** is the exterior border surrounding each letter or symbol. PowerPoint allows you to change the outline color, weight, and style. You also can add an **effect**, which helps add emphasis or depth to the characters. Some effects are shadows, reflections, glows, bevels, and 3-D rotations.

To Insert WordArt

1 DOWNLOAD & SELECT SLIDES | 2 INSERT & FORMAT PICTURES | 3 INSERT & FORMAT SHAPES
4 FORMAT SLIDE BACKGROUNDS | **5 INSERT & FORMAT WORDART** | 6 REVIEW, REVISE, & PRINT SLIDES

The basketball camp is a very popular event among boys and girls in the community, and the sessions fill every year. Parents need to register their student early to reserve a place. You want to emphasize this concept, and the last slide in the presentation is an excellent location to urge your audience to take action. *Why? Audience members remember the first and last things they see and hear.* You quickly can add a visual element to the slide by selecting a WordArt style from the WordArt Styles gallery and then applying it to some text. The following steps insert WordArt.

1
• Display the Insert tab and then click the WordArt button (Insert tab | Text group) to display the WordArt gallery (Figure 2–55).

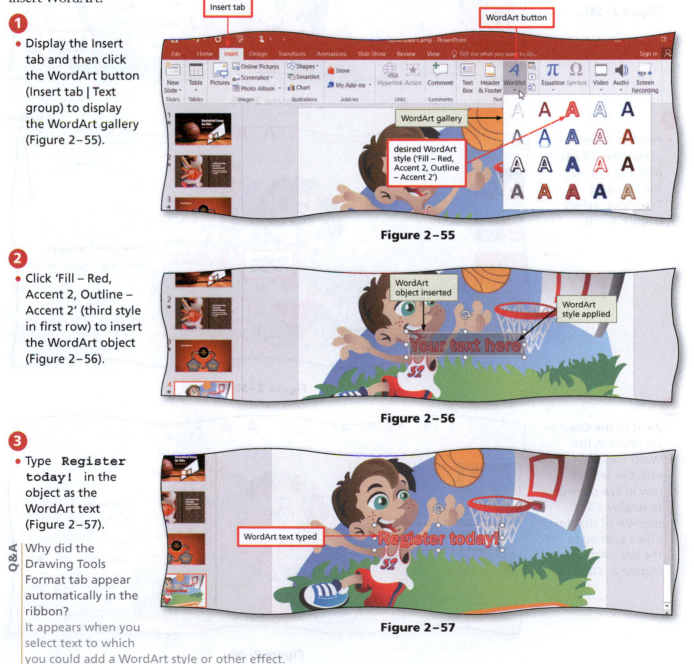

Figure 2–55

2
• Click 'Fill – Red, Accent 2, Outline – Accent 2' (third style in first row) to insert the WordArt object (Figure 2–56).

Figure 2–56

3
• Type **Register today!** in the object as the WordArt text (Figure 2–57).

Q&A
Why did the Drawing Tools Format tab appear automatically in the ribbon?
It appears when you select text to which you could add a WordArt style or other effect.

Figure 2–57

To Change the WordArt Shape

Why? The WordArt text is useful to emphasize the need to register children early for camp. You further can emphasize this text by changing its shape. PowerPoint provides a variety of graphical shapes that add interest to WordArt text. The following steps change the WordArt shape to Chevron Up.

1

- With the WordArt object still selected, click the Text Effects button (Drawing Tools Format tab | WordArt Styles group) to display the Text Effects menu (Figure 2–58).

Figure 2–58

2

- Point to Transform in the Text Effects menu to display the WordArt Transform gallery (Figure 2–59).

Figure 2–59

3

- Point to the Chevron Up effect in the Warp area (first effect in second row in Warp area) to display a live preview of that text effect applied to the WordArt object (Figure 2–60).

Figure 2–60

Experiment

- Point to various effects in the Transform gallery and watch the format of the text and borders change.

Q&A | How can I see the preview of a Transform effect if the gallery overlays the WordArt letters?
Move the WordArt box to the left or right side of the slide and then repeat Steps 1 and 2.

4

- Click the Chevron Up shape to apply this text effect to the WordArt object.

Q&A | Can I change the shape I applied to the WordArt?
Yes. Position the insertion point in the box and then repeat Steps 1 and 2.

5

- Drag the lower-right sizing handle diagonally toward the lower-right corner of the slide until the crosshair is positioned approximately as shown in Figure 2–61.

crosshair indicates lower-right WordArt location

Figure 2–61

6

- Release to resize the WordArt object.
- Drag the WordArt object toward the right side of the slide until it is positioned approximately as shown in Figure 2–62.

WordArt object moved to desired location

Figure 2–62

To Apply a WordArt Text Fill

1 DOWNLOAD & SELECT SLIDES | 2 INSERT & FORMAT PICTURES | 3 INSERT & FORMAT SHAPES
4 FORMAT SLIDE BACKGROUNDS | 5 INSERT & FORMAT WORDART | 6 REVIEW, REVISE, & PRINT SLIDES

Various texture fills are available to give your WordArt characters a unique look. You used a texture fill to add interest to the Slide 3 background. The following steps add the Medium wood texture as a fill for the WordArt characters. *Why? The brown fill coordinates well with the red WordArt outline and is similar to the color of the basketball court in the Slide 1 and Slide 2 backgrounds.*

❶
- With the WordArt object selected, click the Text Fill arrow (Drawing Tools Format tab | WordArt Styles group) to display the Text Fill gallery.
- Point to Texture in the Text Fill gallery to display the Texture gallery.

❷
- If necessary, scroll down and then point to the Medium wood texture (last texture in last row) to display a live preview of that texture applied to the WordArt object (Figure 2–63).

Figure 2–63

🔍 Experiment
- Point to various styles in the Texture gallery and watch the fill change.

❸
- Click the Medium wood texture to apply this texture as the fill for the WordArt object.

Q&A Can I apply this texture simultaneously to text that appears in more than one place on my slide?
Yes. You can select one area of text, press and then hold the CTRL key while you select the other text, and then apply the texture.

To Change the Weight of the WordArt Outline

1 DOWNLOAD & SELECT SLIDES | 2 INSERT & FORMAT PICTURES | 3 INSERT & FORMAT SHAPES
4 FORMAT SLIDE BACKGROUNDS | 5 INSERT & FORMAT WORDART | 6 REVIEW, REVISE, & PRINT SLIDES

The letters in the WordArt style applied have an outline around the edges. You can increase the width of the outlines. **Why?** *The thicker line will emphasize this characteristic and add another visual element.* As with fonts, lines also are measured in points, and PowerPoint gives you the option to change the line **weight**, or thickness, starting with ¼ point (pt) and increasing in ¼-point increments. Other outline options include modifying the color and the line style, such as changing to dots or dashes or a combination of dots and dashes. The following steps change the WordArt outline weight to 6 pt.

1

- With the WordArt object still selected, click the Text Outline arrow (Drawing Tools Format tab | WordArt Styles group) to display the Text Outline gallery.
- Point to Weight in the gallery to display the Weight list.
- Point to 6 pt to display a live preview of this line weight on the WordArt text outline (Figure 2–64).

Figure 2–64

Q&A Can I make the line width more than 6 pt?
Yes. Click More Lines and increase the amount in the Width box.

Experiment

- Point to various line weights in the Weight list and watch the line thickness change.

2

- Click 6 pt to apply this line weight to the WordArt text outline.

Q&A Must my text have an outline?
No. To delete the outline, click No Outline in the Text Outline gallery.

To Change the Color of the WordArt Outline

1 DOWNLOAD & SELECT SLIDES | 2 INSERT & FORMAT PICTURES | 3 INSERT & FORMAT SHAPES
4 FORMAT SLIDE BACKGROUNDS | **5 INSERT & FORMAT WORDART** | 6 REVIEW, REVISE, & PRINT SLIDES

Why? The WordArt outline color and the boy's shorts are similar, so you can add contrast by changing one of these slide elements. The following steps change the WordArt outline color.

1

- With the WordArt object still selected, display the Text Outline gallery.
- Point to Black, Background 1 (first color in Theme Colors row) to display a live preview of this outline color (Figure 2–65).

Figure 2–65

Experiment

• Point to various colors in the gallery and watch the outline colors change.

2

• Click Black, Background 1 to apply this color to the WordArt outline.

• Click outside of the WordArt box to deselect this slide element (Figure 2–66).

Figure 2–66

Reviewing and Revising Individual Slides

The text, pictures, and shapes for all slides in the Basketball Camp presentation have been entered. Once you complete a slide show, you might decide to change elements. PowerPoint provides several tools to assist you with making changes. They include finding and replacing text, inserting a synonym, checking spelling, and printing speaker notes. The following pages discuss these tools.

Replace Dialog Box

BTW

Finding and Replacing Text

When finding and replacing text, you do not need to display the slide that contains the word for which you are searching. You can perform this action when any slide is displayed. To see the results of the search and replace action, however, you need to display the slide where the change occurred.

At times, you might want to change all occurrences of a word or phrase to another word or phrase. For example, an instructor may have one slide show to accompany a lecture for several introductory classes, and he wants to update slides with the particular class name and section that appear on several slides. He manually could change the characters, but PowerPoint includes an efficient method of replacing one word with another. The Find and Replace feature automatically locates specific text and then replaces it with desired text.

In some cases, you may want to replace only certain occurrences of a word or phrase, not all of them. To instruct PowerPoint to confirm each change, click the Find Next button in the Replace dialog box instead of the Replace All button. When PowerPoint locates an occurrence of the text, it pauses and waits for you to click either the Replace button or the Find Next button. Clicking the Replace button changes the text; clicking the Find Next button instructs PowerPoint to disregard that particular instance and look for the next occurrence of the Find what text.

To Find and Insert a Synonym

1 DOWNLOAD & SELECT SLIDES | 2 INSERT & FORMAT PICTURES | 3 INSERT & FORMAT SHAPES
4 FORMAT SLIDE BACKGROUNDS | 5 INSERT & FORMAT WORDART | 6 REVIEW, REVISE, & PRINT SLIDES

Why? *When reviewing your slide show, you may decide that a particular word does not express the exact usage you intended or that you used the same word on multiple slides.* In these cases, you could find a **synonym**, or word similar in meaning, to replace the inappropriate or duplicate word. PowerPoint provides a **thesaurus**, which is a list of synonyms and antonyms, to help you find a replacement word.

In this project, you want to find a synonym to replace the word, acquaintances, on Slide 2. The following steps locate an appropriate synonym and replace the word.

1

- Display Slide 2 and then place the insertion point in the word, acquaintances.

- Right-click to display a shortcut menu related to the word, acquaintances. Then, point to Synonyms on the shortcut menu to display a list of synonyms for this word (Figure 2–67).

Q&A
How do I locate a synonym for multiple words?
You need to select all the words and then right-click to display the shortcut menu.

If I am using a touch screen, how do I find a synonym?
Tap the Thesaurus button (Review tab | Proofing group) to display the Thesaurus pane

for the selected word. Then, in the pane, tap the arrow next to the word to display a shortcut menu.

Figure 2–67

2

- Click the synonym you want (friends) on the Synonyms submenu to replace the word, acquaintances, in the presentation with the word, friends (Figure 2–68).

Q&A
What if a suitable word does not display in the Synonyms submenu?
You can display the Thesaurus pane by clicking Thesaurus on the Synonyms submenu. A complete thesaurus with synonyms displays in the pane along with an

antonym, which is a word with an opposite meaning.

Figure 2–68

Other Ways

1. Click Thesaurus (Review tab | Proofing group)

2. Press SHIFT+F7

To Add Notes

1 DOWNLOAD & SELECT SLIDES | 2 INSERT & FORMAT PICTURES | 3 INSERT & FORMAT SHAPES
4 FORMAT SLIDE BACKGROUNDS | 5 INSERT & FORMAT WORDART | **6 REVIEW, REVISE, & PRINT SLIDES**

Why? As you create slides, you may find material you want to state verbally and do not want to include on the slide. After adding these comments, you can print a set of speaker notes that will print below a small image of the slide. You can type and format comments in the **Notes pane** as you work in Normal view and then print this information as **notes pages**. The Notes pane is hidden until you click the Notes button on the status bar to open the pane. If you want to close the Notes pane, click the Notes button again. Charts, tables, and pictures added to the Notes pane also print on these pages. The following steps add text to the Notes pane on Slides 2, 3, and 4.

Note: In the following step, the word, skills, has been misspelled intentionally as skils to illustrate the use of PowerPoint's spell check feature. Your slides may contain different misspelled words, depending upon the accuracy of your typing.

1

- If necessary, click the Notes button on the status bar to display the Notes pane for Slide 2.

Q&A | Why might I need to click the Notes button?

By default, the Notes pane is closed when you begin a new presentation. Once you display the Notes pane for any slide, the Notes pane will remain open unless you click the Notes button to close it.

- Click the Notes pane and then type **Every morning begins with a group session that covers the day's agenda. The coaches then separate the campers into groups to cover fundamental skils. Each morning ends with a contest designed to be fun and competitive.** (Figure 2–69).

Figure 2–69

Q&A | What if I cannot see all the lines I typed?

You can drag the splitter bar up to enlarge the Notes pane. Clicking the Notes pane scroll arrows or swiping up or down on the Notes pane allows you to view the entire text.

2

- Display Slide 3, click the Notes pane, and then type **Campers will gain confidence while learning sportsmanship and strategies.** (Figure 2–70).

Figure 2–70

3

- Display Slide 4 and then type **Space is limited. Every camper will receive a t-shirt, snacks, and water. Parents are encouraged to attend the awards ceremony at the end of the camp session.** in the Notes pane (Figure 2–71).

Figure 2–71

To Find and Replace Text

1 DOWNLOAD & SELECT SLIDES | 2 INSERT & FORMAT PICTURES | 3 INSERT & FORMAT SHAPES
4 FORMAT SLIDE BACKGROUNDS | 5 INSERT & FORMAT WORDART | **6 REVIEW, REVISE, & PRINT SLIDES**

While reviewing your slides, you realize that the camp will be held in the afternoon, not in the morning. To change this word throughout a presentation, you could view each slide, look for the word, morning, delete the word, and then type the replacement word, afternoon. A more efficient and effective method of performing this action is to use PowerPoint's Find and Replace feature. ***Why?*** *This method locates each occurrence of a word or phrase automatically and then replaces it with specified text.* The word, morning, displays three times in the slides and notes. The following steps use Find and Replace to replace all occurrences of the word, morning, with the word, afternoon.

1
- If necessary, display the Home tab and then click the Replace button (Home tab | Editing group) to display the Replace dialog box.
- Type **morning** in the Find what box (Replace dialog box).
- Click the Replace with box and then type **afternoon** in the box (Figure 2–72).

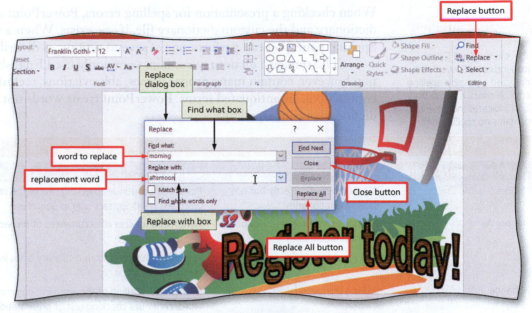

Figure 2–72

2
- Click the Replace All button (Replace dialog box) to instruct PowerPoint to replace all occurrences of the Find what word, morning, with the Replace with word, afternoon (Figure 2–73).

Q&A
If I accidentally replaced the wrong text, can I undo this replacement?
Yes. Press CTRL+Z or click the Undo button on the Quick Access Toolbar to undo all replacements. If you had clicked the Replace button instead of the Replace All button, PowerPoint would undo only the most recent replacement.

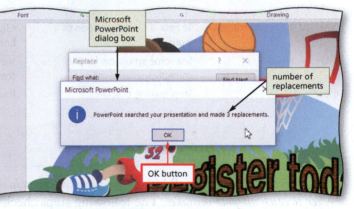

Figure 2–73

3
- Click the OK button (Microsoft PowerPoint dialog box).
- Click the Close button (Replace dialog box).

Other Ways

1. Press CTRL+H

Checking Spelling

After you create a presentation, you should check it visually for spelling errors and style consistency. In addition, you can use PowerPoint's Spelling tool to identify possible misspellings on the slides and in the notes. You should proofread your presentation carefully by pointing to each word and saying it aloud as you point to it. Be mindful of commonly misused words such as its and it's, through and though, and to and too.

PowerPoint checks the entire presentation for spelling mistakes using a standard dictionary contained in the Microsoft Office group. This dictionary is shared with the other Microsoft Office applications such as Word and Excel. A custom dictionary is available if you want to add special words such as proper names, cities, and acronyms.

BTW
Formatting Notes Pane Text
You can format text in the Notes pane in the same manner you format text on a slide. To add emphasis, for example, you can italicize key words or change the font color and size.

When checking a presentation for spelling errors, PowerPoint opens the standard dictionary and the custom dictionary file, if one exists. When a word appears in the Spelling pane, you can perform one of several actions, as described in Table 2–1.

The standard dictionary contains commonly used English words. It does not, however, contain many proper names, abbreviations, technical terms, poetic contractions, or antiquated terms. PowerPoint treats words not found in the dictionaries as misspellings.

Table 2–1 Spelling Pane Buttons and Actions

Button Name/Action	When to Use	Action
Ignore	Word is spelled correctly but not found in dictionaries	PowerPoint continues checking rest of the presentation but will flag that word again if it appears later in document.
Ignore All	Word is spelled correctly but not found in dictionaries	PowerPoint ignores all occurrences of the word and continues checking rest of presentation.
Add	Add word to custom dictionary	PowerPoint opens custom dictionary, adds word, and continues checking rest of presentation.
Change	Word is misspelled	Click proper spelling of the word in Suggestions list. PowerPoint corrects word, continues checking rest of presentation, but will flag that word again if it appears later in document.
Change All	Word is misspelled	Click proper spelling of word in Suggestions list. PowerPoint changes all occurrences of misspelled word and continues checking rest of presentation.
Listen to the pronunciation	To hear the pronunciation of a word	Click the audio speaker icon next to the properly spelled word near the bottom of the Spelling pane.
View synonyms	See some synonyms for the correctly spelled word	View the bullet list of synonyms below the correctly spelled word near the bottom of the Spelling pane.
Close	Stop spelling checker	PowerPoint closes spelling checker and returns to PowerPoint window.

To Check Spelling

1 DOWNLOAD & SELECT SLIDES | 2 INSERT & FORMAT PICTURES | 3 INSERT & FORMAT SHAPES
4 FORMAT SLIDE BACKGROUNDS | 5 INSERT & FORMAT WORDART | **6 REVIEW, REVISE, & PRINT SLIDES**

Why? *Although PowerPoint's spelling checker is a valuable tool, it is not infallible. You should not rely on the spelling checker to catch all your mistakes.* The following steps check the spelling on all slides in the Basketball Camp presentation.

1
• Click Review on the ribbon to display the Review tab.

• Click the Spelling button (Review Tab | Proofing group) to start the spelling checker and display the Spelling pane (Figure 2–74).

Figure 2–74

2

- With the word, skils, selected in the list and in the Notes pane, click the Change button (Spelling pane) to replace the misspelled flagged word, skils, with the selected correctly spelled word, skills, and then continue the spelling check (Figure 2–75).

Figure 2–75

Q&A Could I have clicked the Change All button instead of the Change button?

Yes. When you click the Change All button, you change the current and future occurrences of the misspelled word. The misspelled word, skils, appears only once in the presentation, so clicking the Change or the Change All button in this instance produces identical results.

Occasionally a correctly spelled word is flagged as a possible misspelled word. Why?

Your custom dictionary does not contain the word, so it is seen as spelled incorrectly. You can add this word to a custom dictionary to prevent the spelling checker from flagging it as a mistake.

3

- Replace the misspelled word, lern, with the word, learn.
- Continue checking all flagged words in the presentation. When the Microsoft PowerPoint dialog box appears, click the OK button (Microsoft PowerPoint dialog box) to close the spelling checker and return to the slide where a possible misspelled word appeared.

Other Ways

1. Click Spell Check icon on status bar	2. Right-click flagged word, click correct word	3. Press F7

To Insert a Slide Number

PowerPoint can insert the slide number on your slides automatically to indicate where the slide is positioned within the presentation. The number location on the slide is determined by the presentation theme. You have the option to not display this slide number on the title slide. To insert a slide number on all slides except the title slide, you would follow these steps.

1. Display the Insert tab and then click the Slide Number button (Insert tab | Text group) to display the Header and Footer dialog box.

2. Click the Slide number check box (Header and Footer dialog box) to place a check mark in it.

Q&A Can I prevent the slide number from being displayed on the title slide?

Yes. Click the 'Don't show on title slide' check box (Header and Footer dialog box) to place a check mark in it.

3. Click the 'Apply to All' button (Header and Footer dialog box) to close the dialog box and insert the slide number.

Q&A How does clicking the 'Apply to All' button differ from clicking the Apply button?

The Apply button inserts the slide number only on the currently displayed slide, whereas the 'Apply to All' button inserts the slide number on every slide.

BTW

PowerPoint Help
At any time while using PowerPoint, you can find answers to questions and display information about various topics through PowerPoint Help. Used properly, this form of assistance can increase your productivity and reduce your frustrations by minimizing the time you spend learning how to use PowerPoint. For instructions about PowerPoint Help and exercises that will help you gain confidence in using it, read the Office and Windows module at the beginning of this book.

Other Ways

1. Click 'Header & Footer' button (Insert tab | Text group), click Slide tab, if necessary (Header and Footer dialog box), click Slide number and 'Don't show on title slide' check boxes, click 'Apply to All' button

To Add a Transition between Slides

A final enhancement you will make in this presentation is to change the transition from Fade to Wipe for all slides and increase the transition duration. The following steps apply this transition to the presentation.

1 Click Transitions on the ribbon and then click the Wipe transition (Transitions tab | Transition to This Slide group) to apply this transition.

2 Click the Duration up arrow in the Timing group four times to change the transition speed from 01.00 to 02.00.

3 Click the Preview Transitions button (Transitions tab | Preview area) to view the new transition and time.

4 Click the 'Apply To All' button (Transitions tab | Timing group) to apply this transition and speed to all four slides in the presentation (Figure 2–76).

Q&A Can I apply a particular transition or duration to one slide and then change the transition or timing for a different slide in the presentation?

Yes. Select a slide and then select a transition and duration. Do not click the 'Apply To All' button. Repeat this process to apply the transition and duration to individual slides.

Figure 2–76

How can I use handouts to organize my speech?

As you develop a lengthy presentation with many visuals, handouts can help you organize your material. Print handouts with the maximum number of slides per page. Use scissors to cut each thumbnail and then place these miniature slide images adjacent to each other on a flat surface. Any type on the thumbnails will be too small to read, so the images will need to work with only the support of the verbal message you provide. You can rearrange these thumbnails as you organize your speech. When you return to your computer, you can rearrange the slides on your screen to match the order of your thumbnail printouts. Begin speaking the actual words you want to incorporate in the body of the talk. This process of glancing at the thumbnails and hearing yourself say the key ideas of the speech is one of the best methods of organizing and preparing for the actual presentation. Ultimately, when you deliver your speech in front of an audience, the images on the slides or on your note cards should be sufficient to remind you of the accompanying verbal message.

To Print Speaker Notes

Why? Comments added to slides in the Notes pane give the speaker information that supplements the text on the slide. They will print with a small image of the slide at the top and the comments below the slide. The following steps print the speaker notes.

1

- Display Slide 1, click File on the ribbon to open the Backstage view, and then click the Print tab in the Backstage view to display Slide 1 in the Print gallery.

- Click 'Full Page Slides' in the Settings area to display the Print gallery (Figure 2–77).

Q&A Why does the preview of my slide appear in black and white?

Your printer determines how the preview appears. If your printer is not capable of printing color images, the preview will not appear in color.

Figure 2–77

2

- Click Notes Pages in the Print Layout area to select this option and then click the Next Page button three times to display a preview of Slide 4 (Figure 2–78).

Q&A Can I preview Slides 1, 2, or 3 now?
Yes. Click the Previous Page button to preview the other slides.

Figure 2–78

3

- Verify that the printer listed on the Printer Status button will print a hard copy of the presentation. If necessary, click the Printer Status button to display a list of available printer options and then click the desired printer to change the currently selected printer.
- Click the Print button in the Print gallery to print the notes pages on the currently selected printer.
- When the printer stops, retrieve the hard copy.

Q&A I am not using a color printer, so why do the background images display in the figures but not in my printout?
Graphics are displayed depending upon the settings in the Print gallery. For example, the background will print if Color is specified whereas it will not with a Grayscale or Pure Black and White setting.

Other Ways

1. Press CTRL+P, select desired options

To Save and Print the Presentation

It is a good practice to save a presentation before printing it, in the event you experience difficulties printing. For a detailed example of the procedure summarized below for saving and printing a presentation, refer to the Office and Windows module at the beginning of this book.

1 Save the presentation again on the same storage location with the same file name.

2 Print the presentation.

Q&A Do I have to wait until my presentation is complete to print it?
No, you can follow these steps to print a presentation at any time while you are creating it.

3 Because the project now is complete, you can exit PowerPoint.

BTW

Conserving Ink and Toner

If you want to conserve ink or toner, you can instruct PowerPoint to print draft quality documents by clicking File on the ribbon to open the Backstage view, clicking the Options tab in the Backstage view to display the PowerPoint Options dialog box, clicking Advanced in the left pane (PowerPoint Options dialog box), scrolling to the Print area in the right pane, not placing a check mark in the High quality check box, and then clicking the OK button. Then, use the Backstage view to print the document as usual.

BTW

Distributing a Document

Instead of printing and distributing a hard copy of a document, you can distribute the document electronically. Options include sending the document via email; posting it on cloud storage (such as OneDrive) and sharing the file with others; posting it on social media, a blog, or other website; and sharing a link associated with an online location of the document. You also can create and share a PDF or XPS image of the document, so that users can view the file in Acrobat Reader or XPS Viewer instead of in PowerPoint.

BTW

Printing Document Properties

PowerPoint 2016 does not allow you to print document properties. This feature, however, is available in other Office 2016 apps, including Word and Excel.

Summary

In this module, you have learned how to insert and format pictures, add and format shapes, insert and format WordArt, add and format slide backgrounds, find and replace text, check spelling, add notes, and print speaker notes.

What decisions will you need to make when creating your next presentation?

Use these guidelines as you complete the assignments in this module and create your own slide show decks outside of this class.

1. Determine if an online theme can help you design and develop the presentation efficiently and effectively.

2. Identify personal pictures that would create interest and promote the message being presented.

3. Consider modifying pictures.

    a) Add corrections.

    b) Add styles.

    c) Add effects.

    d) Add and format borders.

4. Locate shapes that supplement the verbal and written message.

    a) Size and position them aesthetically on slides.

    b) Add styles.

5. Develop WordArt that emphasizes major presentation messages.

    a) Modify the shape.

    b) Change the weight and color to coordinate with slide elements.

6. Format individual slide backgrounds.

    a) Add and modify fills.

    b) Insert a picture background.

7. Change fonts to emphasize particular slide components.

8. Search for synonyms that help express your thoughts.

9. Create speaker notes.

10. Check spelling.

Apply Your Knowledge

Reinforce the skills and apply the concepts you learned in this module.

Changing the Background and Adding Photos and WordArt

Note: To complete this assignment, you will be required to use the Data Files. Please contact your instructor for information about accessing the Data Files.

Instructions: Run PowerPoint. Open the presentation called Apply 2–1 Bees, which is located in the Data Files. The four slides in the presentation discuss bee stings. The document you open is an unformatted presentation. You are to add pictures, apply picture styles, add WordArt, change slide layouts, and apply a transition so the slides look like Figure 2–79.

(a) Slide 1

Figure 2–79

Perform the following tasks:

1. On the title slide, use your name in place of Student Name and then bold and italicize this text (Figure 2–79a).

2. If requested to do so by your instructor, change your first name to your mother's first name on the title slide.

3. Increase the title text font size to 96 point and change the font to Bernard MT Condensed. Apply the WordArt style, Fill – White, Outline – Accent 1, Shadow (in first row). Change text fill color to Yellow (in Standard Colors row). Change text outline to Black, Text 1 (in first Theme Colors row) and then change the outline weight to 2¼ pt. Apply the Transform text effect, Arch Up (in Follow Path row) to this text.

4. Apply the Beveled Oval, Black picture style to the picture on Slide 1 and then move the picture to the center of the slide as shown in Figure 2–79a. Use the vertical Smart Guide to align the picture in this location.

5. Create a background on Slide 1 by inserting the photo, Spring, which is located in the Data Files.

6. On Slide 2, change the layout to Title and Content. Increase the title text font to 54 point, change the font color to Green (in Standard Colors row), and then bold this text. Increase the list font size to 32 point, as shown in Figure 2–79b.

7. Create a background on Slides 2 and 3 by inserting the Light Gradient – Accent 4 gradient fill (in first Preset gradients row).

8. On Slide 2, insert the picture, Bee2, move it to the right side of the slide, and then apply the Soft Edge Rectangle picture style to the picture.

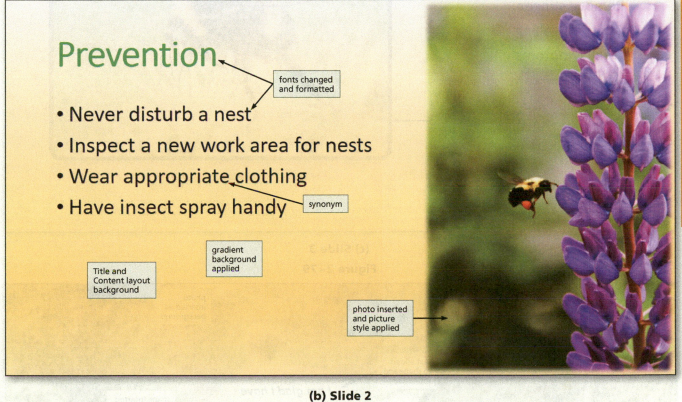

(b) Slide 2

Figure 2–79

9. On Slide 2, type `Wear long pants and a long-sleeved shirt when hiking or working outside.` in the Notes pane.

10. Replace the word, proper, with the synonym, appropriate.

11. On Slide 3 (Figure 2–79c), increase the title text font to 54 point, change the font color to Green (in Standard Colors row), and then bold this text. Increase the list font size to 24 point. Insert the photo, Bee3, and then apply the Reflected Bevel, Black picture style and change the picture brightness to Brightness: +20% Contrast: 0% (Normal) (in Brightness/Contrast area).

12. Type `Apply ice to control swelling.` in the Notes pane.

13. Create a new Slide 4 with the blank layout. Create a background on Slide 4 by inserting the photo, Hiking. Insert the illustration, Bee4. Resize this illustration and move it to the woman's right arm, as shown in Figure 2–79d.

14. On Slide 4, insert the Oval Callout shape (in first row in Callouts area) and then move it to the right side of the woman's head. Apply the Subtle Effect – Gold, Accent 4 (in fourth row) shape style to the callout. Size the shape as shown in the figure. Type `I am glad I have insect repellent in my backpack` in the shape. Bold and italicize this text and then change the font size to 20 point, as shown in Figure 2–79d.

15. Apply the Wind transition in the Exciting category to all slides. Change the duration to 2.50 seconds.

Continued >

Apply Your Knowledge *continued*

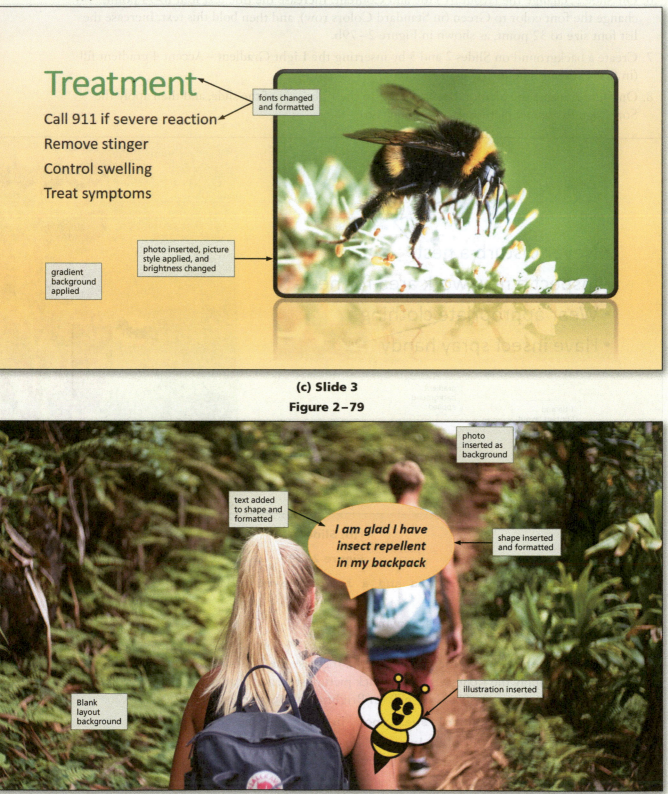

(c) Slide 3

Figure 2–79

(d) Slide 4

Figure 2–79

16. Save the presentation using the file name, Apply 2–1 Bee Stings.

17. Submit the revised document in the format specified by your instructor.

18. ❀ In Step 4 you applied the Beveled Oval, Black picture style to the photo on Slide 1. How did this style enhance the photo and the slide?

Extend Your Knowledge

Extend the skills you learned in this module and experiment with new skills. You may need to use Help to complete the assignment.

Changing Slide Backgrounds, Inserting Shapes and WordArt, and Finding and Replacing Text

Note: To complete this assignment, you will be required to use the Data Files. Please contact your instructor for information about accessing the Data Files.

Instructions: Run PowerPoint. Open the presentation, Extend 2–1 Monarch, which is located in the Data Files. You will create backgrounds including inserting a photo to create a background, apply a WordArt Style and effect, add shapes, and find and replace text to create the presentation.

Perform the following tasks:

1. Change the document theme to Basis and choose the orange variant (third variant).

2. Find and replace the words, stay alive, with the word, survive, on all slides.

3. On all slides, create a background by inserting the photo, Sky. Change the transparency to 25%.

4. On the title slide (Figure 2–80a), apply the WordArt style, Fill - Black, Text 1, Outline – Background 1, Hard Shadow – Accent 1 (second style in third row), to the title text, and then increase the font size to 72 point. Apply the WordArt Glow text effect, Red, 18 pt glow, Accent color 3 (in Glow Variations area), and then italicize this text. Also, align the text in the middle of the text box by clicking the Align Text button (Home tab | Paragraph group) and then selecting Middle in the Align Text gallery. You may need to use Help for assistance in aligning this text.

(a) Slide 1

Figure 2–80

Continued >

Extend Your Knowledge *continued*

5. If requested to do so by your instructor, add your current or previous pet's name as the Slide 1 subtitle text in place of Student Name.

(b) Slide 2

Figure 2–80

(c) Slide 3

Figure 2–80

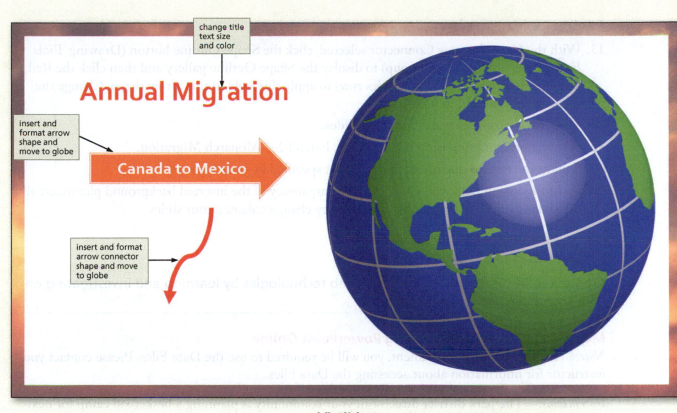

change title
text size
and color

insert and
format arrow
shape and
move to globe

Canada to Mexico

insert and format
arrow connector
shape and move
to globe

Annual Migration

(d) Slide 4

Figure 2–80

6. On Slide 1, move the butterfly illustration in the upper-left corner to the lower-left corner of the slide. Change the butterfly illustration in the upper-right corner of the slide to the illustration, Monarch2. Increase the size of this illustration to approximately 6.26" × 5.44" and move it to the lower-right side of the slide as shown in Figure 2–80a. *Hint*: Use the Size group on the Picture Tools Format tab to enter these measurements for the illustration.

7. On Slides 2 and 3, increase the font size of the first-level paragraphs to 20 point and the one second-level paragraph on Slide 3 to 16 point. Also, change the color of this text to Black, Text 1 (in first Theme Colors row) and then bold this text.

8. On Slide 2 (Figure 2–80b), increase the size of the illustration to approximately 4.14" × 5.53", apply the Reflected Bevel, Black picture style, and then move it under the title text.

9. On Slide 3 (Figure 2–80c), increase the size of the illustration to approximately 4.35" × 5.2", apply the Half Reflection, 8 pt offset reflection picture effect (Reflection Variations area), and then move this illustration to the upper-right corner of the slide.

10. On Slides 2, 3, and 4, decrease the size of the title text to 40 point and then bold this text.

11. On Slide 4 (Figure 2–80d), insert the Right Arrow shape (in Block Arrows area) and position it on the globe illustration near the Canada–United States border. Size the shape as shown in the figure. Type **Canada to Mexico** in the shape. Bold this text and then change the font size to 24 point. Apply the Light 1 Outline, Colored Fill – Orange, Accent 4 shape style (in third Theme Styles row) to the shape.

12. On Slide 4, insert a Curved Arrow Connector shape by displaying the Shapes gallery, clicking this shape (in Lines area), and then positioning the pointer over central Canada in the globe illustration. Then, click and drag the pointer to central Mexico. Size this arrow so it is approximately 0.84" × 1.91". Hint: You can size a shape in the same manner as you size a picture or illustration.

Continued >

Extend Your Knowledge *continued*

13. With the Curved Arrow Connector selected, click the Shape Outline button (Drawing Tools Format tab | Shape Styles group) to display the Shape Outline gallery and then click the Red, Accent 1 style (in first Theme Styles row) to apply this style to this arrow shape. Change the shape outline weight to 6 pt.

14. Apply an appropriate transition to all slides.

15. Save the presentation using the file name, Extend 2–1 Monarch Migration.

16. Submit the revised document in the format specified by your instructor.

17. ✳ In this assignment, you changed the transparency of the inserted background picture on all the slides to 25%. How did this transparency change enhance your slides?

Expand Your World

Create a solution that uses cloud and web technologies by learning and investigating on your own from general guidance.

Modifying a Presentation Using PowerPoint Online

Note: To complete this assignment, you will be required to use the Data Files. Please contact your instructor for information about accessing the Data Files.

Instructions: The park district director in your community is planning a basketball camp for next summer. He has asked you to help him promote this event, and he wants to focus on the skills boys and girls will learn and develop. You inform him that you have created a Basketball Camp presentation for your computer class, and he would like you to customize the content of these slides slightly to promote the summer camp.

Perform the following tasks:

1. Run a browser. Search for the text, PowerPoint Online, using a search engine. Visit several websites to learn about PowerPoint Online. Navigate to the Office Online website. You will need to sign in to your Microsoft account. Run PowerPoint Online.

2. Locate the Basketball Camp presentation in the Recent list and then click the file name to open the file. Click the Edit Presentation button and then click 'Edit in PowerPoint Online' and display the ribbon. Modify the presentation you created for the Basketball Camp presentation by adding the name and address of the nearest park district headquarters on the title slide. In addition, add the date that is the first Saturday in June next year and a starting time of 1 p.m.

3. If requested by your instructor, add the name of one of your high school teachers as the park district director's name on the title slide.

4. Save the presentation using the file name, Expand 2–1 Basketball Camp.

5. Submit the assignment in the format specified by your instructor.

6. ✳ Other than the content the director asked you to include on the title slide, how does the presentation you created using PowerPoint Online differ from the presentation you created in the Module 2 project? Which tabs are not available in PowerPoint Online? View the Home, Design, and Transitions tabs. Do you think the formatting functions, themes, and transitions are adequate to develop effective presentations? Why or why not?

In the Labs

Design, create, modify, and/or use a presentation following the guidelines, concepts, and skills presented in this module. Labs 1 and 2, which increase in difficulty, require you to create solutions based on what you learned in the module; Lab 3 requires you to apply your creative thinking and problem-solving skills to design and implement a solution.

Lab 1: Creating a Presentation, Inserting Photos, Applying Picture Styles, and Inserting Shapes

Note: To complete this assignment, you will be required to use the Data Files. Please contact your instructor for information about accessing the Data Files.

Problem: Your astronomy class is studying the dwarf planet, Pluto, and the New Horizon probe that has been taking photographs of this planet. Prepare the PowerPoint presentation shown in Figure 2–81.

Perform the following tasks:

1. Run PowerPoint. Create a new presentation using the Celestial theme.

2. On Slide 1, insert the photo, Pluto1, as shown in Figure 2–81a. Apply the Metal Oval picture style to the picture, decrease the size of the picture slightly, and then move it to the left side of the slide as shown in the figure.

3. Type **Pluto Up Close** as the Slide 1 title text. Press the ENTER key after the words, PLUTO and UP, so the text is displayed on three lines. Change the font to Britannic Bold and increase the font size to 88 point. Apply the WordArt style Gradient Fill – Gray (first style in

(a) Slide 1

Figure 2–81

Continued >

In the Labs continued

second row). Change the text outline color to Black, Background 1 (in Theme Colors row) and the text outline weight to 3 pt. Also, apply the Perspective Heroic Extreme Left 3-D Rotation (in Perspective area) to this text. Type `New Horizons Probe` as the subtitle text. Change the font to Arial, decrease the font size to 16 point, and then bold this text.

4. Insert four new slides. Create Slides 2 and 5 with the Two Content layout, Slide 3 with the Panoramic Picture with Caption layout, and Slide 4 with the Title Only layout.

5. Using Figures 2–81b through 2–81e as a guide, type the title and content text. On Slide 2, change the title font to Arial, increase the font size to 44 point, and then change the font color to Red (in Standard Colors row). Use the Format Painter to apply these formatting changes to the title text on Slides 4 and 5.

6. On Slide 3, change the font size of the two paragraphs to 24 point and then bold this text.

7. On Slide 5, change the bulleted list font size to 28 point and then bold this text.

8. Using Figures 2–81b through 2–81e as a guide, insert all illustrations on Slides 2 through 5. The pictures and illustration to be inserted, which are available in the Data Files, are called Pluto2 (for Slide 2), Solar System (for Slide 3), Pluto3 (for Slide 4), and Solar System2 (for Slide 5).

9. Size the pictures and then use the Smart Guides to position these images. You may want to zoom the slides to help you align these graphic elements.

10. On Slide 2, apply the Bevel Perspective picture style to the picture, change the picture border color to Red, and then change the border weight to 3 pt, as shown in Figure 2–81b.

(b) Slide 2

Figure 2–81

11. On Slide 2, insert the Diamond shape located in the Basic Shapes area to the right of the title text. Apply the Subtle Effect – Olive Green, Accent 4 shape style (in Theme Styles area) to the shape, type **`Found in 1930`** in the shape, and then bold this text. Insert the 5-Point Star shape located in the Stars and Banners area in the lower-right corner of the slide. Apply the Subtle Effect – Blue, Accent 2 shape style (in Theme Styles area) to the shape, type **`Named after Roman god`** in the shape, and then bold this text. Adjust the size and position of these two shapes, as shown in the figure.

12. On Slide 3, insert the Sun shape located in the Basic Shapes area on the lower-right corner of the slide. Apply the Intense Effect – Gold, Accent 5 shape style (in Theme Styles area) to the shape. Size the shape as shown in the figure. Type the text, **`Pluto takes 248 earth years to orbit the sun`** in the shape and then bold this text, as shown in Figure 2–81c.

(c) Slide 3

Figure 2–81

13. On Slide 4, insert the Oval shape. Select this shape, hold down the SHIFT key, and then draw a circle .75" × .75", as shown in Figure 2–81d. *Hint*: Use the Size group in the Drawing Tools Format tab to enter the exact measurement of the shape. Change the shape fill gradient to Linear Down (in first Light Variations area). Then copy and paste this shape four times. Move the five shapes around the Pluto illustration, as shown in the figure.

14. On Slide 5, apply the Simple Frame, White picture style to the illustration. Insert the Left Arrow shape located in the Block Arrows area to the right of the illustration. Change the shape fill to Red. Size the shape as shown in the figure. Type **`Pluto`** in the shape and then bold this text, as shown in Figure 2–81e.

15. On Slide 2, type **`Pluto was discovered on February 18, 1930, by Clyde Tombaugh of the Lowell Observatory.`** in the Notes pane.

16. On Slide 3, type **`It takes five hours for the sun's rays to reach Pluto. It takes only eight minutes for the sun's rays to reach Earth.`** in the Notes pane.

Continued >

In the Labs *continued*

(d) Slide 4

Figure 2–81

(e) Slide 5

Figure 2–81

17. If requested by your instructor, type the name of the city or county in which you were born into the title placeholder on Slide 3.

18. Apply the Vortex transition in the Exciting category to all slides. Change the duration to 3.0 seconds.

19. Check the spelling and correct any errors. Save the presentation using the file name, Lab 2–1 Pluto Up Close.

20. Print the notes pages. *to a PDF file*

21. Submit the document in the format specified by your instructor. *submit pdf & ppt*

22. ✷ In Step 2, you applied the Metal Oval picture style to the picture. How did this improve the design of the slide? Why did you put a 3 pt red border on the picture on Slide 2?

Lab 2: Creating a Presentation Using an Online Theme Template, Shapes, and WordArt

Note: To complete this assignment, you will be required to use the Data Files. Please contact your instructor for information about accessing the Data Files.

Problem: Your local library has hired a singer for the summer reading program. Her weekly show is centered around music and art, and one of her songs is about the colors of the rainbow. In addition to her backdrop of rainbow colors, you decide to develop a presentation to teach the children more about rainbows. You create the presentation shown in Figure 2–82.

Perform the following tasks:

1. Run PowerPoint and then search for an online template by typing **nature** in the 'Search for online templates and themes' box. Choose the template called Nature presentation, illustrated landscape design (widescreen).

2. Delete Slides 12 and 13, delete Slides 6 through 10, and then delete Slides 3 and 4. Duplicate Slide 2 and then move Slide 4 to the end of the presentation.

3. Type the title and text content for all slides, as shown in Figures 2–82a through 2–82e.

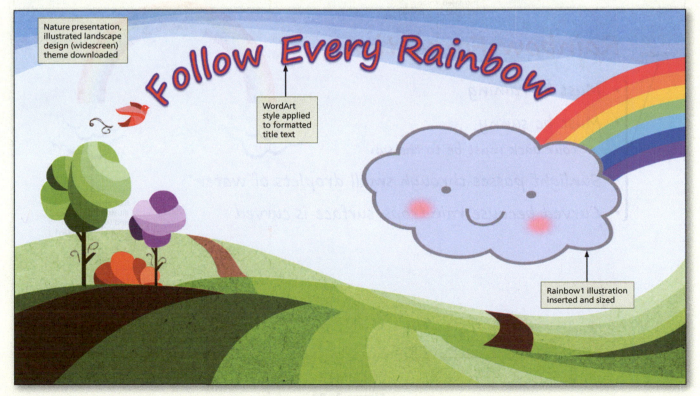

(a) Slide 1

Figure 2–82

Continued >

In the Labs *continued*

title text formatted and color changed

font colors changed

Always appear in this order

Rainbow2 illustration inserted, sized, and formatted

(b) Slide 2

Figure 2–82

title font size increased, color changed, and bolded

font formatted

Rainbow3 illustration inserted and sized and brightness changed

(c) Slide 3

Figure 2–82

4. Insert the illustrations shown in Figures 2–82b through 2–82d from the Data Files. The illustrations are called Rainbow1 (for Slide 1), Rainbow2 (for Slide 2), Rainbow3 (for Slide 3), and People (for Slide 4). Size the illustrations using Figure 2–82 as a guide.

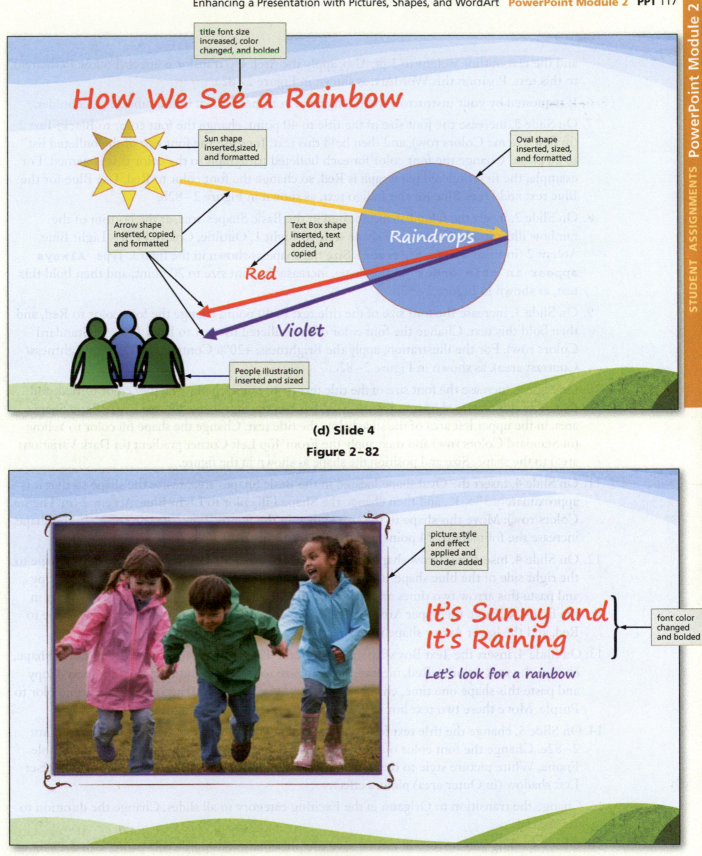

(d) Slide 4

Figure 2–82

(e) Slide 5

Figure 2–82

5. On the title slide, select the title text and then apply the WordArt style Fill – White, Outline – Accent 1, Shadow (fourth style in first row). Increase the font size to 72 point. Change the text fill to Red (in Standard Colors row), the text outline color to Purple (in Standard Colors row),

Continued >

In the Labs *continued*

and the text outline weight to 3 pt. Also, apply the Arch Up transform effect (Follow Path area), to this text. Position this WordArt, as shown in Figure 2 – 82a.

~~6. If requested~~ *skip* by your instructor, add the name of your hometown in the subtitle placeholder.

7. On Slide 2, increase the font size of the title to 40 point, change the font color to Black, Text 2 (in first Theme Colors row), and then bold this text. Increase the font size of the bulleted list to 28 point. Change the font color for each bulleted paragraph to the color that is named. For example, the first bulleted paragraph is Red, so change the font color to Red. Use Blue for the Blue text and Dark Blue for the Indigo text, as shown in Figure 2 – 82b.

8. On Slide 2, insert the Cloud shape, located in the Basic Shapes area, at the bottom of the rainbow illustration. Change the shape style to Light 1, Outline, Colored Fill – Light Blue, Accent 2 (in third Theme Styles row). Size the shape as shown in the figure. Type **Always appear in this order** in the shape, increase the font size to 20 point, and then bold this text, as shown in Figure 2 – 82b.

9. On Slide 3, increase the font size of the title text to 40 point, change the font color to Red, and then bold this text. Change the font color of the bulleted list text to Dark Blue (in Standard Colors row). For the illustration, apply the Brightness: +20% Contrast: +40% (in Brightness/ Contrast area), as shown in Figure 2 – 82c.

10. On Slide 4, increase the font size of the title text to 40 point, change the font color to Red, and then bold this text, as shown in Figure 2 – 82d. Insert the Sun shape, located in the Basic Shapes area, in the upper left area of the slide below the title text. Change the shape fill color to Yellow (in Standard Colors row) and then apply the From Top Left Corner gradient (in Dark Variations area) to the shape. Size and position the shape as shown in the figure.

11. On Slide 4, insert the Oval shape located in the Basic Shapes area, resize the shape so that it is approximately 3" × 3", and then change the Shape Fill color to Light Blue, Accent 2 (in Theme Colors row). Move this shape to the area shown in the figure. Type **Raindrops** in the shape, increase the font size to 24 point, and then bold this text.

12. On Slide 4, insert the Arrow shape, located in the Lines area, from the edge of the sun shape to the right side of the blue shape, as shown in Figure 2 – 82d. Change the weight to 6 pt. Copy and paste this arrow two times and use the sizing handles to position the arrows, as shown in the figure. Change the upper Arrow shape outline color to Yellow, the middle Arrow shape to Red, and the lower Arrow shape to Purple.

13. On Slide 4, insert the Text Box shape, located in the Basic Shapes area, type **Red** in the shape, change the font color to Red, increase the font size to 24 point, and then bold this text. Copy and paste this shape one time, change the text to **Violet,** and then change the font color to Purple. Move these two text box shapes to the areas shown in the figure.

14. On Slide 5, change the title text font color to Red and then bold this text, as shown in Figure 2 – 82e. Change the font color of the text to Purple and then bold this text. Apply the Simple Frame, White picture style to the picture. Add a 3 pt Purple border and then apply the Offset Left shadow (in Outer area) picture effect.

15. Change the transition to Origami in the Exciting category to all slides. Change the duration to 2.5 seconds.

16. Check spelling and correct all errors. Save the presentation using the file name, Lab 2–2 About Rainbows.

17. Submit the revised document in the format specified by your instructor.

18. ✳ You searched for an online rainbow theme. Do you think any of the other themes would have worked well for your presentation? Does choosing specific slide layouts while beginning the exercise help save time creating the presentation?

skip

Lab 3: Consider This: Your Turn

Design and Create a Presentation about Learning to Knit and Crochet

Note: To complete this assignment, you will be required to use the Data Files. Please contact your instructor for information about accessing the Data Files.

Part 1:   More than 50 million people knit or crochet to create fun and useful items, to relax, or to exchange ideas with fellow hobbyists at a regional guild or group. The local craft store in your community is offering a series of classes on knitting and crocheting techniques, and the manager has asked you to help promote the event. The introductory course includes instruction on selecting yarn, hooks, and needles; reading patterns; and making basic stitches. The intermediate and advanced courses include knitting in the round; making sleeves, button holes, and cables; and bead and filet crocheting. Classes are scheduled for four weeks on consecutive Saturdays beginning the first week of every month. All students will learn new skills and complete a fashionable project, which could include creating afghans, hats, and scarves for community residents in need. Use the concepts and techniques presented in this module to prepare a presentation to promote the classes. Select a suitable theme, and include a title slide, bulleted lists, shapes, and WordArt. The presentation should contain photos and illustrations appropriately resized. Six photos and illustrations are available in the Data Files: Green Yarn, Mitten, Two Mittens, Penguin, Quilt, and Scarf. Apply picture styles and effects. Add a title slide and closing slide to complete your presentation. Format the title slide with a shape. Format the background with at least one picture and apply a background texture to at least one slide. Review and revise your presentation as needed. Submit your assignment in the format specified by your instructor.

Part 2:   ✳ You made several decisions while creating the presentation in this assignment: where to place text, how to format the text (such as font, font size, and where to use WordArt), which graphical image(s) to use, what styles and effects to apply, where to position the graphical images, how to format the graphical images, and which shapes to use to add interest to the presentation. What was the rationale behind each of these decisions? When you reviewed the document, what further revisions did you make and why? Where would you recommend showing this slide show?

3 Reusing a Presentation and Adding Media and Animation

Objectives

You will have mastered the material in this module when you can:

- Color a photo
- Add an artistic effect to a photo
- Align paragraph text
- Change views
- Ungroup, change the color of, and regroup an illustration
- Copy a slide element from one slide to another
- Insert and edit a video clip

- Insert an audio clip
- Control audio and video clips
- Insert entrance, emphasis, and exit effects
- Control animation timing
- Change theme colors
- Change a theme and variant on one slide
- Print handouts

BTW

Media in Presentations

Well-produced video and audio clips add value to a presentation when they help explain a concept that cannot be captured in a photo or illustration. Before you insert these files on a slide, however, consider whether they really add any value to your overall slide show. Audiences quickly tire of extraneous movement and sounds on slides, and they will find such media clips annoying. The audience's attention should focus primarily on the presenter; extraneous or inappropriate media files may divert their attention and, in turn, decrease the quality of the presentation.

Introduction

At times, you will need to revise a PowerPoint presentation. Changes may include inserting and adding effects to photos, altering the colors of photos and illustrations, and updating visual elements displayed on a slide. Applying a different theme, changing fonts, and substituting graphical elements can give a slide show an entirely new look. Adding media, including sounds, video, and music, can enhance a presentation and help audience members retain the information being presented. Adding animation can reinforce important points and enliven a presentation.

In this module, you will learn how to create the slides shown in Figure 3–1. The following roadmap identifies general activities you will perform as you progress through this module.

Project — Presentation with Video, Audio, Animation, and Photos with Effects

The project in this module follows graphical guidelines and uses PowerPoint to create the presentation shown in Figure 3–1. The slides in this revised presentation, which discusses the Spokes Bike Club, have a variety of audio and visual elements. For example, the photos in the slides' backgrounds have artistic effects applied that soften the images and help the audience focus on other elements on the slides. The bicycle wheel photo has colors that blend well with the background. The bullet list is animated with entrance, emphasis, and exit effects. The video has been edited to play only one portion and has effects to add audience interest. Bicycle riding sounds integrate with the visual elements.

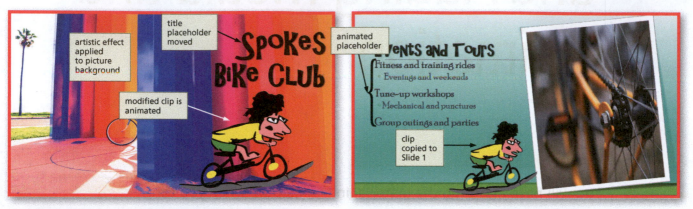

(a) Slide 1 (Title Slide with Picture Background, Modified Clip, and Animated Clip)

(b) Slide 2 (Bulleted List)

(c) Slide 3 (Picture Background and Video Clip)

(d) Slide 4 (Video Playing Full Screen)

Figure 3–1

For an introduction to Windows and instructions about how to perform basic Windows tasks, read the Office and Windows module at the beginning of this book, where you can learn how to resize windows, change screen resolution, create folders, move and rename files, use Windows Help, and much more.

Overall, the slides have myriad media elements and effects that are exciting for your audience to watch and hear.

In this module, you will learn how to create the slides shown in Figure 3–1. The following roadmap identifies general activities you will perform as you progress through this module:

1. **INSERT** and **ADD EFFECTS** to photos, including changing colors and styles.
2. **MODIFY PLACEHOLDERS** on the slides by moving and changing sizes.

3. **MODIFY** and **COPY** an **ILLUSTRATION** to customize its appearance.

4. **ADD MEDIA** files to slides.

5. **ANIMATE SLIDE CONTENT** with entrance, emphasis, and exit effects.

6. **CUSTOMIZE SLIDE ELEMENTS** by changing a theme and variant on one slide and changing the theme colors.

Inserting Photos and Adding Effects

The Spokes Bike Club presentation consists of three slides that have some text, a clip art image, a formatted background, and a transition applied to all slides. You will insert a photo into one slide and then modify it and another photo by adding artistic effects and recoloring. You also will copy the clip art from Slide 2 to Slide 1 and modify the objects in this clip. In Module 2, you inserted photos, made corrections, and added styles and effects; the new effects you apply in this module will add to your repertoire of photo enhancements that increase interest in your presentation.

In the following pages, you will perform these tasks:

1. Insert the first photo into Slide 1.

2. Recolor the Slide 1 photo.

3. Add an artistic effect to the Slide 3 photo.

4. Send the Slide 1 photo back behind all other slide objects.

To Insert and Resize a Photo into a Slide without Content Placeholders

The first step is to insert a photo into Slide 1. This photo is available in the Data Files. Please contact your instructor for information about accessing the required file. The following steps insert a photo into Slide 1.

1 Run PowerPoint and then open the presentation, Spokes, from the Data Files.

2 Save the presentation using the file name, Spokes Bike Club.

3 With Slide 1 displaying, click Insert on the ribbon to display the Insert tab and then click the Pictures button (Insert tab | Images group) to display the Insert Picture dialog box.

4 If necessary, navigate to the photo location (in this case, the Module 03 folder in the Data Files folder).

5 Click Hidden Bike to select the file.

6 Click the Insert button (Insert Picture dialog box) to insert the photo into Slide 1.

7 Drag the sizing handles to resize the photo so that it covers the entire slide. You can click the Height and Width arrows (Picture Tools Format tab | Size group) to adjust the picture size so that it is approximately 7.5" x 13.33" (Figure 3–2).

BTW

PowerPoint Screen Resolution

If you are using a computer or mobile device to step through the project in this module and you want your screens to match the figures in this book, you should change your screen's resolution to 1366 x 768. For information about how to change a computer's resolution, refer to the Office and Windows module at the beginning of this book.

BTW

Organizing Files and Folders

You should organize and store files in folders so that you easily can find the files later. For example, if you are taking an introductory technology class called CIS 101, a good practice would be to save all PowerPoint files in a PowerPoint folder in a CIS 101 folder. For a discussion of folders and detailed examples of creating folders, refer to the Office and Windows module at the beginning of this book.

For an introduction to Office and instructions about how to perform basic tasks in Office apps, read the Office and Windows module at the beginning of this book, where you can learn how to run an application, use the ribbon, save a file, open a file, print a file, exit an application, use Help, and much more.

Figure 3–2

BTW

Touch Screen Differences

The Office and Windows interfaces may vary if you are using a touch screen. For this reason, you might notice that the function or appearance of your touch screen differs slightly from this module's presentation.

Adjusting Photo Colors

PowerPoint allows you to adjust colors to match or add contrast to slide elements by coloring photos. The Color gallery has a wide variety of preset formatting combinations. The thumbnails in the gallery display the more common color saturation, color tone, and recolor adjustments. **Color saturation** changes the intensity of colors. High saturation produces vivid colors; low saturation produces gray tones. **Color tone** affects the coolness, called blue, or the warmness, called orange, of photos. When a digital camera does not measure the tone correctly, a **color cast** occurs, and, as a result, one color dominates the photo. **Recolor** effects convert the photo into a wide variety of hues. The more common are **grayscale**, which changes the color photo into black, white, and shades of gray, and **sepia**, which changes the photo colors into brown, gold, and yellow, reminiscent of a faded photo. You also can fine-tune the color adjustments by clicking the Picture Color Options and More Variations commands in the Color gallery.

To Color a Photo

1 INSERT & ADD EFFECTS | 2 MODIFY PLACEHOLDERS | 3 MODIFY & COPY ILLUSTRATIONS
4 ADD MEDIA | 5 ANIMATE SLIDE CONTENT | 6 CUSTOMIZE SLIDE ELEMENTS

The Office theme and text on Slides 1 and 2 are simple and fulfill the need to communicate the presentation's bicycling message. The photos on Slides 1 and 3 help set the tone of riding on an open road and enjoying the freedom that biking brings. You may want to add an effect to photos. *Why? An effect adds variety to the presentation and helps enhance ordinary photos.* The following steps recolor the Slide 1 photo to intensify the bright colors.

1

- With Slide 1 displaying and the Hidden Bike photo selected, click the Color button (Picture Tools Format tab | Adjust group) to display the Color gallery (Figure 3–3).

Q&A Why does the Adjust group look different on my screen?
Your monitor is set to a different resolution. See the Office 2016 and Windows 10 module for an explanation of screen resolution and the appearance of the ribbon.

Why are gray borders surrounding the thumbnails in the Color Saturation, Color Tone, and Recolor areas in the gallery?
The gray borders show the color saturation, tone, and recolor settings currently in effect for the image on Slide 1.

Figure 3–3

2

- Point to Saturation: 400% (last thumbnail in Color Saturation row) to display a live preview of this adjustment on the photo.

Experiment

- Point to various thumbnails in the Color Saturation area and watch the saturation change on the photo in Slide 1.

- Click Saturation: 400% to apply this saturation to the Hidden Bike photo (Figure 3–4).

Q&A Could I have applied this recoloring to the photo if it had been a background instead of a file inserted into the slide?
No. Artistic effects and recoloring cannot be applied to backgrounds.

Figure 3–4

Other Ways

1. Click Format Picture on shortcut menu, click Picture icon, click Picture Color, use Saturation slider (Format Picture pane)

To Add an Artistic Effect to a Photo

1 INSERT & ADD EFFECTS | 2 MODIFY PLACEHOLDERS | 3 MODIFY & COPY ILLUSTRATIONS
4 ADD MEDIA | 5 ANIMATE SLIDE CONTENT | 6 CUSTOMIZE SLIDE ELEMENTS

Artists use a variety of techniques to create effects in their paintings. They can vary the amount of paint on their brushstroke, use fine bristles to add details, mix colors to increase or decrease intensity, and smooth their paints together to blend the colors. You, likewise, can add similar effects to your photos using PowerPoint's built-in artistic effects. *Why? The completed Slide 3 will have both a photo and a video, so applying an artistic effect to the photo will provide a contrast between the two images.* The following steps add an artistic effect to the Slide 3 photo.

1

- Display Slide 3 and select the photo.
- Click the Artistic Effects button (Picture Tools Format tab | Adjust group) to display the Artistic Effects gallery (Figure 3–5).

Figure 3–5

2

- Point to Cement (first thumbnail in fourth row) to display a live preview of this effect on the photo.

🅿 **Experiment**

- Point to various artistic effects and watch the hues change on the photo in Slide 3.
- Click Cement to apply this artistic effect to the photo (Figure 3–6).

Figure 3–6

Q&A Can I adjust a photo by recoloring and applying an artistic effect?
Yes. You can apply both a color and an effect. You may prefer at times to mix these adjustments to create a unique image.

Other Ways

1. Click Format Picture on shortcut menu, click Effects icon, click Artistic Effects

To Change the Stacking Order

1 INSERT & ADD EFFECTS | 2 MODIFY PLACEHOLDERS | 3 MODIFY & COPY ILLUSTRATIONS
4 ADD MEDIA | 5 ANIMATE SLIDE CONTENT | 6 CUSTOMIZE SLIDE ELEMENTS

The objects on a slide stack on top of each other, much like individual cards in a deck. To change the order of these objects, you use the Bring Forward and Send Backward commands. **Bring Forward** moves an object toward the top of the stack, and **Send Backward** moves an object underneath another object. When you click the Bring Forward arrow, PowerPoint displays a menu with an additional command, **Bring to Front**, which moves a selected object to the top of the stack. Likewise, when you click the Send Backward arrow, the **Send to Back** command moves the selected object underneath all objects on the slide. The following steps arrange the Slide 1 photo. *Why? On this slide, the photo is on top of the placeholders, so you no longer can see the text. If you send the photo to the bottom of the stack on the slide, the letters will become visible.*

1

- Display Slide 1 and then select the Hidden Bike photo.
- Click the Picture Tools Format tab and then click the Send Backward arrow (Picture Tools Format tab | Arrange group) to display the Send Backward menu (Figure 3–7).

Q&A How can I see objects that are not on the top of the stack?
Press TAB or SHIFT + TAB to display each slide object.

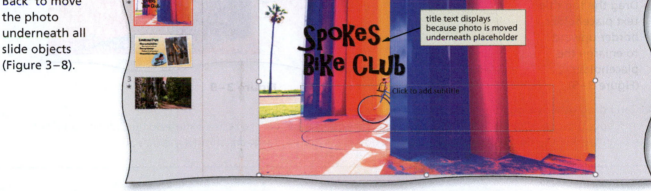

Figure 3–7

2

- Click 'Send to Back' to move the photo underneath all slide objects (Figure 3–8).

Figure 3–8

Other Ways

1. Click Send Backward arrow (Picture Tools Format tab | Arrange group), press K

2. Right-click photo, point to 'Send to Back' on shortcut menu, click 'Send to Back'

Modifying Placeholders

You have become familiar with inserting text and graphical content in the three types of placeholders: title, subtitle, and content. These placeholders can be moved, resized, and deleted to meet desired design requirements. In addition, placeholders can be added to a slide when needed. After you have modified the placeholder locations, you can view thumbnails of all your slides simultaneously by changing views.

In the following pages, you will perform these tasks:

1. Resize the Slide 1 title text placeholder.

2. Align the Slide 1 title text.

3. Move the Slide 1 title text placeholder.

4. Delete the Slide 1 subtitle text placeholder.

5. Change views.

BTW

The Ribbon and Screen Resolution
PowerPoint may change how the groups and buttons within the groups appear on the ribbon, depending on the computer or mobile device's screen resolution. Thus, your ribbon may look different from the ones in this book if you are using a screen resolution other than 1366 x 768.

To Resize a Placeholder

When the Slide 1 title placeholder is selected, the AutoFit button displays on the left side of the placeholder because the two lines of text exceed the placeholder's borders. PowerPoint attempts to reduce the font size when the text does not fit, and you can click this button to resize the existing text in the placeholder so the spillover text will fit within the borders. The following step increases the Slide 1 title text placeholder size. *Why? The two lines of text exceed the placeholder's borders, so you can resize the placeholder and fit the letters within the rectangle.*

1

- With Slide 1 displaying, click somewhere in the title text paragraphs to position the insertion point in the placeholder. Click the border of the title text placeholder to select it and then point to the top-middle sizing handle.

- Drag the top title text placeholder border upward to enlarge the placeholder (Figure 3–9).

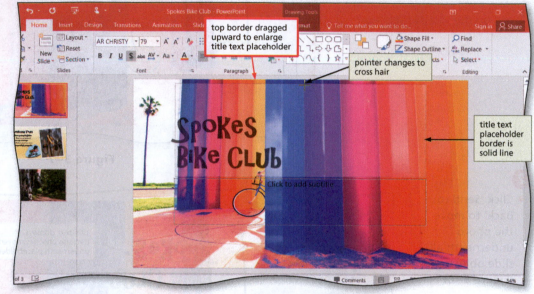

Figure 3–9

Q&A Can I drag other sizing handles to enlarge or shrink the placeholder?

Yes, you also can drag the left, right, top, and corner sizing handles to resize a placeholder. When you drag a corner sizing handle, the box keeps the same proportion and simply enlarges or shrinks the overall shape.

To Align Paragraph Text

The presentation theme determines the formatting characteristics of fonts and colors. It also establishes paragraph formatting, including the alignment of text. Some themes **center** the text paragraphs between the left and right placeholder borders, while others **left-align** the paragraph so that the first character of a text line is near the left border or **right-align** the paragraph so that the last character of a text line is near the right border. The paragraph also can be **justified** so that the text is aligned to both the left and right borders. When PowerPoint justifies text, it adds extras spaces between the words to fill the entire line.

The words, Spokes Bike Club, are left-aligned in the Slide 1 title text placeholder. Later, you will add an illustration on the right side of the slide below this text, so you desire to right-align the paragraph. *Why? Both the text and the picture will be located on the right side of the slide, so the alignments complement each other.* The following steps change the alignment of the Slide 1 title text placeholder.

1
- With the Home tab displayed, click somewhere in the title text paragraph of Slide 1 to position the insertion point in the text to be formatted (Figure 3–10).

Figure 3–10

2
- Click the Align Right button (Home tab | Paragraph group) to move the text to the right side of the title text placeholder (Figure 3–11).

Q&A What if I want to return the paragraph to left-alignment? Click the Align Left button (Home tab | Paragraph group).

Figure 3–11

Other Ways

1. Right-click paragraph, click Align Right button on mini toolbar
2. Right-click paragraph, click Paragraph on shortcut menu, click Alignment arrow (Paragraph dialog box), click Right, click OK button
3. Click Paragraph dialog box launcher (Home tab | Paragraph group), click Alignment arrow (Paragraph dialog box), click Right, click OK button
4. Press CTRL+R

---

1 INSERT & ADD EFFECTS | 2 MODIFY PLACEHOLDERS | 3 MODIFY & COPY ILLUSTRATIONS
4 ADD MEDIA | 5 ANIMATE SLIDE CONTENT | 6 CUSTOMIZE SLIDE ELEMENTS

To Move a Placeholder

Why? *If you desire to have a placeholder appear in a different area of the slide, you can move it to a new location.* The theme layouts determine where the text and content placeholders display on the slide. The Slide 1 title text placeholder currently displays in the middle third of the slide, but the text in this placeholder would be more aesthetically pleasing if it were moved to the upper-right corner of the slide. The following step moves the Slide 1 title text placeholder.

1
- Click the border of the Slide 1 title text placeholder to select it.
- With the title text placeholder border displaying as a solid line or fine dots, point to an area of the left border between the middle and lower sizing handles so that the pointer changes to a four-headed arrow.

title text placeholder dragged to desired location

pointer is four-headed arrow

subtitle text placeholder

Figure 3–12

Q&A Can I click any part of the border to select it?
Yes. You can click any of the four border lines.

How do I know if the placeholder is selected?
The selection handles are displayed.

- Drag the placeholder upward and to the right, as shown in Figure 3–12.
- If requested by your instructor, replace with word, Spokes, with the name of the city in which you were born.

To Delete a Placeholder

1 INSERT & ADD EFFECTS | **2 MODIFY PLACEHOLDERS** | 3 MODIFY & COPY ILLUSTRATIONS
4 ADD MEDIA | 5 ANIMATE SLIDE CONTENT | 6 CUSTOMIZE SLIDE ELEMENTS

When you run a slide show, empty placeholders do not display. You may desire to delete unused placeholders from a slide. **Why?** *So they are not a distraction when you are designing slide content.* The subtitle text placeholder on Slide 1 is not required for this presentation, so you can remove it. The following steps remove the Slide 1 subtitle text placeholder.

1
- Click a border of the subtitle text placeholder so that it displays as a solid or finely dotted line (Figure 3–13).

2
- Press the DELETE key to remove the subtitle text placeholder.

subtitle text placeholder is selected

Figure 3–13

Q&A Can I also click the Cut button to delete the placeholder?
Yes. Generally, however, the Cut button is used when you desire to remove a selected slide element, place it on the Clipboard, and then paste it in another area. The DELETE key is used when you do not want to reuse that particular slide element.

Other Ways

1. Select placeholder, press BACKSPACE
2. Right-click placeholder border, click Cut on shortcut menu

TO ADD A TEXT BOX

You occasionally may need to insert a small amount of text in an area of a slide where no content placeholder is located. A text box allows you to emphasize or set off text that you consider important for your audience to read. To add a text box to a slide, you would perform the following steps.

1. Click the Text Box button (Insert tab | Text group), click the slide, and then drag the object to the desired location on the slide.

2. Click inside the text box to add or paste text.

3. If necessary, change the look and style of the text box characters by using formatting features (Home tab | Font group).

Changing Views

You have been using **Normal view** to create and edit your slides. Once you completed your slides in projects for previous modules, you reviewed the final products by displaying each slide in **Slide Show view**, which occupies the full computer screen. You were able to view how the transitions, graphics, and effects will display in an actual presentation before an audience.

PowerPoint has other views to help review a presentation for content, organization, and overall appearance. **Slide Sorter view** allows you to look at several slides at one time. **Reading view** is similar to Slide Show view because each slide displays individually, but the slides do not fill the entire screen. Using this view, you easily can progress through the slides forward or backward with simple controls at the bottom of the window. Switching between Slide Sorter, Reading, and Normal views helps you review your presentation, assess whether the slides have an attractive design and adequate content, and make sure they are organized for the most impact. After reviewing the slides, you can change the view to Normal so that you may continue working on the presentation.

To Change Views

1 INSERT & ADD EFFECTS | **2 MODIFY PLACEHOLDERS** | **3 MODIFY & COPY ILLUSTRATIONS**
4 ADD MEDIA | **5 ANIMATE SLIDE CONTENT** | **6 CUSTOMIZE SLIDE ELEMENTS**

Why? *You have made several modifications to the slides, so you should check for balance and consistency.* The following steps change the view from Normal view to Slide Sorter view, then Reading view, and back to Normal view.

❶

● Click the Slide Sorter view button on the right side of the status bar to display the presentation in Slide Sorter view (Figure 3–14).

Q&A Why is Slide 1 selected?
It is the current slide in the Slides tab.

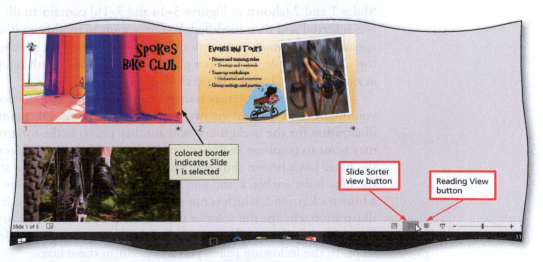

colored border indicates Slide 1 is selected

Slide Sorter view button

Reading View button

Figure 3–14

● Click the Reading
View button on
the right side of
the status bar to
display Slide 1 of
the presentation
in Reading view
(Figure 3–15).

Figure 3–15

3

● Click the Next button two times to advance through the presentation.
● Click the Previous button two times to display Slide 2 and then Slide 1.
● Click the Menu button to display commonly used commands (Figure 3–16).

4

● Click End Show to return to Slide Sorter view, which is the view you were using before Reading view.
● Click the Normal view button to display the presentation in Normal view.

Figure 3–16

Modifying and Copying an Illustration

Slides 1 and 2 (shown in Figures 3–1a and 3–1b) contain an illustration of a biker that was inserted and then modified. You may want to modify an illustration for various reasons. Many times, you cannot find an illustration that precisely represents your topic. For example, you want a picture of a red flower with red petals, but the only available picture has yellow petals.

Occasionally, you may want to remove or change a portion of an illustration or you might want to combine two or more illustrations. For example, you can use one illustration for the background and another photo as the foreground. Other times, you may want to combine an illustration with another type of object. In this presentation, the biker has a brown shirt, and you want to change the color to yellow. In addition, the bike hubs are black, and you want to change them to yellow. The illustration has a blue background, which is not required to display on the slide. You will ungroup the illustration, change the color of the shirt and hubs, and remove the blue background.

Modifying the clip on Slide 2 and then copying it to Slide 1 requires several steps. In the following pages, you will perform these tasks:

1. Zoom Slide 2 to examine the illustration.

2. Ungroup the illustration.

3. Change objects' color.

4. Delete objects.

5. Regroup the illustration.

6. Copy the illustration from Slide 2 to Slide 1.

To Zoom a Slide

You will be modifying small areas of the illustration, so it will help you select the relevant pieces if the graphic is enlarged. The following step changes the zoom to 90 percent.

1 Display Slide 2 and then drag the Zoom slider or click the Zoom level button or the Zoom In button to change the zoom level to 90%. If necessary, click the Down scroll arrow several times so that the entire graphic is visible (Figure 3–17).

Figure 3–17

To Ungroup an Illustration

1 INSERT & ADD EFFECTS | 2 MODIFY PLACEHOLDERS | **3 MODIFY & COPY ILLUSTRATIONS**
4 ADD MEDIA | 5 ANIMATE SLIDE CONTENT | 6 CUSTOMIZE SLIDE ELEMENTS

The next step is to ungroup the biker illustration, also called a clip, on Slide 2. When you **ungroup** an illustration, PowerPoint breaks it into its component objects. A clip may be composed of a few individual objects or several complex groups of objects. These groups can be ungrouped repeatedly until they decompose into individual objects. *Why? Because an illustration is a collection of complex groups of objects, you may need to ungroup a complex object into less complex objects before being able to modify a specific object.* When you ungroup a clip and click the Yes button in the Microsoft PowerPoint dialog box, PowerPoint converts the clip to a PowerPoint object. The following steps ungroup an illustration.

1

- Click the biker clip to select it and then click Format on the ribbon to display the Picture Tools Format tab.
- Click the Group Objects button (Picture Tools Format tab | Arrange group) to display the Group Objects menu (Figure 3–18).

Q&A Why does the Group Objects button look different on my screen? Your monitor is set to a different resolution. See the Office 2016 and Windows 10 module for an explanation of screen resolution and the appearance of the ribbon.

Figure 3–18

2

- Click Ungroup on the Group Objects menu to display the Microsoft PowerPoint dialog box (Figure 3–19).

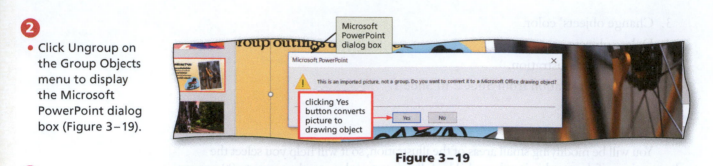

Figure 3–19

3

- Click the Yes button (Microsoft PowerPoint dialog box) to convert the clip to a Microsoft Office drawing.

Q&A What happens if I click the No button?
The clip will remain displayed on the slide as an illustration and will not ungroup.

- Click Format on the ribbon to display the Drawing Tools Format tab. Click the Group Objects button (Drawing Tools Format tab | Arrange group) and then click Ungroup again to display the objects that form the biker clip (Figure 3–20).

Q&A Why does the ribbon change from the Picture Tools Drawing tab to the Drawing Tools Format tab and show different options this time?
The illustration has become a drawing object, so tools related to drawing now display.

Why do all those circles display in the clip?
The circles are sizing handles for each of the clip's objects, which resemble pieces of a jigsaw puzzle.

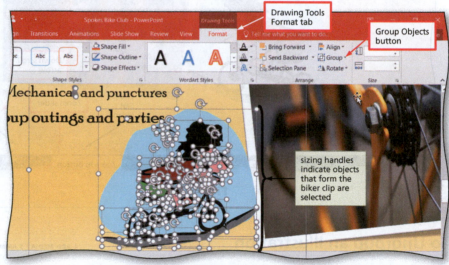

Figure 3–20

Other Ways

1. Right-click clip, point to Group on shortcut menu, click Ungroup   2. Press CTRL+SHIFT+G

To Change the Color of a Clip Object

1 INSERT & ADD EFFECTS | 2 MODIFY PLACEHOLDERS | **3 MODIFY & COPY ILLUSTRATIONS**
4 ADD MEDIA | 5 ANIMATE SLIDE CONTENT | 6 CUSTOMIZE SLIDE ELEMENTS

Now that the biker illustration is ungrouped, you can change the color of the objects. You must exercise care when selecting the correct object to modify. *Why? A clip might be composed of hundreds of objects.* The following steps change the color of the biker's shirt from brown to yellow.

1

- Click an area of the slide that is not part of the clip to deselect all the clip pieces.
- Click the biker's shirt to display sizing handles around the brown colored area (Figure 3–21).

Q&A What if I selected a different area by mistake?
Click outside the clip and retry.

Figure 3–21

2

- Click the Shape Fill arrow (Drawing Tools Format tab | Shape Styles group) to display the Shape Fill gallery.
- Point to Yellow (fourth color in Standard Colors row) to display a live preview of the shirt color (Figure 3–22).

🔍 **Experiment**

- Point to various colors and watch the biker's shirt color change.

Figure 3–22

3

- Click the color Yellow to change the biker's shirt color (Figure 3–23).

Q&A
Why is the bar under the Shape Fill button now yellow?
The button displays the last fill color selected.

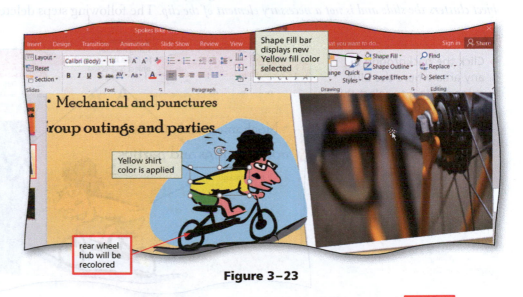

Figure 3–23

4

- Click the rear wheel hub to select it.
- Click the Shape Fill button (Drawing Tools Format tab | Shape Styles group) to change the wheel hub color to Yellow (Figure 3–24).

Q&A
Why did I not need to click the Shape Fill arrow to select this color?
PowerPoint uses the last fill color selected. This color displays in the bar under the bucket icon on the button.

Figure 3–24

5

- Change the front wheel hub color to Yellow (Figure 3–25).

Q&A Can I select multiple objects so I can color them simultaneously?
Yes. While pressing the SHIFT key, click the desired elements to select them.

Yellow front wheel hub color is applied

Figure 3–25

Other Ways

1. Click Shape Fill arrow (Home tab | Drawing group)   2. Right-click object, click Fill button below shortcut menu   3. Right-click object, click Format Shape on shortcut menu, click 'Fill & Line' icon

To Delete a Clip Object

1 INSERT & ADD EFFECTS | 2 MODIFY PLACEHOLDERS | 3 MODIFY & COPY ILLUSTRATIONS
4 ADD MEDIA | 5 ANIMATE SLIDE CONTENT | 6 CUSTOMIZE SLIDE ELEMENTS

With the biker's shirt and hub colors changed, you want to delete the blue background object. *Why? This object clutters the slide and is not a necessary element of the clip.* The following steps delete this object.

1

- Click the background in any area where the blue color displays to select this object (Figure 3–26).

Q&A Can I select multiple objects so I can delete them simultaneously?
Yes. While pressing the SHIFT key, click the unwanted elements to select them.

solid border and sizing handles indicate background object is selected

blue background color

Figure 3–26

2

- Press the DELETE key to delete this object (Figure 3–27).

six sweat droplets will be deleted

blue background is removed

Figure 3–27

3

- Click one black sweat droplet, press the SHIFT key, and then click the other five sweat droplets to select all six objects (Figure 3–28).

Q&A What can I do if I am having difficulty selecting just these six objects?
Try increasing the zoom, or select a few objects at a time and then delete them.

- Press the DELETE key to delete these objects.

Figure 3–28

To Regroup Objects

1 INSERT & ADD EFFECTS | 2 MODIFY PLACEHOLDERS | 3 MODIFY & COPY ILLUSTRATIONS
4 ADD MEDIA | 5 ANIMATE SLIDE CONTENT | 6 CUSTOMIZE SLIDE ELEMENTS

When you ungrouped the biker clip, you eliminated the embedding data or linking information that tied all the individual pieces together. If you attempt to move or size this clip now, you might encounter difficulties because it consists of multiple objects and is no longer one unified piece. Dragging or sizing affects only a selected object, not the entire collection of objects, so you must use caution when objects are not completely regrouped. You can **regroup** all of the ungrouped objects so they are reassembled into a single unit. The individual pieces of the biker clip now will be regrouped. *Why? When they are regrouped, they cannot be accidentally moved or manipulated.* The following steps regroup these objects into one object.

1

- Position the selection pointer (the left-pointing arrow) in the lower-left corner of the biker illustration and then drag diagonally to the upper-right corner of the illustration so that the entire illustration is covered with a gray box (Figure 3–29).

Q&A Must I drag diagonally from left to right?
No. You can drag in any direction as long as the gray box covers all the clip.

Figure 3–29

2

- Release the mouse to display all the selected pieces of the illustration.
- Click the Drawing Tools Format tab, and then click the Group Objects button (Drawing Tools Format tab | Arrange group) to display the Group Objects menu (Figure 3–30).

3

- Click Regroup to recombine all the clip objects.

4

- Use the Zoom slider to change the zoom level to 60%.

Figure 3–30

Other Ways
1. Right-click selected clip, point to Group on shortcut menu, click Regroup

To Copy a Clip from One Slide to Another

1 INSERT & ADD EFFECTS | 2 MODIFY PLACEHOLDERS | 3 MODIFY & COPY ILLUSTRATIONS
4 ADD MEDIA | 5 ANIMATE SLIDE CONTENT | 6 CUSTOMIZE SLIDE ELEMENTS

The biker clip on Slide 2 also can display in its modified form on the title slide. You first must copy it using the Office Clipboard and then paste it in the desired location. The **Office Clipboard** is a temporary storage location that can hold a maximum of 24 text or graphics items copied from any Office program. *Why? You have made modifications to the illustration that you would like to duplicate on the title slide.* The same procedure of copying and pasting objects works for copying and pasting text from one placeholder to another. The following steps copy this slide element from Slide 2 to Slide 1.

1

- With the biker illustration on Slide 2 selected, display the Home tab and then click the Copy button (Home tab | Clipboard group) (Figure 3–31).

2

- Display Slide 1 and then click the Paste button (Home tab | Clipboard group), shown in Figure 3–31, to insert the biker illustration into the title slide.

Figure 3–31

Q&A | Is the clip deleted from the Office Clipboard when I paste it into the slide?
No.

3

- Increase the biker illustration size by dragging one of the corner sizing handles outward until the biker is the size shown in Figure 3–32 (approximately 5.24" x 6.55" as indicated on the Drawing Tools Format tab). Drag the biker to the location shown in this figure.

clip resized and moved to desired location

Figure 3–32

Break Point: If you wish to take a break, this is a good place to do so. Be sure to save the Spokes Bike Club file again and then you can quit PowerPoint. To resume at a later time, start PowerPoint, open the file called Spokes Bike Club, and continue following the steps from this location forward.

Adding Media to Slides

Media files can enrich a presentation if they are used correctly. Video files can be produced with a camera and editing software, and sound files can come from the Internet, files stored on your computer, or an audio track on a CD. To hear the sounds, you need a sound card and speakers or headphones on your system.

Once an audio or video clip is inserted into a slide, you can specify options that affect how the file is displayed and played. For example, you can have the video play automatically when the slide is displayed, or you can click the video frame when you are ready to start the playback. You also can have the video fill the entire slide, which is referred to as **full screen**. If you decide to play the slide show automatically and have it display full screen, you can drag the video frame to the gray area off the slide so that it does not display briefly before going to full screen. You can select the 'Loop until Stopped' option to have the video repeat until you click the next slide, or you can choose to not have the video frame display on the slide until you click the slide.

If your video clip has recorded sounds, the volume controls give you the option to set how loudly this audio will play. They also allow you to mute the sound so that your audience will hear no background noise or music.

In the following pages, you will perform these tasks:

1. Insert a video file into Slide 3.
2. Trim the video file to shorten the play time.
3. Add video options that determine the clip's appearance and playback.
4. Insert an audio file into Slide 1.
5. Add audio options that determine the clip's appearance and playback.
6. Resize the Slide 3 video clip.
7. Add a video style to the Slide 3 clip.
8. Add a border to the Slide 3 clip and then change the border weight and color.

To Insert a Video File

Slide 3 has another photo of a biker, and you have a video clip of a person riding a bike through a wooded area. You want to use a majority of the clip and eliminate a few seconds from the beginning and end. PowerPoint allows you to insert this clip into your slide and then trim the file. *Why? You want to play just a portion of the video when you preview the clip or run the slide show.* This clip is available in the Data Files. The following steps insert this video clip into Slide 3.

1
- Display Slide 3 and then display the Insert tab. Click the Insert Video button (Insert tab | Media group) to display the Insert Video menu (Figure 3–33).

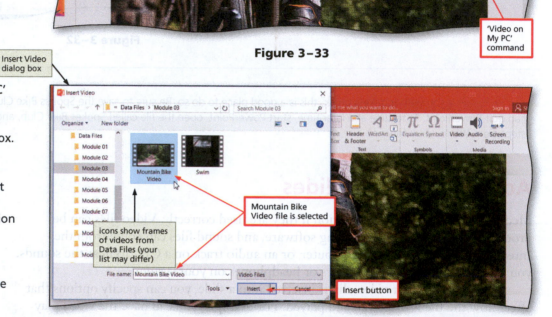

Figure 3–33

2
- Click 'Video on My PC' on the Insert Video menu to display the Insert Video dialog box.
- If the list of files for Module 03 is not displayed in the Insert Video dialog box, navigate to the location where the files are located.
- Click Mountain Bike Video to select the file (Figure 3–34).

Figure 3–34

3
- Click the Insert button (Insert Video dialog box) to insert the video clip into Slide 3 (Figure 3–35).

Can I adjust the color of a video clip?

Yes. You can correct the brightness and contrast, and you also can recolor a video clip using the same methods you learned in this module to color a photo.

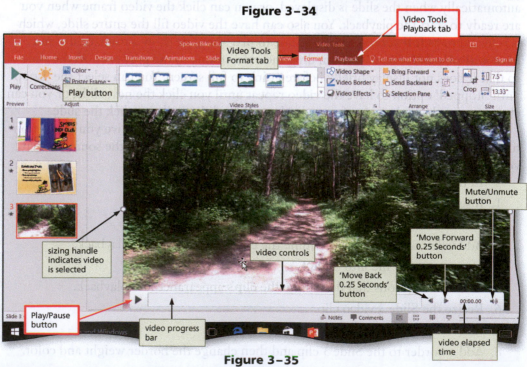

Figure 3–35

To Trim a Video File

Why? The Mountain Bike Video file has a running time of slightly more than 32 seconds. Much of the video is the same view of the bike path through the woods, so you decide to delete a few seconds from the beginning and the end to shorten the duration. PowerPoint's **Trim Video** feature allows you to trim the beginning and end of your clip by designating your desired Start Time and End Time. These precise time measurements are accurate to one-thousandth of a second. The start point is indicated by a green marker, and the end point is indicated by a red marker. The following steps trim the Mountain Bike Video clip.

❶

- With the video clip selected on Slide 3, click the Play/Pause button in the video controls underneath the video to play the entire video.

Q&A

Can I play the video by clicking the Play button in the Preview group?
Yes. This Play button plays the entire clip. You may prefer to click the Play/Pause button displayed in the video controls to stop the video and examine one of the frames.

Figure 3–36

- Click Playback on the ribbon to display the Video Tools Playback tab.
- Click the Trim Video button (Video Tools Playback tab | Editing group) to display the Trim Video dialog box (Figure 3–36).

❷

- Point to the start point, which is indicated by the green marker on the right side, so that the pointer changes to a two-headed arrow.
- Slide or drag the green marker to the right until the Start Time is approximately 00:05.991 (Figure 3–37).

Figure 3–37

3

- Point to the end point, which is indicated by the red marker on the right side, so that the pointer changes to a two-headed arrow.
- Slide or drag the red marker to the left until the End Time is 00:29.100 (Figure 3–38).

Q&A Can I specify the start or end times without dragging the markers?
Yes. You can enter the time in the Start Time or End Time boxes, or you can click the Start Time or End Time box arrows. You also can click the Next Frame and Previous Frame buttons (Trim Video dialog box).

Figure 3–38

4

- Click the Play/Pause button (Trim Video dialog box) to review the shortened video clip.
- Click the OK button (Trim Video dialog box) to set the Start Time and End Time and to close the Trim Video dialog box.

Other Ways

1. Right-click clip, click Trim on shortcut menu

To Add Video Options

1 INSERT & ADD EFFECTS | 2 MODIFY PLACEHOLDERS | 3 MODIFY & COPY ILLUSTRATIONS
4 ADD MEDIA | 5 ANIMATE SLIDE CONTENT | 6 CUSTOMIZE SLIDE ELEMENTS

Once the video clip is inserted into Slide 3, you can specify that the video plays automatically when the slide is displayed. *Why? When you are giving your presentation, you do not want to click the mouse to start the video.* You also can adjust the volume of the sound recorded on the file. The following steps add the option of playing the video full screen automatically and also decrease the volume of the clip.

1

- With the Video Tools Playback tab displaying, click the Start arrow (Video Tools Playback tab | Video Options group) to display the Start menu (Figure 3–39).

Q&A What does the On Click option do?
The video clip would begin playing when a presenter clicks the frame during the slide show.

Figure 3–39

2

- Click Automatically in the Start menu to run the video clip automatically when the slide is displayed.

3

- Click the 'Play Full Screen' check box (Video Tools Playback tab | Video Options group) to place a check mark in it.
- Click the Volume button (Video Tools Playback tab | Video Options group) to display the Volume menu (Figure 3–40).

4

- Click Medium on the Volume menu to set the audio volume.

Q&A Will the Mute option silence the video's background sounds?
Yes. Click Mute if you do not want your audience to hear any recorded sounds.

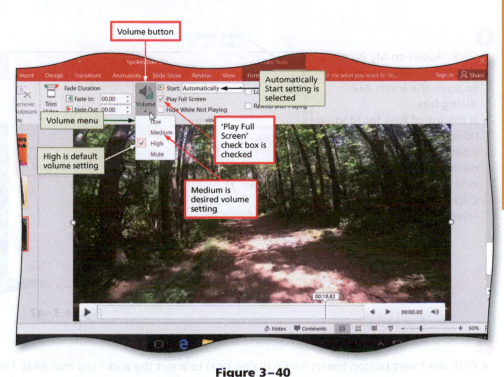

Figure 3–40

To Insert an Audio File

1 INSERT & ADD EFFECTS | 2 MODIFY PLACEHOLDERS | 3 MODIFY & COPY ILLUSTRATIONS
4 ADD MEDIA | 5 ANIMATE SLIDE CONTENT | 6 CUSTOMIZE SLIDE ELEMENTS

If you have a digital audio recorder or an app on your smartphone or mobile device, you can record sounds to insert into your presentation. The following steps insert an audio clip into Slide 1. *Why? An audio clip of pedaling sounds adds interest to the start of your presentation when Slide 1 is displayed.*

1

- Display Slide 1 and then click Insert on the ribbon to display the Insert tab.
- Click the Insert Audio button (Insert tab | Media group) to display the Insert Audio menu (Figure 3–41).

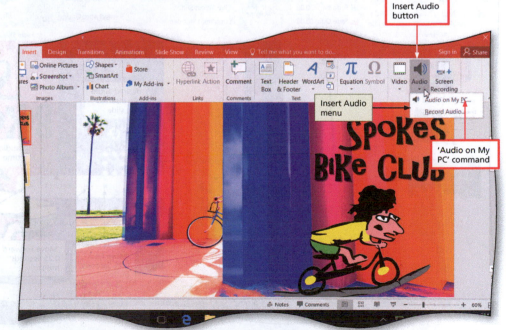

Figure 3–41

2

- Click 'Audio on My PC' on the Insert Audio menu to open the Insert Audio dialog box.
- If the list of files for Module 03 is not displayed in the Insert Audio dialog box, navigate to the location where the files are located.
- Click Pedaling Sounds to select the file (Figure 3–42).

Figure 3–42

3

- Click the Insert button (Insert Audio dialog box) to insert the audio clip into Slide 1 (Figure 3–43).

Q&A

Why does a sound icon display on the slide?
The icon indicates an audio file is inserted.

Do the audio control buttons have the same functions as the video control buttons that displayed when I inserted the Mountain Bike Video clip?
Yes. The controls include playing and pausing the sound, moving back or forward 0.25 seconds, audio progress, elapsed time, and muting or unmuting the sound.

Figure 3–43

4

- Drag the sound icon to the lower-left corner of the slide (Figure 3–44).

Q&A Must I move the icon on the slide?

No. Although your audience will not see the icon when you run the slide show, it is easier for you to see the audio controls in this area of this slide.

Figure 3–44

To Add Audio Options

Once an audio clip is inserted into a slide, you can specify options that control playback and appearance. As with the video options you applied to the Mountain Bike Video clip, the audio clip can play either automatically or when clicked, it can repeat the clip while a particular slide is displayed, and you can drag the sound icon off the slide and set the volume. The following steps add the options of starting automatically, playing until the slide no longer is displayed, and hiding the sound icon on the slide. *Why? You do not want to click the screen to start the sound, so you do not need to see the icon. In addition, you want the pedaling sound to repeat while the slide is displayed to coordinate with the bicycle picture prominently shown and to keep the audience's attention focused on the topic of riding a bike.*

1

- If necessary, click Playback on the ribbon to display the Audio Tools Playback tab. Click the Start arrow (Audio Tools Playback tab | Audio Options group) to display the Start menu (Figure 3–45).

2

- Click Automatically in the Start menu.

Q&A Does the On Click option function the same way for an audio clip as On Click does for a video clip?

Yes. If you were to select On Click, the sound would begin playing only after the presenter clicks Slide 1 during a presentation.

Figure 3–45

3

- Click the 'Loop until Stopped' check box (Audio Tools Playback tab | Audio Options group) to place a check mark in it.

Q&A What is the difference between the 'Loop until Stopped' option and the 'Play Across Slides' option?
The audio clip in the 'Loop until Stopped' option repeats for as long as one slide is displayed. In contrast, the 'Play Across Slides' option would play the clip only once, but it would continue to play while other slides in the presentation are displayed. Once the end of the clip is reached, the sound would end and not repeat.

4

- Click the 'Hide During Show' check box (Audio Tools Playback tab | Audio Options group) to place a check mark in it (Figure 3–46).

Q&A Why would I want the icon to display during the show?
If you had selected the On Click option, you would need to find this icon on the slide and click it to start playing the clip.

Can I adjust the sound's volume?
Yes. You can adjust the volume or mute the sound by clicking the Volume button (Audio Tools Playback tab | Audio Options group) or by clicking the Mute/Unmute button on the Media Controls bar and using the volume slider.

Figure 3–46

BTW

Ideal Decibels for Creativity
When you need to be creative, move to an environment filled with moderate background noise, such as a coffee shop. Researchers at the University of British Columbia state that a noise level of approximately 70 decibels, which is the sound of a quiet conversation or highway noise from afar, fosters original ideas. Anything louder than this ambient noise level decreases the thought process.

TO TRIM AN AUDIO FILE

PowerPoint's **Trim Audio** feature allows you to set the beginning and end of a clip. You select the desired sound to play by designating a Start Time and End Time, which are accurate to one-thousandth of a second. As with the video file markers, the Start Time is indicated by a green marker and the End Time is indicated by a red marker. To trim an audio file, you would perform the following steps.

1. Select the sound icon on the slide and then click the Trim Audio button (Audio Tools Playback tab | Editing group).

2. Drag the green marker to the right until the desired Start Time is displayed.

3. Drag the red marker to the left until the desired End Time is displayed.

4. Click the Play/Pause button (Trim Audio dialog box) to review the shortened audio clip.

5. Click the OK button to set the Start Time and End Time and to close the Trim Audio dialog box.

To Resize a Video

The default Mountain Bike Video frame size can be changed. You resize a video clip in the same manner that you resize photos and illustrations. The following steps will decrease the Mountain Bike Video frame using a sizing handle. *Why? You want to fit the video near the center of the slide.*

1

- Display Slide 3 and select the video frame. Click Format on the ribbon to display the Video Tools Format tab (Figure 3–47).

Figure 3–47

2

- With the video selected, drag any corner sizing handle diagonally inward until the frame is resized to approximately 5.5" x 9.78".
- Drag the clip to the location shown in Figure 3–48.

Figure 3–48

To Add a Video Style

The video styles are similar to the photo styles you applied in Module 2 and include various shapes, angles, borders, and reflections. The following steps apply a video style to the Mountain Bike Video clip on Slide 3. *Why? The Mountain Bike Video clip on Slide 3 displays full screen when it is playing, but you decide to increase the visual appeal of the clip when it is not playing by applying a video style.*

1

- With the video selected and the Video Tools Format tab displaying, click the More button in the Video Styles gallery (Video Tools Format tab | Video Styles group) (shown in Figure 3–48) to expand the gallery.
- Point to Reflected Perspective Right in the Intense area of the Video Styles gallery (sixth style in first row) to display a live preview of that style applied to the video frame on the slide (Figure 3–49).

Figure 3–49

Experiment

- Point to various photo styles in the Video Styles gallery and watch the style of the video frame change in the document window.

3

- Click Reflected Perspective Right in the Video Styles gallery to apply the style to the selected video and then move the video to the location displayed in Figure 3–50.

Q&A
Can I preview the movie clip?
Yes. Point to the clip and then click the Play button on the ribbon (Preview group) or the Play/Pause button on the video controls below the video.

Figure 3–50

To Add a Video Border

You have added borders to photos, and this design element can be added to video frames. The following steps apply a border to the Mountain Bike Video clip. *Why? A border adds visual interest and distinguishes the video frame from the photo background.*

1

- With the video clip selected, click the Video Border button (Video Tools Format tab | Video Styles group) and then point to Weight on the Video Border gallery to display the Weight gallery.

2

- Point to 2¼ pt to display a live preview of this line weight on the video frame (Figure 3–51).

🔍 **Experiment**

- Point to various line weights in the Weight gallery and watch the line thickness change.

3

- Click 2¼ pt to add this line weight to the video.

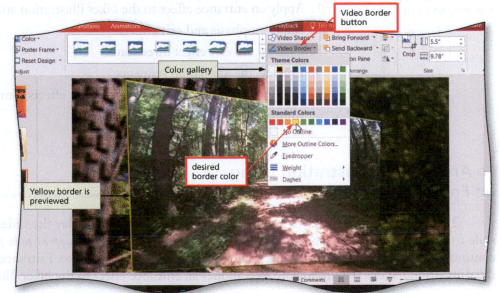

Figure 3–51

To Change a Video Border Color

1 INSERT & ADD EFFECTS | 2 MODIFY PLACEHOLDERS | 3 MODIFY & COPY ILLUSTRATIONS
4 ADD MEDIA | 5 ANIMATE SLIDE CONTENT | 6 CUSTOMIZE SLIDE ELEMENTS

Once you have added a border to a video, you can modify the default color. The following steps change the video border color to yellow. *Why? Yellow is used as an accent color in many components of the Spokes Bike Club slides.*

1

- With the video clip selected, click the Video Border button (Video Tools Format tab | Video Styles group) and then point to Yellow (fourth color in Standard Colors row) to display a live preview of this border color on the video frame (Figure 3–52).

🔍 **Experiment**

- Point to various colors in the gallery and watch the line colors change.

3

- Click Yellow to change the video border color.

Figure 3–52

Other Ways

1. Click Format Video on shortcut menu, click Fill & Line icon, click Color button

Break Point: If you wish to take a break, this is a good place to do so. Be sure to save the Spokes Bike Club file again and then you can quit PowerPoint. To resume at a later time, start PowerPoint, open the file called Spokes Bike Club, and continue following the steps from this location forward.

Animating Slide Content

Animation includes special visual and sound effects applied to text or other content. You already are familiar with one form of animation: transitions between slides. To add visual interest and clarity to a presentation, you can animate various parts of an individual slide, including pictures, shapes, text, and other slide elements. For example, each paragraph on the slide can spin as it is displayed. Individual letters and shapes also can spin or move in various motions. PowerPoint has a variety of built-in animations that will fade, wipe, or fly-in text and graphics.

Custom Animations

BTW

Animation Effect Icon Colors
Animation effects allow you to control how objects enter, move on, and exit slides. Using a traffic signal analogy may help you remember the sequence of events. Green icons indicate when the animation effect starts on the slide. Yellow icons represent the object's motion; use them with caution so they do not distract from the message you are conveying to your audience. Red icons indicate when the object stops appearing on a slide.

You can create your own **custom animations** to meet your unique needs. Custom animation effects are grouped in categories: entrance, exit, emphasis, and motion paths. **Entrance effects**, as the name implies, determine how slide elements first appear on a slide. **Exit effects** work in the opposite manner as entrance effects: They determine how slide elements disappear. **Emphasis effects** modify text and objects displayed on the screen. For example, letters may darken or increase in font size. The entrance, exit, and emphasis animations are grouped into categories: Basic, Subtle, Moderate, and Exciting. You can set the animation speed to Very Fast, Fast, Medium, Slow, or Very Slow.

The Slide 2 illustration shows a person riding a bike. When the slide is displayed, the audience will see this biker enter from the lower-left corner, move across the slide, stop beside the bicycle picture, rock slightly, and then continue across the slide toward the right corner.

In the following pages, you will perform these tasks:

1. Apply an entrance effect to the biker illustration and then change the direction.
2. Apply emphasis and exit effects.
3. Change the exit effect direction.
4. Preview the animation sequence.
5. Modify the entrance, emphasis, and exit effects' timing.
6. Animate text paragraphs.

To Animate an Illustration Using an Entrance Effect

1 INSERT & ADD EFFECTS | 2 MODIFY PLACEHOLDERS | 3 MODIFY & COPY ILLUSTRATIONS
4 ADD MEDIA | 5 ANIMATE SLIDE CONTENT | 6 CUSTOMIZE SLIDE ELEMENTS

The biker you modified will not appear on Slide 2 when you display the slide. Instead, it will enter the slide from the lower-left corner. *Why? The biker is facing right, so he will appear to be pedaling forward.* It will then continue across the slide until it reaches the lower-right side of the photo. Entrance effects are colored green in the Animation gallery. The following step applies an entrance effect to the biker illustration in Slide 2.

1
- Display Slide 2, select the biker clip, and then click Animations on the ribbon to display the Animations tab.
- Click the Fly In animation in the Animation gallery (Animations tab | Animation group) to display a live preview of this animation and to apply this entrance animation to the biker illustration (Figure 3–53).

Q&A Are more entrance animations available?
Yes. Click the More button in the Animation gallery to see additional animations. You can select one of the 13 entrance animations that are displayed, or you can click the 'More Entrance Effects' command to expand the selection. You can click any animation to see a preview of the effect.

Why does the number 1 appear in a box on the left side of the clip?
The 1 is a sequence number and indicates Fly In is the first animation that will appear on the slide when you click the slide.

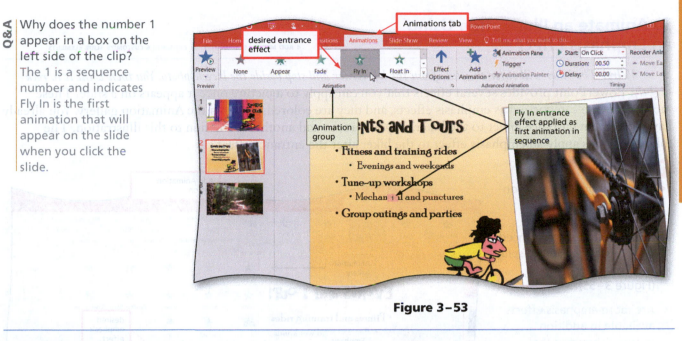

Figure 3–53

To Change Animation Direction

1 INSERT & ADD EFFECTS | 2 MODIFY PLACEHOLDERS | 3 MODIFY & COPY ILLUSTRATIONS
4 ADD MEDIA | 5 ANIMATE SLIDE CONTENT | 6 CUSTOMIZE SLIDE ELEMENTS

Why? By default, the illustration appears on the slide by entering from the bottom edge, and you want it to enter from the left. You can modify this direction and specify that it enters from another side or from a corner. The following steps change the biker entrance animation to enter from the left.

1
• Click the Effect Options button (Animations tab | Animation group) to display the Direction gallery (Figure 3–54).

Why does a pink box appear around the From Bottom arrow?
From Bottom is the default entrance direction applied to the animation.

Figure 3–54

2
• Click the From Left arrow to see a preview of this animation and apply this direction to the entrance animation.

Can I change this entrance effect?
Yes. Repeat Step 1 to select another direction.

To Animate an Illustration Using an Emphasis Effect

Why? *The biker will enter the slide from the left corner and stop beside the bicycle photo. You then want it to rock slightly.* PowerPoint provides several effects that you can apply to a picture once it appears on a slide. These movements are categorized as emphasis effects, and they are colored yellow in the Animation gallery. You already have applied an entrance effect to the biker, so you want to add another animation to this illustration. The following steps apply an emphasis effect to the biker after the entrance effect.

1

- Select the biker illustration and then click the Add Animation button (Animations tab | Advanced Animation group) to display the Animation gallery (Figure 3–55).

Q&A

Are more emphasis effects available in addition to those shown in the Animation gallery?
Yes. To see additional emphasis effects, click 'More Emphasis Effects' in the lower portion of the Animation gallery. The effects are arranged in the Basic, Subtle, Moderate, and Exciting categories.

Figure 3–55

2

- Click Teeter (third effect in the first Emphasis row) to see a preview of this animation and to apply this emphasis effect to the biker illustration (Figure 3–56).

Q&A

Do I need to use both an entrance and an emphasis effect, or can I use only an emphasis effect?
You can use one or the other effect, or both effects.

Why does the number 2 appear in a box below the number 1 on the left side of the illustration?
The 2 in the numbered tag indicates a second animation is applied in the animation sequence.

Figure 3–56

To Animate an Illustration Using an Exit Effect

The animated biker will enter the slide from the lower-left corner, stop beside the bicycle photo, and then teeter. It then will continue across the slide and exit in the lower-right corner. To continue this animation sequence, you first need to apply an exit effect. As with the entrance and emphasis effects, PowerPoint provides a wide variety of effects that you can apply to remove an illustration from a slide. These exit effects are colored red in the Animation gallery. You already have applied the Fly In entrance effect, so you will apply the Fly Out exit effect. **Why?** *It would give continuity to the animation sequence.* The following steps add this exit effect to the biker illustration after the emphasis effect.

1
- Select the biker illustration and then click the Add Animation button (Animations tab | Advanced Animation group) again to display the Animation gallery.
- Scroll down to display all the exit effects in the gallery (Figure 3–57).

Q&A Are more exit effects available in addition to those shown in the Animation gallery?
Yes. To see additional exit effects, click 'More Exit Effects' in the lower portion of the Animation gallery. The effects are arranged in the Basic, Subtle, Moderate, and Exciting categories.

Figure 3–57

2
- Click Fly Out to see a preview of this animation and to add this exit effect to the sequence of biker illustration animations (Figure 3–58).

Q&A How can I tell that this exit effect has been applied?
The Fly Out effect is displayed in the Animation gallery (Animations tab | Animation group), and the number 3 is displayed to the left of the biker illustration.

How can I delete an animation effect?
Click the number associated with the animation you wish to delete and then press the DELETE key.

Figure 3–58

To Change Exit Animation Direction

The default direction for a picture to exit a slide is To Bottom. In this presentation, you want the biker to exit in the lower-right corner. *Why? To give the impression it is continuing down a bike path across the slide.* The following steps change the exit animation direction from To Bottom to To Right.

1 Click the Effect Options button (Animations tab | Animation group) to display the Direction gallery (Figure 3–59).

2 Click the To Right arrow to apply this direction to the exit animation effect.

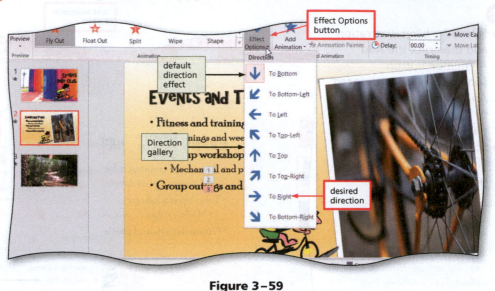

Figure 3–59

To Preview an Animation Sequence

1 INSERT & ADD EFFECTS | 2 MODIFY PLACEHOLDERS | 3 MODIFY & COPY ILLUSTRATIONS
4 ADD MEDIA | 5 ANIMATE SLIDE CONTENT | 6 CUSTOMIZE SLIDE ELEMENTS

Why? Although you have not completed developing the presentation, you should view the animation you have added to check for continuity and verify that the animation is displaying as you expected. By default, the entrance, emphasis, and exit animations will be displayed when you run the presentation and click the slide. The following step runs the presentation and displays the three animations.

1

• Click the Preview button (Animations tab | Preview group) to view all the Slide 2 animations (Figure 3–60).

Q&A

Why does a red square appear in the middle of the circle on the Preview button when I click that button?
The red square indicates the animation sequence is in progress. Ordinarily, a green arrow is displayed in the circle.

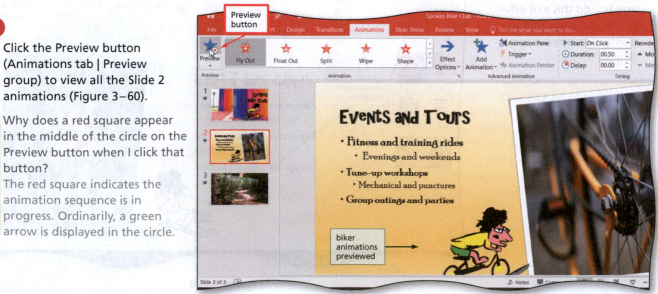

Figure 3–60

To Modify Entrance Animation Timing

The three animation effects are displayed quickly. To create a dramatic effect, you can change the timing. The default setting is to start each animation with a click, but you can change this setting so that the entrance effect is delayed until a specified number of seconds has passed. The following steps modify the start, delay, and duration settings for the entrance animation. *Why? You want the slide title text to display and then, a few seconds later, the biker to start to move across the slide slowly.*

1

- Click the tag numbered 1 on the left side of the biker illustration and then click the Start arrow (Animations tab | Timing group) to display the Start menu (Figure 3–61).

2

- Click After Previous to change the start option.

Q&A

Why did the numbered tags change from 1, 2, 3 to 0, 1, 2?
The first animation now occurs automatically without a click. The first and second clicks now will apply the emphasis and exit animations.

What is the difference between the With Previous and After Previous settings?
The With Previous setting starts the effect simultaneously with any prior animation; the After Previous setting starts the animation after a prior animation has ended. If the prior animation is fast or a short duration, it may be difficult for a viewer to discern the difference between these two settings.

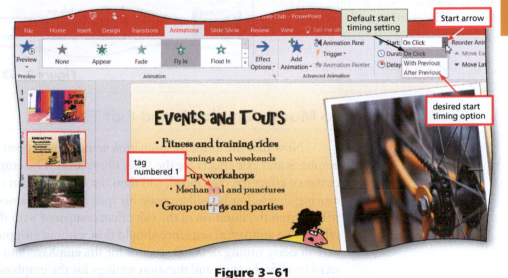

Figure 3–61

3

- Click the Duration up arrow (Animations tab | Timing group) several times to increase the time from 00.50 second to 02.00 seconds (Figure 3–62).
- Click the Preview button to view the animations.

Q&A

What is the difference between the duration time and the delay time?
The duration time is the length of time in which the animation occurs; the delay time is the length of time that passes before the animation begins.

Can I type the speed in the Duration box instead of clicking the arrow to adjust the speed?
Yes. Typing the numbers allows you to set a precise timing.

Figure 3–62

4

- Click the Delay up arrow (Animations tab | Timing group) several times to increase the delay time from 00.00 seconds to 03.00 seconds (Figure 3–63).

- Click the Preview button to view the animations.

Q&A Can I adjust the delay time I just set? Yes. Click the Delay up or down arrows and run the slide show to display Slide 2 until you find the time that best fits your presentation.

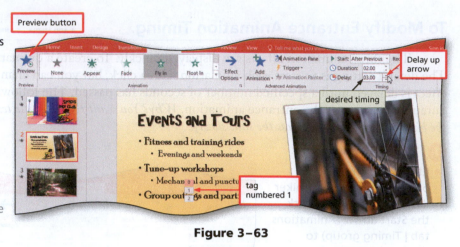

Figure 3–63

To Modify Emphasis and Exit Timings

Now that the entrance animation settings have been modified, you can change the emphasis and exit effects for the biker illustration. The emphasis effect can occur once the entrance effect has concluded, and then the exit effect can commence. The biker will start moving slowly, but he will increase his speed after he pauses briefly. You, consequently, will shorten the duration of the exit effect compared with the duration of the entrance effect. The animation sequence should flow without stopping, so you will not change the default delay timing of 00.00 seconds for the emphasis and exit effects. The following steps modify the start and duration settings for the emphasis and exit animations.

1 Click the tag numbered 1, which represents the emphasis effect, on the left side of the biker illustration.

2 Click the Start arrow (Animations tab | Timing group) to display the Start menu and then click After Previous to change the start option.

3 Click the Duration up arrow (Animations tab | Timing group) several times to increase the time to 02.00 seconds.

4 Click the tag numbered 1, which now represents the exit effect, click the Start arrow, and then click After Previous.

5 Click the Duration up arrow twice to increase the time to 01.00 seconds.

6 Preview the Slide 2 animation (Figure 3–64).

Figure 3–64

To Animate Content Placeholder Paragraphs

The biker illustration on Slide 2 has one entrance, one emphasis, and one exit animation. You decide to add similar animations to the five bulleted paragraphs in the Slide 2 content placeholder. *Why? For a special effect, you can add several emphasis animations to one slide element.* The following steps add one entrance and two emphasis animations to the bulleted list paragraphs.

1

- Double-click the Slide 2 content placeholder border so that it displays as a solid line (Figure 3–65).

Figure 3–65

2

- Click the More button (shown in Figure 3–65) in the Animation group (Animations tab | Animation group) to expand the Animation gallery (Figure 3–66).

Figure 3–66

3

- Click the Fade entrance effect in the Animation gallery (second effect in first row) to add and preview this animation.
- Change the Start option to With Previous.
- Change the Duration time to 02.00 seconds (Figure 3–67).

Q&A Do I need to change the delay time?
No. The paragraphs can start appearing on the slide when the biker exit effect is beginning.

Figure 3–67

④

- Click the Add Animation button (Animations tab | Advanced Animation group), scroll down to display the entire Emphasis area, and then click the Font Color emphasis animation effect (last effect in third row).
- Change the Start option to After Previous (Figure 3–68).
- Preview the Slide 2 animation.

Figure 3–68

⑤

- Click the Add Animation button, scroll down to display the entire Emphasis area again, and then click the Underline emphasis animation effect (first effect in the fourth row).

Q&A Why do the animation effects display differently in the Animation gallery on my screen?
The width of the Animation gallery and the order of the animations may vary, especially if you are using a tablet.

- Change the Start option to With Previous (Figure 3–69).

Q&A Why is a second set of animation numbered tags starting with 0 displaying on the left side of the content placeholder?
They represent the three animations associated with the paragraphs in that placeholder.

Figure 3–69

Customizing Slide Elements

PowerPoint's varied themes and layouts help give presentations a unified and aesthetically pleasing look. You may, however, desire to modify the default settings to give your slides a unique quality. One of the easier methods of developing a custom show is to change a theme for one or more slides, not an entire presentation. Similarly, you can change the variant for one or more slides to give a coordinating look to the slides in your deck. One other method of altering your slides slightly is to change the default colors associated with a particular theme.

The animated elements on Slide 2 help emphasize the events and tours that members of the Spokes Bike Club can experience. Changing the theme colors for that slide to yellow coordinates with the yellow slide elements.

To Change the Theme and Variant on One Slide

The Office theme applied to the presentation is appropriate for this topic. The font and placeholder locations are simple and add variety without calling attention to the design elements. The following steps change the theme and variant for Slide 2. *Why? To call attention to the material in the bulleted list on Slide 2, you can apply an equally effective theme that has a design element on the bottom that resembles a bike path. You then can modify this new theme by changing the variant on one slide.*

1

- With Slide 2 displaying, display the Design tab and then click the More button (Design tab | Themes group) to expand the Theme gallery.
- Point to the Retrospect theme to see a preview of that theme on Slide 2 (Figure 3–70).

🔎 **Experiment**

- Point to various document themes in the Themes gallery and watch the colors and fonts change on Slide 2.

Figure 3–70

2

- Right-click the Retrospect theme to display a shortcut menu (Figure 3–71).

Figure 3–71

3

- Click 'Apply to Selected Slides' to apply the Retrospect theme to Slide 2.
- Right-click the green variant (second variant in row) to display a shortcut menu (Figure 3–72).

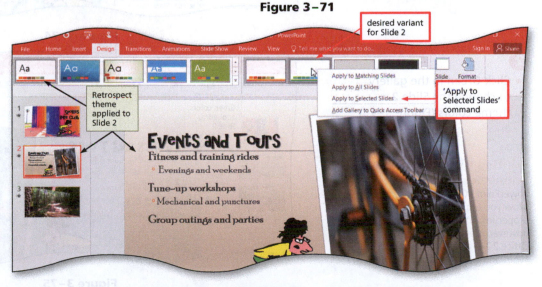

Figure 3–72

4

- Click 'Apply to Selected Slides' to apply the green variant to Slide 2 (Figure 3–73).

Figure 3–73

To Change the Theme Colors

1 INSERT & ADD EFFECTS | 2 MODIFY PLACEHOLDERS | 3 MODIFY & COPY ILLUSTRATIONS
4 ADD MEDIA | 5 ANIMATE SLIDE CONTENT | 6 CUSTOMIZE SLIDE ELEMENTS

Every theme has 10 standard colors: two for text, two for backgrounds, and six for accents. The following steps change the theme colors for the Spokes Bike Club slides. *Why? You can change the look of your presentation and add variety by applying the colors from one theme to another theme.*

1

- Click the More button (shown in Figure 3–73) in the Variants group to expand the gallery.
- Point to Colors in the menu to display the Colors gallery (Figure 3–74).

Experiment

- Point to various color rows in the gallery and watch the colors change on Slide 2.

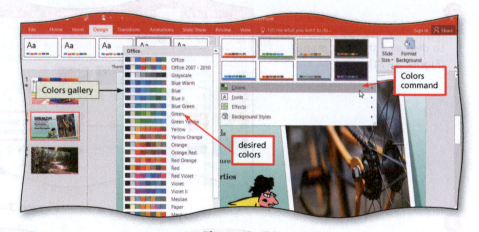

Figure 3–74

2

- Click Green in the gallery to change the Slide 2 theme colors (Figure 3–75).

BTW

Printing Document Properties

PowerPoint 2016 does not allow you to print document properties. This feature, however, is available in other Office 2016 apps, including Word and Excel.

Figure 3–75

To Run a Slide Show with Media

All changes are complete, so you now can view the Spokes Bike Club presentation. The following steps start Slide Show view.

1 Click the 'Start From Beginning' button on the Show tab to display the title slide and listen to the bicycle engine sound. Allow the audio clip to repeat several times.

2 Press the SPACEBAR to display Slide 2. Watch the biker and bulleted list animations.

3 Press the SPACEBAR to display Slide 3. Watch the video clip.

4 Press the SPACEBAR to end the slide show and then press the SPACEBAR again to exit the slide show.

To Preview and Print a Handout

1 INSERT & ADD EFFECTS | 2 MODIFY PLACEHOLDERS | 3 MODIFY & COPY ILLUSTRATIONS
4 ADD MEDIA | 5 ANIMATE SLIDE CONTENT | 6 CUSTOMIZE SLIDE ELEMENTS

Printing handouts is useful for reviewing a presentation. You can analyze several slides displayed simultaneously on one page. Additionally, many businesses distribute handouts of the slide show before or after a presentation so attendees can refer to a copy. Each page of the handout can contain reduced images of one, two, three, four, six, or nine slides. The three-slides-per-page handout includes lines beside each slide so that your audience can write notes conveniently. The following steps preview and print a presentation handout with two slides per page. *Why? Two of the slides are predominantly pictures, so your audience does not need full pages of those images. The five bulleted paragraphs on Slide 2 can be read easily on one-half of a sheet of paper.*

1
- Click File on the ribbon to open the Backstage view and then click the Print tab.
- Click the Previous Page button to display Slide 1 in the Print gallery.
- Click 'Full Page Slides' in the Settings area to display the Full Page Slides gallery (Figure 3–76).

Q&A Why does the preview of my slide appear in black and white?
Your printer determines how the preview appears. If your printer is not capable of printing color images, the preview will appear in black and white.

Figure 3–76

BTW

Conserving Ink and Toner
If you want to conserve ink or toner, you can instruct PowerPoint to print draft quality documents by clicking File on the ribbon to open the Backstage view, clicking the Options tab in the Backstage view to display the PowerPoint Options dialog box, clicking Advanced in the left pane (PowerPoint Options dialog box), scrolling to the Print area in the right pane, not placing a check mark in the High quality check box, and then clicking the OK button. Then, use the Backstage view to print the document as usual.

2

- Click 2 Slides in the Handouts area to select this option and display a preview of the handout (Figure 3–77).

Q&A The current date displays in the upper-right corner of the handout, and the page number displays in the lower-right corner of the footer. Can I change their location or add other information to the header and footer?
Yes. Click the 'Edit Header & Footer' link at the bottom of the Print gallery, click the Notes and Handouts tab (Header and Footer dialog box), and then decide what content to include on the handout page.

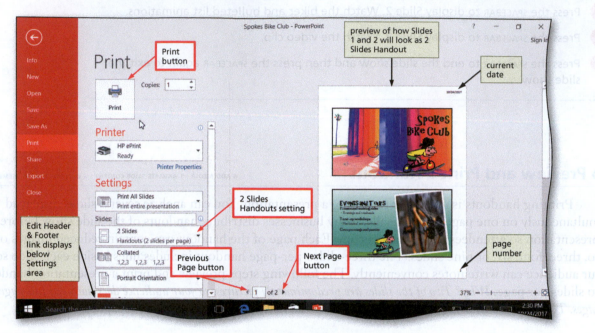

Figure 3–77

3

- Click the Next Page and Previous Page buttons to display previews of the two pages in the handout.
- Click the Print button in the Print gallery to print the handout.
- When the printer stops, retrieve the printed handout.
- Save the presentation again in the same storage location with the same file name.
- Because the project now is complete, you can exit PowerPoint.

Summary

In this module, you have learned how to adjust photo colors and effects, modify placeholders, modify and copy illustrations, add and format media, animate slide content, customize slides, and print a handout.

BTW

Distributing a Document
Instead of printing and distributing a hard copy of a document, you can distribute the document electronically. Options include sending the document via email; posting it on cloud storage (such as OneDrive) and sharing the file with others; posting it on social media, a blog, or other website; and sharing a link associated with an online location of the document. You also can create and share a PDF or XPS image of the document, so that users can view the file in Acrobat Reader or XPS Viewer instead of in PowerPoint.

What decisions will you need to make when creating your next presentation?

Use these guidelines as you complete the assignments in this module and create your own slide show decks outside of this class.

1. Determine if adjusting photo colors and effects can increase visual appeal.

   a) Change color saturation.

   b) Change tones.

   c) Recolor the image.

2. Vary paragraph alignment.

   a) Themes dictate whether paragraph text is aligned left, center, or right in a placeholder, but you can modify these design decisions when necessary. Moving placeholders and changing paragraph alignment can help create a unique slide.

   b) Different effects are achieved when text alignment shifts in a presentation.

3. Use multimedia selectively.

   a) Locate video, music, and sound files that are appropriate for your audience and that you have permission to use.

   b) Use media files only when necessary, however, because they draw the audience's attention away from the presenter and toward the slides.

   c) Using too many multimedia files can be overwhelming.

4. Use animation sparingly.

   a) PowerPoint audience members usually take notice the first time an animation is displayed on the screen, so be certain the animation will help focus on the precise points being presented during a particular time of the presentation.

   b) Avoid using animation for the sake of using animation. Use animation only when necessary to add emphasis.

   c) Animation overuse annoys and desensitizes audience members.

   d) Carefully decide how text or a slide element enters and exits a slide and how it is displayed once it is present on the slide.

5. Use handouts to organize your speech and to distribute to audiences.

   a) Determine if a handout with two slides per page will help unify your message when you distribute copies to an audience.

Apply Your Knowledge

Reinforce the skills and apply the concepts you learned in this module.

Resizing a Photo by Entering Exact Measurements, Formatting a Video Border, Trimming a Video File, Resizing and Moving a Placeholder, and Animating a Photo and Title

Note: To complete this assignment, you will be required to use the Data Files. Please contact your instructor for information about accessing the Data Files.

Instructions: Run PowerPoint. Open the presentation called Apply 3-1 Cats, which is located in the Data Files. The four slides in the presentation, shown in Figure 3–78, discuss the factors you should consider when adopting a cat. The local pet store is holding a special event for cat adoptions. The document you open is composed of slides containing pictures and a video. You will apply artistic effects or modify some of these graphic elements. You also will move placeholders. In addition, you will animate photos and a title using an entrance effect.

Continued >

Apply Your Knowledge *continued*

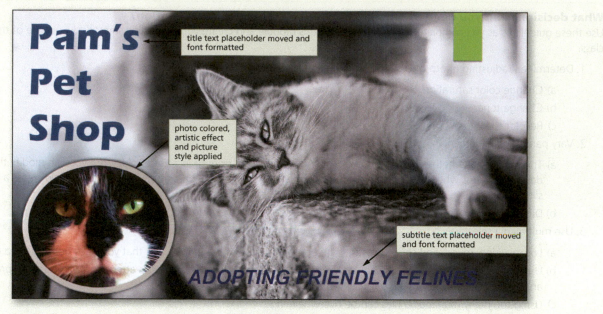

(a) Slide 1

Figure 3–78a

Perform the following tasks:

1. On Slide 1 (Figure 3–78a), move the title text placeholder to the upper area of the slide, the subtitle text placeholder to the lower area of the slide, and the green-eyed cat picture to the bottom left corner of the slide, as shown in the figure. Color the green-eyed cat picture by selecting Saturation: 200% from the Color Saturation area, and apply the Paint Brush artistic effect to the picture, as shown in figure. Decrease the picture size to 3.35"×3.88" and apply the Metal Oval picture style to the picture. Apply the Float In animation entrance effect, change the duration to 2.50, and then change the Start timing setting to With Previous.

2. On Slide 1, change the title font to Eras Bold ITC, increase the font size to 72 point, and then change the font color to Dark Blue, Background 2 (in Theme Colors row). Change the size of the title text placeholder to 3.73"×3.75" and then move it to the left area of the slide using the Smart Guides to line it up with the left edge of the picture, as shown in the figure. Apply the Fly In animation and then change the direction to From Right to the title text font and change the duration to 2.00. Change the Start timing setting to After Previous.

3. On Slide 1, change the subtitle font to Arial, increase the font size to 36 point, change the font color to Dark Blue (in Standard Colors row), and then bold and italicize this text.

4. On Slide 2 (Figure 3–78b), change the title text font to Arial, increase the font size to 44 point, bold this text, and then change the font color to Light Green (in Standard Colors row). Align this text left. Use the Format Painter to format the title text font on Slides 3 and 4 with the same features as the title text font on Slide 2.

5. Increase the size of the bulleted list font on Slide 2 to 24 point and then bold this text. Apply the Grow & Turn entrance effect to the bulleted list and then change the duration to 1.75. Change the Start timing setting to After Previous.

6. On Slide 2, increase the size of the right cat picture to approximately 4.12"×4.29" and then apply the Bevel Rectangle picture style to the cat picture. Decrease the size of the kitten picture in the center of the slide to approximately 4.24"×4.98" and then apply the Soft Edge Oval picture style to the kitten picture. Move the cat and kitten pictures to the locations shown in the figure.

7. On Slide 3 (Figure 3–78c), increase the size of the video to 5"×8.88". Apply the Rotated, Gradient video style in the Moderate area to the video, change the border weight to 6 pt, and

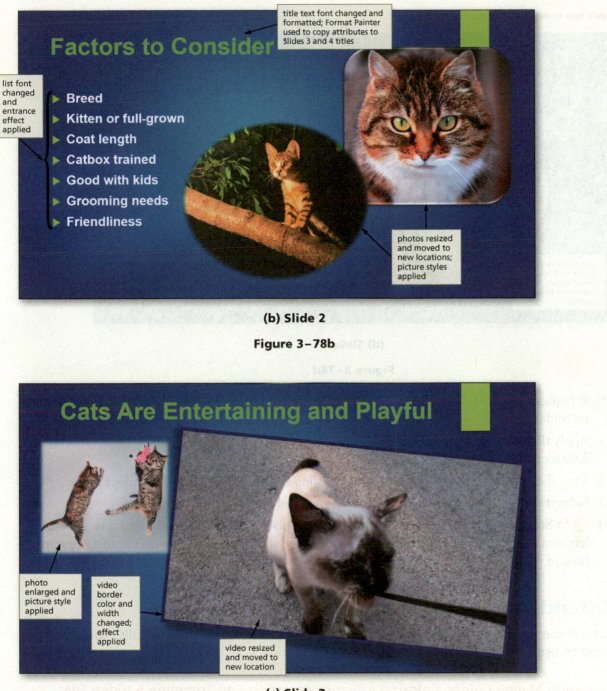

(b) Slide 2

Figure 3–78b

(c) Slide 3

Figure 3–78c

then change the border color to Dark Blue (in Standard Colors row). Move the video to the location shown in the figure. Trim the video so that the Start Time is 00:15.073. Start this video automatically.

8. Increase the size of the picture to approximately 3.1"×3.51" on Slide 3. Apply the Soft Edge Rectangle picture style to the picture.

9. On Slide 4 (Figure 3–78d), reset the picture to its original color and style by clicking the Reset Picture button (Picture Tools Format tab | Adjust group). Increase the size of the picture to approximately 5.75"×10.21", apply the Beveled Oval, Black picture style, and then move the picture to the location shown in the figure.

Continued >

Apply Your Knowledge *continued*

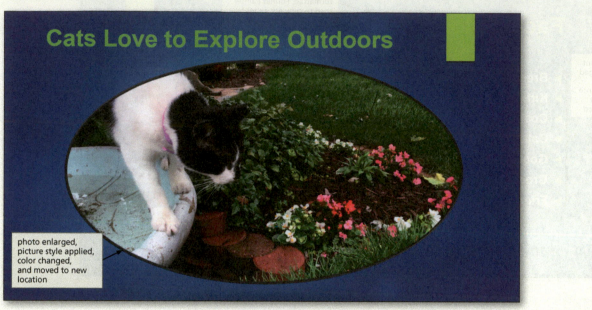

(d) Slide 4

Figure 3–78d

10. If requested by your instructor, add your mother's first name as a second line under the subtitle on Slide 1.

11. Apply the Clock transition in the Exciting category to all the slides. Change the duration to 3.00 seconds.

12. View the presentation and then save the file using the file name, Apply 3–1 Adopt a Cat.

13. Submit the revised document in the format specified by your instructor.

14. ✳ In Step 2, you changed the size of the title text placeholder and then moved it to the upper left area of the slide. How did this style improve the slide? On Slide 3, you trimmed the start time of the video. Why?

Extend Your Knowledge

Extend the skills you learned in this module and experiment with new skills. You may need to use Help to complete the assignment.

Changing Theme Colors, Coloring a Picture, Inserting and Trimming a Video File, Adding a Text Box, and Animating an Illustration

Note: To complete this assignment, you will be required to use the Data Files. Please contact your instructor for information about accessing the Data Files.

Instructions: Run PowerPoint. Open the presentation called Extend 3-1 Swimming, which is located in the Data Files. You will change theme colors, insert a video file, trim a video file, and insert a text box to create the presentation shown in Figure 3–79.

Perform the following tasks:

1. Change the theme variant to Black on Slide 1 only. Change the theme color to Blue II on Slide 3 only.

2. On Slide 1 (Figure 3–79a), change the title text font to Britannic Bold, increase the font size to 48 point, change the font color to Yellow (in Standard Colors row), and then center the text.

(a) Slide 1

Figure 3–79a

Change the font case to UPPERCASE. (*Hint*: The Change Case button is located in the Font group (Home tab | Font group).) Move the title text placeholder to the top of the slide, as shown in the figure. Delete the subtitle text placeholder.

3. Increase the size of the picture on Slide 1 to approximately 6.19" × 11", apply the Moderate Frame, White picture style, and then move the picture to the center of the slide, using the vertical Smart Guide to help you align this picture. Recolor the picture using the Blue, Accent color 3 Dark color (in Recolor area). Adjust the title text placeholder so that the text is below the picture border.

4. On Slide 1, apply the Grow/Shrink Emphasis effect to the Teardrop shape and then change the duration to 3.00. Change the Start timing setting to After Previous.

5. On Slide 2 (Figure 3–79b), change the title text font to Franklin Gothic Heavy, increase the font size to 40 point, change the font color to Dark Blue (in Standard Colors row), and then center the text. Use the Format Painter to apply these attributes to the title text font on Slide 4.

6. Apply the Bevel Perspective picture style to the picture. Increase the size of the picture to approximately 5.01" × 7.63" and then position it on the right side of the slide.

7. On Slide 2, apply the Zoom Entrance effect to the bulleted list, change the duration to 2:00, and then change the Start timing setting to After Previous.

8. On Slide 3 (Figure 3–79c), insert the video file called Swim, which is located in the Data Files. Increase the size of the video to approximately 6.41" × 8.74" and move the video to the location shown in the figure. Apply the Simple Frame, White video style and then change the Video Border color to Yellow (in Standard Colors row). Trim the video so that the End Time is 00:14.151. Start this video automatically.

9. Insert a text box on the left side of Slide 3 and type `Video highlights from one of our swim meets` in the text box, change the font to Arial, change font size to 24 point, and then bold and italicize this text. Adjust the size of the text box so that it measures approximately 2.52" × 2.01", and then use the horizontal Smart Guide to center the text box between the left end of the slide and the left edge of the video file.

Continued >

Extend Your Knowledge *continued*

change and format title text font; use Format Painter to copy attributes to Slide 4 title

BENEFITS OF JOINING AQUATIC CENTER

animate bulleted list

- JOIN A SWIM TEAM
- LEARN UNDERWATER HOCKEY
- SET PERSONAL GOALS
- MAKE A COMMITMENT
- MEET NEW FRIENDS

enlarge photo and apply picture style

(b) Slide 2

Figure 3–79b

change theme color to Blue II

Video

Insert text box and then type and format text

video file inserted, resized, trimmed, video style applied, and video border color and weight changed

(c) Slide 3

Figure 3–79c

10. On Slide 4 (Figure 3–79d), increase the size of the swimmer picture to approximately 3.88" × 6.29" and apply the Beveled Oval, Black picture style to the picture. Change the border color to Light Green (in Standard Colors row) and then change the border weight to 6 pt. Position this picture on the left side of the slide under the title using the Smart Guides to align the picture with the left, right, and bottom edges of the placeholder.

11. On Slide 4, apply the Float Out exit effect to the flippers illustration and then change the duration to 5.00. Change the Start timing setting to After Previous.

12. If requested by your instructor, insert a text box on Slide 3 under the text box and add the time of day you were born.

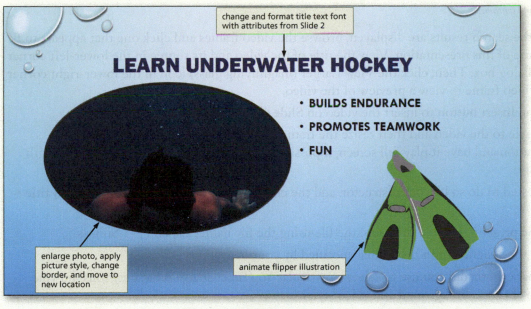

(d) Slide 4

Figure 3–79d

13. Apply an appropriate transition to all slides.

14. View the presentation and then save the file using the file name, Extend 3-1 Galaxy Aquatic Center.

15. Submit the revised document in the format specified by your instructor.

16. ✸ In this assignment, you inserted a video file and trimmed it. How did this enhance the presentation?

Expand Your World

Create a solution that uses cloud or web technologies by learning and investigating on your own from general guidance.

Inserting Video Files from the Web

Instructions: The Spokes Bike Club presentation you created in the module has a video you inserted from the Data Files. The bicyclist in this video mounted a camera on his helmet and recorded his ride through the forest. Using a helmet can help reduce head and brain injury risk and increase rider visibility to motorists and other cyclists. Many organizations promoting bicycling safety have created videos describing how to select and fit a bicycle helmet, and these videos are posted to online websites. PowerPoint allows you to insert online videos easily in a manner similar to how you inserted the Mountain Bike Video clip. You are going to search for and then insert one of these online videos into the Spokes Bike Club presentation.

Perform the following tasks:

1. In PowerPoint, open the Spokes Bike Club file, insert a new Slide 4 with the Title and Content layout, and then type **Helmet Safety Tips** as the title text. Use the Format Painter to copy the title text font formatting from Slide 2 to the new Slide 4 title. Center this title text.

2. Format the Slide 4 background with a gradient or texture fill.

3. Click the Insert Video icon in the content placeholder to display the Insert Video dialog box. Click the YouTube button in the dialog box and then type **bicycling helmet safety** as the search text in the Search YouTube search box.

Continued >

4. When the search results are displayed, browse the video frames and click one that appears to fit the theme of this presentation. View the title of the video and its source in the lower-left corner of the dialog box. Then, click the View Larger (magnifying glass) icon in the lower-right corner of the video frame to view a preview of the video.

5. Click the Insert button to insert the video on Slide 4.

6. Add a style to the video and then resize the frame. Start this file automatically during the presentation and have it play full screen, if possible. If necessary, trim the video to the length you desire.

7. If requested to do so by your instructor, add the city where you were born to the Slide 4 title text.

8. View the presentation and then save the file using the file name, Expand 3-1 Spokes.

9. Submit the assignment in the format specified by your instructor.

10. ✸ What criteria did you use to select a particular YouTube video? What decisions did you make to choose a background and video style?

In the Labs

Design, create, modify, and/or use a presentation following the guidelines, concepts, and skills presented in this module. Labs 1 and 2, which increase in difficulty, require you to create solutions based on what you learned in the module; Lab 3 requires you to apply your creative thinking and problem-solving skills to design and implement a solution.

Lab 1: Changing the Stacking Order, Inserting an Audio File, and Animating a Photo, Illustration, and Title

Note: To complete this assignment, you will be required to use the Data Files. Please contact your instructor for information about accessing the Data Files.

Problem: Your local library is featuring information about national parks. Your travel club is planning to visit Yellowstone National Park next year, and you decide to gather some general information to present to the club. You create the slides shown in Figure 3–80.

Perform the following tasks:

1. Run PowerPoint. Open the presentation called Lab 3-1 Yellowstone, which is located in the Data Files. On Slide 1, increase the size of the waterfall picture to 7.5" × 11.54" and then move the picture to the left side of the slide, as shown in Figure 3–80a.

2. On Slide 1, select the title text placeholder. Display the Animation gallery, click 'More Entrance Effects,' and then apply the Expand entrance effect (in Subtle area) to the title text. Change the Start timing option to With Previous and the duration to 03.00 seconds. Bring the title text Forward so that the eagle's wings do not block the title.

3. On Slide 1, decrease the size of the eagle illustration to approximately 4.43" × 5.3" and then move it to the position shown in the figure. Apply the Fly In entrance effect with the From Bottom-Right direction to the illustration and then change the start timing option to After Previous and the duration to 02.50 seconds. Add the Fly Out exit animation with the To Left direction to the eagle illustration and then change the Start timing option to After Previous and the duration to 3.00 seconds.

entrance effect applied to title text

photo size increased and picture style applied

illustration size decreased, moved to front of photo, and entrance effect applied

Established in 1872
America's first national park
Located in Wyoming
    (Small portion in Montana and Idaho)
Spans 3,468.4 square miles

(a) Slide 1

Figure 3–80a

4. On Slide 2 (Figure 3–80b), change the size of the video so that it measures approximately 5.93" × 8.9". Change the video style to the Canvas, White style (in Intense area) and then change the border weight to 6 pt. Have the video start Automatically. Trim the video by changing the Start Time to 00:28.008 and changing the End Time to 00:50.55. Move the video to the location shown in the figure.

5. On Slide 3 (Figure 3–80c), increase the size of the picture to approximately 6.26" × 8.23" and then apply the Moderate Frame, Black picture style to the picture. Move the picture to the location shown in the figure. Start the audio file Automatically and hide this file during the show. Trim the audio file so that the Start Time is at 01:00 and the End Time is at 02:00.

Video trimmed and size, style, and border weight changed

OLD FAITHFUL
ERUPTS APPROXIMATELY EVERY 91 MINUTES

(b) Slide 2

Figure 3–80b

Continued >

In the Labs *continued*

picture style applied
to resized photo

TWO GEYSERS ERUPTING TOGETHER

Old Faithful Geyser

Beehive Geyser

audio file
trimmed, volume
changed, and
sound icon hidden
during show

(c) Slide 3

Figure 3–80c

6. On Slide 4 (Figure 3–80d), apply the Moderate Frame, Black picture style to the bear picture. Apply the Metal Oval picture style to the wolf picture. Move the two pictures to the locations shown, and bring the wolf picture forward, as shown in the figure.

7. Apply the Fade entrance effect to the two pictures. Change the Start timing option to After Previous and the duration to 02.50.

8. Insert the audio file called Wolves, which is located in the Data Files. Change the volume to Medium, start Automatically, and hide the audio file during the show.

9. On Slide 5 (Figure 3–80e) apply the Metal Oval picture style to the four fish pictures. Apply the Bounce entrance effect to the upper left picture and then change the Start timing option to After Previous and the duration to 5.25. Apply these same animation effects to the remaining three pictures in a clockwise order.

picture styles
applied to photos
and entrance
effects added

▶ **Wolves**

▶ **Grizzly bears**

▶ **Herds of bison**

▶ **Elk**

▶ **And much more**

audio file inserted and
hidden during show

YELLOWSTONE HAS ABUNDANT WILDLIFE

(d) Slide 4

Figure 3–80d

(e) Slide 5

Figure 3–80e

10. Apply the Wind transition in the Exciting category to all the slides. Change the duration to 2.50 seconds.

11. If requested by your instructor, insert a text box on Slide 2 and add the name of the street where you lived as a child.

12. View the presentation and then save the file using the file name, Lab 3–1 Visiting Yellowstone.

13. Submit the document in the format specified by your instructor.

14. ✹ On Slide 1, why did you bring the title text to the front of the eagle illustration? Why did you choose the Bounce entrance effect with a 05.25 duration on the four fish pictures on Slide 5?

Lab 2: Adding Audio Options, Ungrouping a Clip, Changing the Color of a Clip Object, Deleting a Clip Object, and Regrouping Objects

Note: To complete this assignment, you will be required to use the Data Files. Please contact your instructor for information about accessing the Data Files.

Problem: You work at a nature center and are asked to do a PowerPoint presentation on how to attract hummingbirds to your yard. You create the presentation shown in Figure 3–81.

Perform the following tasks:
1. Run PowerPoint. Open the presentation called Lab 3-2 Hummingbirds, which is located in the Data Files. On Slide 1 (Figure 3–81a), change the volume of the audio file to High and then select Start Automatically, 'Play Across Slides', 'Loop until Stopped', 'Rewind after Playing', and 'Hide During Show'.

2. Copy the hummingbird illustration from Slide 2 (Figure 3–81b) to Slide 1 and then delete it from Slide 2. Decrease the size of this illustration so that it measures approximately

Continued >

In the Labs *continued*

1.71" × 1.87" and then move it to the location shown in Figure 3–81a. Apply the Fly In 'From Top–Right' entrance effect to the illustration, change the Start timing setting to After Previous, and then change the duration to 02.50.

3. Increase the title text font on Slide 1 to 72 point, bold the text, and then change the color of the title text font to Red (in Standard Colors). Decrease the size of the title text placeholder to approximately 1.65" × 7.62" and then position the title on top of the red rectangle. Apply the Fly In entrance effect with the From Top direction to the title, change the Start timing option to After Previous, and then change the duration to 02.50.

4. On Slide 1, change the shape fill color of the red rectangle to Lime, Accent 1 (in first Theme Colors row). Decrease the size of the rectangle shape to approximately 1.7" × 6.96", as shown in the figure. Increase the font size of the three paragraphs in the rectangle shape to 28 point and then bold this text.

5. On Slide 1, apply the Appear entrance effect to the first paragraph in the list and then change the start timing option to After Previous and the duration to 02.50. Apply the same animation settings for the second and third paragraphs in the list.

6. On Slide 2 (Figure 3–81b), move the video to the right side of the slide, increase the size to approximately 5.84" × 8.2", apply the Beveled Oval, Black video style (in Moderate area) to the video, change the video border color to Red (in Standard Colors), and then change the border weight to 3 pt. Trim the video so that the End Time is 00:17.88. Change the volume to High and then start the video automatically.

7. On Slide 2 (Figure 3–81b), apply the Float In entrance effect to the title text and then change the direction to Float Down. Change the start timing option to With Previous and the duration to 03.00.

8. On Slide 3 (Figure 3–81c), apply the Shape entrance effect to the title text and then change the Start timing option to With Previous and the duration to 3.00.

9. On Slide 3, select the hummingbird and flowers illustration and zoom in to view the three pink flowers. Ungroup this illustration. Select the three pink flowers and change their fill color to Red (in Standard Colors). Delete the three green leaves in the middle of the dark green stem.

(a) Slide 1

Figure 3–81a

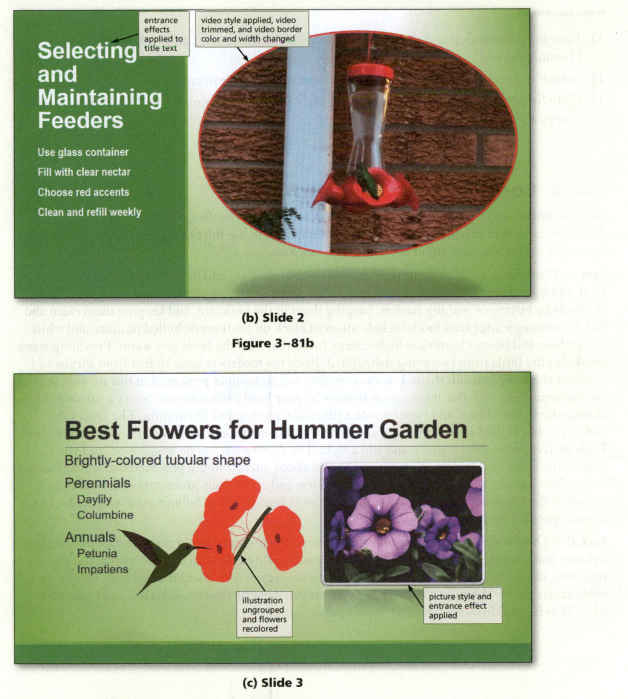

(b) Slide 2

Figure 3–81b

(c) Slide 3

Figure 3–81c

Regroup the illustration, increase the size to approximately 3.14" × 4.85", and then zoom out and move it to the area shown in the figure.

10. On Slide 3, apply the Reflected Bevel, White picture style to the flower picture. Resize the picture to approximately 3.1" × 4.17" and then move it to the right side of the slide, as shown in the figure. Apply the Zoom entrance effect to this picture. Change the Start timing option to On Click and the duration to 2.00.

11. If requested by your instructor, insert a text box at the lower-right corner of Slide 2 and type the color of your eyes in the text box.

12. Change the transition to None for all slides.

Continued >

In the Labs *continued*

13. View the presentation and then save the file using the file name, Lab 3–2 Attracting Hummingbirds.

14. Submit the revised document in the format specified by your instructor.

15. ✳ In Step 9, you changed the color of the three flowers from pink to red. Why? Why did you change the volume of the audio file to High?

Lab 3: Consider This: Your Turn

Design and Create a Presentation about Winter Bird Feeding

Note: To complete this assignment, you will be required to use the Data Files. Please contact your instructor for information about accessing the Data Files.

Part 1: Winter storms in cold climates can affect wild birds. Ice and deep snow reduce the natural food supply, and birds, consequently, have a difficult time surviving and thriving. People can help the birds by buying or making feeders, hanging them in the backyard, and keeping them clean and full. Nutritious winter seed foods include mixes of black oil sunflowers, hulled peanuts, and white millet. Suet and peanut butter are high-energy foods that help the birds stay warm. Providing water also helps the birds from becoming dehydrated. Place the feeders at least 10 feet from shrubs and compact the snow beneath them. Use the concepts and techniques presented in this module to create a presentation with this information to show at your local garden center. Select a suitable theme, change the theme colors, and then include a title slide, photos, and illustration. The Data Files contain a video called Birds in Winter and photos and illustrations called Bird Feeder, Red Jay, and Birds in Tree. Trim the video file and add a style. The illustration can be ungrouped, and you can change the color of it and the photos to add some visual interest to the presentation. Add animation to the slide content using effects and timing. Review and revise your presentation as needed and then save the file using the file name, Lab 3-3 Winter Bird Feeding. Submit your assignment in the format specified by your instructor.

Part 2: ✳ You made several decisions while creating the presentation in this assignment: selecting a theme and changing the theme colors, coloring and adding effects to the illustration and photos, trimming the video and adding a style, and adding animation. What was the rationale behind each of these decisions? When you reviewed the document, what further revisions did you make and why? Where would you recommend showing this slide show?

Index

Note: **Boldfaced** page numbers indicate key terms

A

account, signing in, OFF 6–8
active tab, **OFF 19**
add-in, **PA-10**
address bar, **OFF 30**
Adobe Reader, OFF 26
animation
  changing entrance direction, PPT 151
  changing exit direction, PPT 154
  content placeholder paragraphs, PPT 157–158
  custom, PPT 150–158
  effect icon colors, PPT 150
  modifying emphasis and exit animation timings, PPT 156
  modifying entrance animation timing, PPT 155–156
  presentation with, PPT 121–122
  previewing sequence, PPT 154
  slide content, PPT 150–158
  using emphasis effect, PPT 152
  using entrance effect, PPT 150–151
  using exit effect, PPT 153
animation emphasis effects, **PA-8**
app(s), **OFF 2**
  exiting Office, OFF 42, OFF 53
  Office Mix, PA-12
  running and using. *See* running apps
  switching between, OFF 32
Apply to All button *vs.* Apply button, PPT 99
audio
  adding options, PPT 145–146
  inserting file, PPT 143–145
  presentation with, PPT 121–122
  trimming file, PPT 146
augmented reality with Office Mix, teaching, PA-13
automatic spelling correction, PPT 17
automatically updated properties, **PPT 44**

B

backgrounds, slide
  formatting background picture fill transparency, PPT 88
  inserting picture to create, PPT 87–88
  in specific order, PPT 86
BACKSPACE key, error correction, OFF 23
Backstage view, **OFF 24**
  closing, OFF 33
  closing Office using, OFF 49–50
  creating new documents from, OFF 48
  Info tab in, OFF 24
  opening recent files using, OFF 50
Berlin theme, PPT 4–5, PPT 9
bevel effects, PPT 71
black slide, **PPT 37**
blinking bar, OFF 23
brightness, **PPT 66**
Bring Forward, **PPT 126**
Bring to Front, **PPT 126**
bulleted list, **PPT 13**
  adding new text slide with, PPT 12–13
  creating text slide with multilevel, PPT 13–19
  deleting bullets on slide, PPT 16
  presentation with pictures and, PPT 2–3
  removing extra, PPT 17

C

card, **PA-6**
centering text, **PPT 128**
characters
  in file name, OFF 34
  formatting in presentation, PPT 9–12
  inserting special, PPT 71
clip, PPT 133, **PA-11**
  changing color of object, PPT 134–136
  copying from one slide to another, PPT 138–139
  deleting object, PPT 136–137
  to regroup objects, PPT 137–138
codec (compressor/decompressor), **PPT 139**

color(s), **PPT 9**
  adjusting photo, PPT 124–127
  animation effect icon, PPT 150
  changing color of clip object, PPT 134–136
  changing picture border, PPT 69–70
  changing text, PPT 11–12
  changing theme, PPT 160
  changing video border, PPT 149
  WordArt outline, PPT 93–94
color cast, **PPT 124**
color saturation, **PPT 124**
color tone, **PPT 124**
command, **OFF 10**
'Connect to Internet' button, OFF 6
contextual tabs, OFF 14
contrast, **PPT 66**
Cortana, **OFF 59, PA-14**
  in Microsoft Edge, PA-14–16
Creative Commons license, **PA-7**
creativity, ideal decibels for, PPT 146
custom animations, **PPT 150**, PPT 150–158
custom dictionary, PPT 97
custom layout, **PPT 19**

D

decibels for creativity, PPT 146
deck, **PPT 1**
demoting text, **PPT 15**
desktop (Windows 10), OFF 8
dialog box(es)
  navigating in, **OFF 35**, OFF 35–39
  replacing, PPT 94–97
Dialog Box Launcher, **OFF 17**
Docs.com, Microsoft, **PA-8**
document(s)
  distributing, PPT 47, PPT 102, PPT 162
  electronic image of, OFF 26
document properties, **OFF 24**, **PPT 44**, PPT 44–45
  changing, OFF 24–25, PPT 44–45
  printing, PPT 44, PPT 102, PPT 160
  purpose, OFF 24
drag and drop, **PPT 39**